Language, Society and Identity in early Iceland

Publications of the Philological Society, 45

**WILEY-
BLACKWELL**

Language, Society and Identity in
early Iceland

Publications of the Philological Society, 45

WILEY
BLACKWELL

Language, Society and Identity in early Iceland

Stephen Pax Leonard

Publications of the Philological Society, 45

WILEY-
BLACKWELL

This edition first published 2012

© 2012 The Philological Society

Blackwell Publishing was acquired by John Wiley & Sons in February 2007. Blackwell's publishing program has been merged with Wiley's global Scientific, Technical, and Medical business to form Wiley-Blackwell.

Registered Office

John Wiley & Sons Ltd, The Atrium, Southern Gate, Chichester, West Sussex, PO19 8SQ, United Kingdom

Editorial Offices

350 Main Street, Malden, MA 02148-5020, USA

9600 Garsington Road, Oxford, OX4 2DQ, UK

The Atrium, Southern Gate, Chichester, West Sussex, PO19 8SQ, UK

For details of our global editorial offices, for customer services, and for information about how to apply for permission to reuse the copyright material in this book please see our website at www.wiley.com/wiley-blackwell.

The right of Stephen Pax Leonard to be identified as the author of this work has been asserted in accordance with the UK Copyright, Designs and Patents Act 1988.

Wiley also publishes its books in a variety of electronic formats. Some content that appears in print may not be available in electronic books.

Designations used by companies to distinguish their products are often claimed as trademarks. All brand names and product names used in this book are trade names, service marks, trademarks or registered trademarks of their respective owners. The publisher is not associated with any product or vendor mentioned in this book. This publication is designed to provide accurate and authoritative information in regard to the subject matter covered. It is sold on the understanding that the publisher is not engaged in rendering professional services. If professional advice or other expert assistance is required, the services of a competent professional should be sought.

Library of Congress Cataloging-in-Publication Data

Library of Congress Cataloging-in-Publication Data is available for this work.

ISBN 978-1-1182-9496-3

A catalogue record for this book is available from the British Library.

Set in Times by SPS (P) Ltd., Chennai, India

Printed in Singapore

1 2012

CONTENTS

ACKNOWLEDGEMENTS

An interdisciplinary work of this kind has meant that I have benefited from the knowledge and expertise of a great number of scholars working in neighbouring disciplines such as history, anthropology and archaeology as well as linguistics itself. This monograph is based on my D.Phil thesis and was written principally in Oxford, but also in Oslo, Reykjavík and Akureyri. I have been exceptionally fortunate in being able to have met and worked with the leaders of their respective fields in all of these places. An additional benefit has been that a number of them have become friends.

Special thanks for help and support beyond the call of duty must go to Paul Bibire who has been more than willing throughout to give advice on any number of issues ranging from Icelandic culture to Scandinavian history to the nuts and bolts of word processing. My D.Phil supervisors, Prof. Andreas Willi and Dr Heather O'Donoghue were very generous with their help and support from the very beginning. Andreas gave unstintingly of his time and energy at every stage of the project, reading the various drafts of each chapter word for word, correcting many errors and suggesting much-needed improvements. I have gained tremendously from his intelligence, learning and example. Heather introduced me to Old Icelandic and has provided guidance and direction throughout.

In Oslo, I was supervised by Kjartan Ottósson who offered sound advice and scholarly inspiration for the duration of my five-month stay at the Institutt for lingvistiske og nordiske studier (ILN). Kjartan read the entire text, chapter by chapter, made many useful suggestions and provided additional references. Also in Oslo, Jón Viðar Sigurðsson, was always keen to hear my ideas over a coffee. He read Chapter 4 and we have continued a dialogue on a number of issues. Terje Spurkland read parts of Chapter 3 and improved my poor knowledge of runology. I am also very grateful for a long and fruitful meeting with the archaeologist, Christian Keller, with whom I discussed settlement patterns and population movements for Iceland, the Faroe Islands and mainland Scandinavia. I would like to express my gratitude to all these scholars.

In London, both Richard Perkins and Peter Foote were patient enough to hear my ideas on the emergence of Icelandic social structures. Peter Foote wrote to me, inviting me for lunch at his house in London. The discussion stretched well into the afternoon, and I am grateful for his well-thought out, balanced views and hospitality.

One of the many joys of this research has been the trips to the Stofnun Árna Magnússonar in Reykjavík each summer. I was always made to feel welcome there, and have grown very fond of the place and its traditions. I have discussed my work with a large number of scholars based at Háskóli Íslands and am particularly grateful to Kristján Árnason, Gísli Pálsson, Orri Vésteinsson, Gunnar Karlsson and Helgi Þorláksson and for their time, suggestions and for sharing my enthusiasm for the topic. The Stofnun Árna Magnússonar proved to be an excellent place for meeting scholars from all over the world. It was particularly helpful to discuss *Grágás* with Patricia Pires Boulhosa. She was good company during my stay and I am grateful for her kind hospitality and the interest she continues to show in my work.

My trips to Iceland would not have been the same without Sigurður Pétursson's unsurpassed generosity and excellent sense of humour. I am indebted to Sigurður for willingly fielding so many of my questions on Icelandic culture and for sharing his encyclopedic knowledge which extends to all manner of things, not least English antique chairs.

The summer of 2007 was spent in Iceland conducting fieldwork. Although they are far too numerous to name individually, I would like to thank all my informants for their time, patience and genuine interest in my research. Whilst living in Akureyri that summer, I was based at the Stofnun Vilhjálms Stefánssonar as a Visiting Scholar. The scholars working there were very kind, providing me with all the facilities that I needed, as well as a very friendly, cosy environment in which to conduct my research. The secretary, Lára Ólafsdóttir, was immensely patient with my endless questions. I would like to thank especially Jón Haukur Ingimundarson and Joan Nymand Larsen who work at the Stofnun Vilhjálms Stefánssonar and who produced a feast of Icelandic lamb on my last night.

My research has been funded by the Arts and Humanities Research Council (AHRC). In addition, I was a beneficiary of a Norwegian Government Scholarship for the first five months of 2008. The Icelandic Travel Scholarship at Oxford University has helped finance a number of stays in Iceland. I would like to extend my thanks to all these funding bodies for making this research possible. In addition, I would like to thank the Faculty of Linguistics, Philology & Phonetics in Oxford for generous provision of guidance and facilities.

Even more important than the financial support has been the friendly atmosphere of Exeter College, Oxford. My friends and the staff at the College made it a marvellous place to live and learn and have given me many very good, life-lasting memories.

Finally, I must add the customary yet sincere caveat that none of the above-named necessarily agrees with everything I say or is to be blamed for any errors and blunders that remain.

LIST OF TABLES AND MAPS

ABBREVIATIONS AND CONVENTIONS

The following abbreviations have been used in this study:
acc. accusative
AM Arnamagnæan Institute, Copenhagen and Árnastofnun, Reykjavík
dat. dative
gen. genitive
Gmc. Germanic
MS. manuscript
nom. nominative
pl. plural
sg. singular

These abbreviations refer to key texts and editions that have been consulted:

DD *Diplomatarium Danicum.* 1 række. 1957–1990. Edited by Weibull, L. *et al.* Vols. 1–7. København: Munksgaard.
Diplomatarium Danicum. 2 række. 1938–1960. Edited by Afzelius, A. *et al.* Vols. 1–12. København: Munksgaard.

DFP Dennis, A., Foote, P. & Perkins, R. 1980. *Laws of Early Iceland.* Winnipeg: University of Manitoba Press; 2000. *Laws of Early Iceland II.* Winnipeg: University of Manitoba Press.

DI *Diplomatarium Islandicum.* 1857–1972. Íslenzkt fornbréfasafn, sem hefir inni að halda bréf, gjörninga, dóma og máldaga og aðrar skrár, er snerta Ísland og íslenzka menn, Vols. 1–16. Kaupmannahöfn & Reykjavík: Hið íslenzka bókmenntafélag.

DN *Diplomatarium Norvegicum.* 1847–1995. Oldbreve til Kundskab om Norges indre og ydre Forhold, Sprog, Slægter, Lovgiving og Rettergang i Middelalderen. Edited by Lange, C. A. & Unger, C. R. Vols. 1–32. Christiania: P. T. Mallings Forlagshandel.

HN *Phelpstead, C. (editor). 2001. A History of Norway and the Passion and Miracles of the Blessed Óláfr,* translated by Kunin, D. Text Series 13. London: Viking Society for Northern Research.

IED *Icelandic – English Dictionary.* 1874. Edited by Cleasby, R., Guðbrandur Vigfússon, Craigie, W. A. Oxford: Clarendon Press.

Íf *Íslenzk fornrit.* 1933 ff. Vols. I–XXXV. Reykjavík: Hið íslenzka fornritafélag.

KLNM *Kulturhistorisk leksikon for nordisk middelalder fra vikingetid til reformationstid.* 1956–78. I–XXII. København: Rosenkilde og Bagger.

NgL *Norges gamle love indtil 1387.* 1846–95. Edited by Keyser, R. & Munch, P. A. *et al.* 5 Vols. Christiania: Trykt hos C. Gröndahl.

ÓTM *Óláfs saga Tryggvasonar en mesta.* 1958–2000. Edited by Ólafur Halldórsson. 3 Vols. Copenhagen: Ejnar Munksgaard.

References to and quotations from the first Icelandic law code, *Grágás*, are based on the Vilhjálmur Finsen editions. This is a work in three volumes, published in 1852 (parts Ia and Ib), 1879 (part II) and 1883 (part III) respectively and reprinted in 1974. As for the saga material, reference is made to the *Íslenzk fornrit* (*Íf*) editions for the more well-known sagas. When quoting from a saga, the abbreviation (*Íf*) is given followed by the volume number in Roman numerals, as in *Íf* XII (*Brennu-Njáls saga*: 56). Given that there are a number of different recensions of *Landnámabók*, it has on occasions been easiest to refer to the text in translation. The English translation used here is that of Hermann Pálsson & Edwards (1972).

Mention should also be made of the Icelandic alphabet and writing conventions. Readers familiar with Old Norse will find this paragraph unnecessary, while it is essential preliminary reading for those without a knowledge of the language. The Roman alphabet was used for writing Old Norse, except for a small number of vowels and consonants. Two symbols, þ (upper case Þ) and ð (upper case Ð), represent the sounds written *th* in English; þ occurs in word-initial position, while ð is found in medial or final position. The following vowels and vocalic ligatures will also be encountered: æ represents a front vowel (approximately equivalent to the *a* in English *pat*); ø and œ are approximately equivalent to the vowel sound in French *feu*. The hooked 'o', rendered here as an ö which is the later standardised way of writing it, is similar to the vowel sound in *hot*. Accent marks over the vowels indicate length.

Personal names of saga characters are given in their normalised Old Icelandic form. This means that names are presented with nominative inflections, if applicable. The same applies to the names of modern Icelandic scholars. Given that most Icelanders of the present day have no surnames, it is conventional to refer to them by their first name after first mention (so Finnur for Finnur Jónsson). This is the convention that I have used here. As well as personal names, place-names are also presented in the Old Icelandic nominative form. The spelling convention used in the Finsen editions of *Grágás* is not always the same as that used in other texts: there are therefore a number of occasions when I need to quote from the Finsen edition using his spelling (such as *búa quiðr*), but elsewhere use the more conventional spelling, (*búakviðr*) ('panel verdict').

1

INTRODUCTION

1.1 AIMS OF THE PRESENT STUDY

In the view of the Icelandic historian Árni Pálsson, the saddest event in the history of Iceland was when the Icelanders lost Norway 'out of their linguistic community and into the hands of the Danes' (*vjer höfðum misst Noreg úr málfjélagi við oss í hendur Dana*). This occurred around 1400 A.D., and the result was that ever since 'we have only had ourselves to communicate with out here on the distant skerry' (*síðan höfum vjer orðið að mælast einir við hjer á útskerinu*) (Árni Pálsson, 1924: 201).[1] It is significant that Icelanders tend to emphasize the *linguistic* consequences of such historical events; central to the understanding of the Icelandic national character is the view that Icelanders see their cultural heritage as language.

This study was prompted by similar observations, and it was these observations which triggered an interest in exploring the Icelanders' linguistic heritage and their identity. Whilst he did not have the identity of the Icelanders in mind, Harris (1980: Preface) points out that, 'language-making [...] is [...] the essential process by which men construct a cultural identity for themselves, and for the communities to which they see themselves as belonging'. It is not my intention to address specifically issues of 'language-making', but the question of how a group of settlers arriving in a *terra nova* construct an identity for themselves lies at the heart of this research.

My basic aim is two-fold: (a) to analyse how the dialect(s) taken to Iceland in the ninth and tenth centuries developed in the context of a new society whose settlers were scattered; (b) to examine how the dialect(s) became relatively homogenous and how language was subsequently used and perceived as an identity marker, reflecting social (and individual) identities in conjunction with the social structures of early Iceland. These topics are discussed in Chapters 3, 4 and 5 and in order to follow this discussion, a number of terms need to be defined from the outset: 'social identity' here refers to the individual's self-perception which is derived from perceived membership of social groups (cf. Section 2.7.1) while a social structure is taken to mean 'the articulation of a set of clearly definable social institutions which were considered to constitute the basic framework of the society concerned' (Leach, 1982: 32). The reason for focusing on

---

[1] Reproduced in Kristján Árnason (2003a: 7).

social structures is that the Icelanders became fully self-conscious as an Icelandic community through the establishment of these. Hence the terminology used to describe them may be expected to reflect this new identity. 'Early Iceland' is not a widely-used term in the literature, but will be used here to refer to the period from the settlement of Iceland (the 'Settlement') in c. 870 A.D. until Iceland's submission to the Norwegian Crown in 1262–64 A.D. Dennis, Foote & Perkins (1980) call their translation of the Old Icelandic legal code, *Grágás*, the 'Laws of Early Iceland' but do not define 'early Iceland' specifically. My use of the term 'early Iceland' encompasses both the 'Settlement Period' (c. 870–930 A.D.) and the 'Commonwealth Period' (930–1262–64 A.D.). Both the Settlement Period (*landnámsöld*) and Commonwealth Period (*þjóðveldisöld*) are widely-used and recognised terms, cf. Björn Þorsteinsson (1953: 77); Gunnar Karlsson (1975: 29). There are a number of occasions when I need to refer to the status of the language at later dates. In order to be able to comment on the process of dialect formation in a new society such as early Iceland and to discuss how language reflected changing identities, it is imperative to focus on the earliest period possible but also to have a time horizon sufficiently long enough for perceptions of language as an identity marker to be fully reflected in the written literature.

It must also be stressed, however, what I do *not* intend to achieve. Whilst I touch inevitably on issues of historical linguistics and the history of Old Icelandic, my intention is *not* to describe language change (neither phonological, syntactic or otherwise) in Norse or Old Icelandic for which studies are already available.[2] The syntax of Old Norse in particular has been much discussed recently and has been the subject of book publications. My focus is purely the question of dialect and in particular identity-formation in early Iceland. My approach to this problem is to reconstruct language in a social context. It would go well beyond the scope of this book and the domain of socio-historical linguistics to examine all aspects of language change (sound change being just one part).

The terms Old Icelandic and Old Norse (or just Norse) are often used interchangeably in the literature. Old Norse is used if I want to refer to the wider culture beyond Iceland; otherwise I use the term Old Icelandic. Old Norse implies all the various dialects of the Germanic language and its culture used in the Scandinavian Middle Ages, so embracing Old Icelandic, Old Faroese, Old Norwegian, Old Danish, Old Swedish and Old Gutnish.

Language *and* identity in early Iceland is a promising area of research for two reasons: (a) the comprehensive chronicling of the Settlement and the establishment of social structures represents an opportunity to study the process of identity-formation in a new society; (b) there is a distinct lack of

---

[2] See Sections 3.2.

research on language and identity in early Iceland *per se*, with scholars tending to discuss only selectively topics such as putative dialect levelling, the use of linguistic labels in early Iceland or the question of identity more generally.[3]

This research will appeal both to scholars of Scandinavian linguistics interested in the language and history of early Iceland, and to sociolinguists (and socio-historical linguists). It will also contribute to the recent theoretical discussion amongst sociolinguists on matters such as new-dialect formation and language isolation. Studies focusing on language development in new societies have thus far seldom addressed the problem of identity-formation. The issue of identity-formation is taken up here and an attempt is made to fill some of the gaps in our knowledge of this topic.

My approach to the problem of identity-formation in early Iceland uses linguistic, historical and where appropriate also archaeological data. The linguistic data alone are insufficient to address the relevant issues fully in this timeframe. Some may feel uneasy that I build up an argument for dialect valuation when some of the facts are missing. I do not share this unease, however. The deductions that I have made are reasonable and based on the most recent compelling work in sociolinguisitics. Careful analysis of historical texts proved to be essential, as did analysing the settlement patterns from an archaeological perspective. It became soon apparent from discussions with linguists, historians and archaeologists in Oxford, Norway and Iceland that their respective views on a number of issues were often radically different. Whilst subscribing to certain sociolinguistic models, I have, where possible, tried to adopt an interdisciplinary approach.

The conclusions will be based on the broadest possible analysis, looking at different registers of the Icelandic language whose sources are described in full in Section 1.6. The research has been undertaken in the context of a number of limitations. The difficulties of analysing language development in a distant historical period are numerous and varied. Also, issues relating to language and identity are invariably complex, and thus it is difficult to offer uncontroversial solutions to a number of the problems. It should also be remembered that my data are inevitably from the written form and yet my inferences often concern the spoken form. In Old Icelandic some registers such as the presentation of the laws for instance were available in oral form. Skaldic poetry (Section 1.6.5) was a spoken form and the sagas represent skaldic poetry as a genre that could be used by Icelandic farmers. The tendency is to think of everyday speech as low-register, but it need not be and need not have been.

---

[3] Studies on dialect mixing/levelling in Icelandic are discussed in Sections 3.6.1 and 3.6.2 whilst literature on linguistic labels is referred to in Section 5.3.1. Sverrir Jakobsson (2005) wrote a monograph on the issue of an Icelandic world-view in the period 1100–1400 A.D.

1.2 ORGANISATION OF STUDY

We turn our attention now to the organisation of the study. It is laid out so as to proceed, where possible, chronologically. Before we discuss the linguistic situation leading up to the Settlement and thereafter, a concise description of the social and historical context in which the Icelandic language develops is given in Sections 1.3 and 1.4. The aim of Section 1.3 is to provide the very basic, but necessary information regarding the Settlement, whilst Section 1.4 intends to place early Iceland's social structures in their correct historical setting. Alongside the Settlement and the establishment of social structures, the reader is introduced to the language of the Icelanders. It is not the intention of Section 1.5 to describe the language fully at this stage, but merely to ensure sufficient knowledge has been provided to follow the more detailed discussion in Chapter 3. The remainder of this chapter, Section 1.6, is devoted to describing the sources which are referred to throughout.

Having supplied the basic historical and linguistic information in Chapter 1, Chapter 2 assesses the relevant sociolinguistic literature and determines which linguistic models are most appropriate for analysing the processes of dialect and identity-formation in early Iceland. Chapter 3 moves on from this theoretical discussion and addresses the first key issue of the study, namely the question of how the dialect(s) taken to Iceland at the time of the Settlement developed. Chapter 3 suggests that the dialects spoken in Norse colonies may have *begun* to 'level' prior to the Settlement. There is not only a plausible historical context for such a development, but this explanation circumvents the problem of reconciling the requisite linguistic development with the settlement pattern of Iceland: dialect levelling requires typically a convergence of speakers on one place, but the settlement pattern is not conducive to convergence with isolated farmsteads dotted around the periphery of Iceland.[4]

Chapter 4 approaches the topic of identity from an alternative perspective, examining how the emergence of social structures in early Iceland may have contributed to the formation of an Icelandic identity. A society such as early Iceland needed means to identify its members – who did and did not belong – and Chapter 4 shows how this is reflected in terminology. There were a multitude of markers of an Icelandic identity of which language was only one; a new identity must also have been based on the elaborate and innovative social structures themselves as well as on the extensive medieval Icelandic literature.

Chapter 5 examines to what degree an Icelandic identity was reflected in the literature. The chapter shows that the evidence is often ambiguous and

---

[4] Section 3.6.3 examines a few of the plausible historical contexts in which convergence of people on one place and thus dialect levelling could have occurred prior to the Settlement.

that there are few texts that portray explicitly an Icelandic identity, although those that do seek an identity in linguistic terms were amongst the earliest documents to be written in the vernacular. Icelandic society appears to have had many of the features which are cross-culturally conducive to a common identity – a common body of law, a uniform vernacular language, a myth of foundation and descent. The notion of ethnic separateness plays, however, little part in the early literature. The conclusions are presented in Chapter 6.

1.3 THE SETTLEMENT OF ICELAND

The period from c. 870 A.D. until the establishment of the *alþingi* ('General Assembly') in 930 A.D. is known as the period of the *landnám* (literally, 'land-taking').[5] During this period, between 10,000 and 60,000 people are thought to have come to Iceland to settle. Estimates vary: Bryce (1901: 266) believes the population of Iceland at the close of the period to have been about 50,000; Herrmann (1914) thinks that Iceland had a population of 60,000 in 965 A.D.; Valtýr Guðmundsson (1924: 34) estimates 60,000–70,000; Gjerset (1925: 19) puts the figure at 25,000 people; Ólafur Lárusson (1944: 16) calculates that the population of Iceland in 930 A.D was approximately 56,000. This figure is based on the fact that we know from the census in 1840 that there were 5,600 farms in Iceland, and assumes that the number of farms did not change greatly over this very long period and that there were on average ten people living on a farm. In a discussion of population in the early period, Gunnar Karlsson (2000: 44–51) uses the same methodology, calculating that there were approximately 5,000 tax-paying farms and that the average household did not number more than eight people: a couple, three children, one elder and two farm hands, male and female. This results in a population figure of 40,000. It is not clear where the figure of 5,000 comes from. Ari's *Íslendingabók* tells us that at the beginning of the twelfth century that the farmers were 38 'hundreds' in number, which equates to 4,560, using the custom of the time to count in long hundreds (120).

The Settlement does not appear to have been an organised venture under a united leadership: the settlers took what land they could until the land became fully settled. An analysis of the personal names and places of origin of the people named in *Landnámabók* shows a considerable preponderance of Norwegian settlers, but it is significant that the Celtic element also looms large. Unlike elsewhere, notably the British Isles, the settlers did not have to accommodate to existing arrangements: they were settling in a land that was effectively empty and thus *terra nullius*. There were no settlements to be

---

[5] *Historia Norvegiæ* (93) states that the Settlement was complete in 50 years.

taken over or avoided, and the social, economic and legal systems established by the settlers were unaffected by the presence of a native population.

It is impossible to give any definitive answer to the question of *why* the settlers were attracted in such large numbers to this far northern island. Jones (1968: 269) sums up the motivation as a 'need for land and pasture', whilst many other scholars would insist that the island was colonised because of the tyranny of Haraldr *inn hárfagri* (Maurer, 1874: 25–6; Bogi Th. Melsteð, 1903: 37–8; Turville-Petre, 1951: 117). These two factors were connected, as Foote & Wilson (1970: 52–3) suggest: the first settlers went to Iceland because of land shortage brought about by King Haraldr's seizure of their land. The Settlement may also be explained by the same expansionist tendency discernible in Viking raids and expeditions at a time of major technological progress in shipbuilding and navigation.

The first written source to mention the existence of Iceland is a book by the Irish monk Dicuil, *De mensura orbis terrae*, which dates back to 825 A.D. (Tierney, 1967: 75). Whilst the veracity of the source may be questioned, Dicuil claims to have met Irish monks who had lived on the island of Thule. Before the period of the *landnám*, Irish monks or hermits known as *papar* had certainly visited the land but, according to *Íslendingabók* (see Section 1.6.1), they quickly abandoned the otherwise unpopulated island when the Norsemen arrived. There is some evidence of the *papar* element in Icelandic place-names, but *papar* place-names are much more common in the Northern and Faroe Islands where the existence of eremitic populations can reasonably be assumed.[6]

1.4 THE ESTABLISHMENT OF SOCIAL STRUCTURES

It is likely that the social structure of the country had its roots in the groupings of these original settlers. Given their ownership of ships, the leaders of the settler groups were people of wealth and standing who were influential in the establishment of social institutions.

Until 930 A.D. the settlers remained without formal political institutions that could ensure social integration. In 930 A.D. the *alþingi*, an annual 'General Assembly' with national legislative and judicial functions, was established, meeting at the same place each summer under the presidency of an elected lawspeaker who memorised and recited the laws over a three-year period, repeating the regulations on assembly procedure each year.

Once the Settlement was complete, the establishment of the rule of law became a priority for the leaders of the new country. A Norwegian

---

[6] Hermann Pálsson (1996: 42–46) discusses the issue of *papar* place-names.

called Úlfljótr spent three years in Norway studying the law, devising subsequently a national law for the settlers to Iceland. We have no direct knowledge of these laws of western Norway in the early tenth century, but we do know that the first Icelandic laws were modelled on the laws of the Norwegian west-coast law province called Gulaþing. In accordance with the Viking Age (c. 793–1066 A.D.) concept of law, Gulaþing embraced both the legislation enacted and also the area in which this legislation applied. Definitions of the Viking Age vary, but this definition is based on the period from the first Viking raid on the abbey on Lindisfarne on 6th January, 793 A.D. until the defeat of Haraldr harðráði by the Saxon King Harold Godwinsson in 1066 A.D. at the Battle of Stamford Bridge. This definition is therefore in accordance with the Viking Age from the English perspective (cf. Viking raids in Ireland).

At the time of the Settlement, Norway was in fact divided into several legal areas. In contrast to this, it appears to have been important for Icelandic society that the whole country was united under one code of law and with one *central* assembly, the *alþingi* at Þingvellir (*Íf* Ii, *Íslendingabók*: 17). This does not mean to say that there were not regional assemblies: there existed in fact an extensive network of local assemblies and courts, dotted around the country as Map 1 (below) shows:

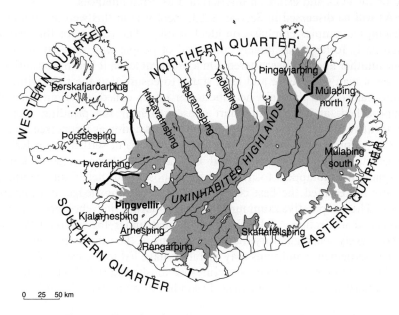

Map 1: The Assemblies of Early Iceland (Source: Gunnar Karlsson, 2000: 25)

Icelandic law describes or prescribes a society which differs in other respects too from other societies in medieval Europe. It had for example a common code of law and system of courts, alongside the *alþingi*, where new laws and changes to existing laws were debated. Perhaps more so than in mainland Scandinavia, law in medieval Iceland appears to have touched virtually all aspects of social intercourse, yet it was enforced by the aggrieved party and not an executive arm of government. The use of force was often the only means of successfully implementing a verdict.

In the Commonwealth Period, Iceland was a society governed by free farmers. At the centre of this society were the *goðar* ('chieftains') to whom the farmers had to declare allegiance.[7] Fundamental to this structure was the fact that nobody had authority over a *goði*, because in formal terms he was bound by nothing but the law. In order to function as a leader the *goði*, who socially and politically was *primus inter pares*, had to secure two sorts of alliance: firstly with other chieftains in the event of some major confrontation, especially in the *alþingi*; and, secondly, with the farmers who had pledged allegiance to him. In this system any free male was by law equal to each other and had an independent legal status, but no public institution protected his rights. He had to be prepared to defend his property and rights, and in any conflict his allegiance to a *goði* enabled him to take his case to court. The result was a society where all dealings between free individuals were politicised, and where one of the most easily identifiable sources of power was conflict management or the ability to settle disputes and establish internal and external alliances.

As will be discussed in Section 4.2.3, there was in this web of politicised dealings a complex emphasis on identification. The reason for this may be that early Iceland was largely composed of people who were strangers to one another and thinly scattered. On a practical level, it became essential to know a man's residence and legal status to ensure that the right witnesses were named and the right neighbours or jurors called, the right chieftain approached, and the right court chosen to hear the pleading. Certain innovative social structures, such as neighbours acting as jurors (see Section 4.3.2), seem to have sprung from these conditions of settlement in Iceland where, to begin with, people did not have any large circle of kin or acquaintance to appeal to. It could be supposed that neighbours acting as jurors represented the best combination of local knowledge and impartiality. The cooperative communes of neighbouring householders (*hreppar*) discussed in Section 4.3.1, which functioned under the national law but were largely self-regulatory, had their origins in the same conditions.

The settlement conditions may therefore have led to the establishment of social structures. The social structures established in 930 A.D. resulted in the emergence of the so-called Icelandic Commonwealth and Iceland

---

[7] The role of the *goðar* is discussed more fully in Section 4.3.4.

remained independent until 1262–64 A.D., when the Icelanders had to swear allegiance to the King of Norway. Thereafter, Iceland was subject to a foreign king (principally the Danish Crown) until the declaration of the Republic of Iceland in 1944. Thus, compared to the total span of time in which the country has been inhabited, its periods of independence are relatively short. This is one reason why the early and self-defining state stands out so markedly in the Icelandic consciousness and historiography. Another reason is the fact that the social and political achievements of the people of the Commonwealth were exceptional. In a short period of time, a combination of social compromise, political ingenuity and legal inventiveness had produced a constitutional and judicial system that was very comprehensive.

1.5 THE LANGUAGE OF THE ICELANDERS

We turn now to the language of the Icelanders itself. Seip (1971: 18–47) and Haugen (1976: 132–33) note that the limited linguistic information that we have for the period prior to the Settlement and just after derives from foreign texts (Old English poems such as *Beowulf* and *Widsith* in which anglicised forms of Scandinavian names appear), loan-words (early Germanic loan-words in Finnish for example), place-names, personal names, skaldic poetry and runic inscriptions. Seip (1971: 47) assumes the oldest skaldic poems date from the period 850–900 A.D. Before and after the Settlement Scandinavians carved runes on wood or stone. The runic inscriptions tend to be short, but 'they provide information on the forebears of present-day speakers of Icelandic' (Stefán Karlsson, 2004: 8).

The language at the time of the Settlement belongs to what Haugen (1976: 132) calls the 'Common Scandinavian' Period (550–1050 A.D.).[8] According to Haugen (1976: 92) and Torp (2002: 19), towards the end of this period, divergences between dialects had become sufficiently conspicuous that the region could be divided into two main areas: East Norse and more conservative West Norse.[9] Haugen (1976: 198) claims that we can speak of two dialects as certain phonological distinctions between East and West Norse in the pre-literary period can be dimly followed in the runic inscriptions.[10] It is improbable, however, that *more* dialect distinctions did not develop in the five centuries since the Age of Migrations (c. 300–700 A.D.), but they do not appear to be visibly recorded in the runic record. The runic inscriptions for this period are sparse, very short and difficult to interpret.

[8] Cf. Seip (1971: 18–47) who breaks this period down into two separate periods: 'Synkopezeit' (c. 600–800 A.D.) and 'Wikingerzeit' (c. 800–1050 A.D.) but whose end-date for the period concurs with Haugen (1976).
[9] See Kjartan G. Ottósson (2002: 787–93) for a more in-depth discussion.
[10] See Section 3.2.2.

The different North Germanic languages emerge in written form with Roman letters over the course of the twelfth and thirteenth centuries, gradually establishing what could be called national written standards. The number of places where manuscripts were produced was rather small, and each major centre had its own tradition of writing. The extent to which these traditions represent actual speech is not always known because scribes (at least in the Middle Ages) did not usually write as they spoke, but as they had been taught to write. However, it is true that dialectal variation in Old High German and Old English was reflected in writing and one could argue that there is no reason why the situation in Scandinavia should have been any different.

To speak of national languages at this point in time may be anachronistic, especially as the Scandinavians themselves appear to have been content to refer to all of them as *dönsk tunga*.[11] Snorri Sturluson in the Prologue to *Heimskringla* says that the chiefs of the Northlands spoke the *dönsk tunga*, (*Íf* XXVI, *Heimskringla*: 3): *Á bók þessi lét ek rita fornar frásagnir um höfðingja þá, er ríki hafa haft á Norðrlöndum ok á danska tungu hafa mælt* 'In this book I have written tales concerning those chiefs who have ruled the Northlands, and who spoke the Danish tongue'. This term refers to a 'variegated picture of dialects in Scandinavia: an abstraction standing for the common elements in what were diverging dialects' (Haugen, 1976: 135).

Despite the fact that the Scandinavians had the same conception of their language, and although Old Icelandic appeared to differ little from its forerunner, West Norse, there was, however, an indigenous Icelandic concern for the Icelandic language.[12] This became explicit when writing became established. The introduction of writing in Iceland was due to the Church. From the linguistic point of view, the most important consequence of the spread of Christianity was that the Latin alphabet (written primarily in the Carolingian minuscule script) became known in areas where people had previously only had access to runes. The whole apparatus of the Church naturally augmented the vocabulary of Icelandic.

A national Icelandic literary tradition soon emerged with its centres of learning located at the bishops' residences at Skálholt and Hólar, and at various monastery scriptoria such as Helgafell, Þingeyrar, Munka-Þverá as well as Haukadalur and Oddi. Ólafur Halldórsson (1966) shows that a large group of manuscripts from the second half of the fourteenth century had been written in the Augustinian monastery at Helgafell; Stefán Karlsson (1999: 138–58) believes that the production of manuscript books was not limited to ecclesiastical foundations. Significantly enough, the laws were among the first themes to be dealt with in writing. This happened all over Scandinavia. The writing down of the laws expressed an acknowledgement of some kind of unified (national) community.

---

[11] Section 5.3.1 discusses the usage of this term.
[12] See Section 1.6.4.

Icelandic was the sole West Norse dialect that succeeded in maintaining its written tradition through the centuries of Danish dominance. There are a number of factors that may account for this: the intense tradition of writing that had made the Icelanders so literate; isolation that escaped immediate control by the Danish rulers; the conservative and unified spoken language.

Finally, it may be stressed that the differences between Old and modern Icelandic are generally few and insignificant, and that distinct dialects are virtually non-existent.[13] Explanations of this conservatism are found in the exceptional literary heritage and practice of the Icelanders, in the fact that communication, and not least the movement of people, between different parts of the country was constant, and in the self-conscious desire of the Icelanders to preserve their ancient language and the link it gave them to the past. The development of Icelandic still owes much to the interest generally taken by the Icelanders in their language and its use, and to the fact that most of the population regard it as an honour to possess a language so little changed from its ancient form. The Icelandic identity is consolidated around the ancient literary heritage and the preservation of the nation's language.

1.6 SOURCES

Reference is made to a wide number of sources throughout the study. In determining which sources to consult I was guided by two key factors: (a) chronology: the earliest texts are likely to be the most reliable for what they tell us of the Settlement and the language spoken (written) at the time and thereafter; (b) the intention to examine reflections of linguistic identity in as many different genres as possible.

One is spoilt by the sheer volume of literature written (almost exclusively) in the vernacular in medieval Iceland. It was decided to put particular emphasis on the Icelandic legal code as a source. There are a number of reasons for this: Icelanders put law at the centre of their society more emphatically than other people in Scandinavia; the law codes were amongst the first documents written down in Iceland and were written in the vernacular; the Icelandic law code was far more varied and extensive than any other Scandinavian law code and gives us a clear picture of Icelandic social structures.[14]

As Dennis, Foote & Perkins (1980: 7) observe, there are difficulties in working with the law codes: 'many of the laws are casuistical in form,

---

[13] Kristján Árnason (1980b) summarises the key differences in the so-called 'phonological dialects'.

[14] *Konungsbók* (see Section 1.6.3) alone is three and a half times the size of the Danish King Erik's Sjælland Law, the largest of the Scandinavian provincial law-books.

defining a conceivable offence, prescribing the punishment for it, stating the procedure for its prosecution and sometimes the grounds and procedure for a defence'. It is not known, however, if there was any truly 'legal' codification in Iceland, or whether the laws acted merely as a set of 'juridical' norms and thus as a practical guide for proper social behaviour. In the present analysis, the manuscripts discussed in Section 1.6.3 are *not* taken to constitute a codified legal text, nor are they a definite sign that things necessarily happened according to what was written in them.

To see how the laws functioned in society, one has to turn to the sagas where the laws are referred to implicitly and explicitly. The difficulty with relying solely on the sagas is that a large part of the saga material was written down centuries after the events that they depict. The standpoint taken here will be that they constitute the small fragments of evidence that we have and the saga-author presents them as if they would sound plausible to his audience and therefore they would not appear immediately false. Any discussion of saga evidence *à propos* identity will thus be based on the assumption that this evidence can be accepted to that degree.[15]

1.6.1 *Historical texts*

The oldest known work of Icelandic historiography, written down centuries before the sagas, is Ari *inn fróði*'s *Íslendingabók*, the 'Book of the Icelanders', preserved in two seventeenth-century copies of a now lost codex from about 1200 A.D. (AM 113a and b fol.).[16] It is clear from the Prologue that Ari wrote the book twice. The first version was drafted between 1122 A.D., when Ketill Þorsteinsson became bishop of Hólar, and 1133 A.D., when Bishop Þorlákr Runólfsson of Skálholt and Sæmundr the Wise both died. The second draft is the text we now possess, probably also written in the lifetime of the two bishops, c. 1130 A.D. (Jónas Kristjánsson, 1988: 120–121) (cf. Finnur Jónsson, 1930: 42–45; Grønlie, 2006: xiii).

Íslendingabók comprises a brief account of the history of Iceland until the death of the Bishop Gizurr (1118 A.D.), giving information on certain major events from the first settlements and in particular on four outstanding settlers, one in each Quarter of the country. The account also includes a complete list of Lawspeakers from the time of the establishment of the *alþingi* in 930 A.D. as well as a list of bishops. Moreover, it is our first evidence for law codes being recorded. Also, *Íslendingabók* contains information on the political institutions of the country, the problems of calendar and the discovery of Greenland. Ari focuses more, however, on the consolidation of Christianity in Iceland,

---

[15] Torfi Tulinius (2000: 260) thinks that the rise of fiction in early thirteenth-century Iceland can be linked to a crisis in identity.

[16] See Einar Arnórsson's (1942) monograph for a complete background on Ari *inn fróði*.

which is perhaps not surprising given that he himself was a man of clerical education.

Ari is very conscientious in his citation of sources and the text appears to have been written with considerable care, scrupulously choosing the most knowledgeable and reliable informants known to the author and openly acknowledging them as authorities for this or that part of the narrative. Ari is preoccupied with the chronology of events and firmly establishes dates by relating them to the life of a known individual as well as to the birth of Christ. He appears to be trying to impress his readership not by citing great names, but by selecting informants whose truthfulness and long memories were beyond doubt. Although 250 years separate writing from the starting point of Icelandic history, there is general agreement that Ari's work is in some sense the official line, not least because it was written under the supervision of two bishops and the learned priest Sæmundr Sigfússon, himself a historian (Meulengracht Sørensen, 1993: 1). Throughout this study I shall refer to *Íslendingabók* as an important source of information about particular aspects of an Icelandic identity.

It is significant that Ari chose not to write in Latin, the language of learned men throughout Christendom. As Jónas Kristjánsson (1988: 121) notes, 'this is all the more surprising since Sæmundr the Wise, one of Ari's mentors and supervisors, had himself apparently written in Latin on one of the subjects included in the first edition of *Íslendingabók*, the lives of the kings of Norway'. Ari was probably the first to write in the vernacular, Icelandic, and the first to write on Icelandic historiography. This tells us that early on Icelanders had a sense of historical reflection, and that they wanted to express it using their own language. Whaley (2000: 162) believes that the value placed on historical knowledge is clear from the fact that many of the greatest scholars of early Iceland were distinguished by the honorific nickname *inn fróði* 'the wise, learned'. Ari was working within a scholarly tradition which had embraced the vernacular as the medium for the dissemination of works in Iceland.

Another important document which is evidence of a historical consciousness is *Landnámabók*, the 'Book of Settlements'. *Landnámabók* has been connected with Ari, and it is not improbable that his genealogical works provided information about the preceding generations, without which the compilers of *Landnámabók* could not have produced such a comprehensive account.[17] The original version is now lost, but its existence is vouched for by the law-man Haukr Erlendsson who compiled his own version.

Landnámabók is preserved in a number of recensions. From the thirteenth century we know of a version of *Landnámabók*, compiled by Styrmir

---

[17] The Prologue to the second edition indicates that originally *Íslendingabók* contained genealogical material.

Kárason who died in 1245 A.D. and who was the prior of the monastery at Viðey. The *Sturlubók* version (preserved in AM 107 fol., a copy from the seventeenth century of a later lost vellum MS) is thought to have been written in approximately 1275–80 A.D. because it was compiled late in life by Sturla Þórðarson who died in 1284 A.D. The *Melabók* (of which only a short fragment is preserved in a MS from around 1400 A.D., AM 445b 4to) and *Hauksbók* versions (AM 371 4to) are believed to date to shortly after 1300 A.D. Two early modern recensions are those by Björn Jónsson of Skarðsá known as *Skarðsárbók* (before 1655 A.D., preserved in AM 104 fol.) and *Þórðarbók* (preserved in AM 106 and 112 fol.) by Þórður Jónsson of Hítardalur who died in 1670 A.D. The former is a conflation of *Sturlubók* and *Hauksbók*. The latter followed *Skarðsárbók* but Þórður also knew *Melabók* in a better condition than it is in now and he sometimes includes material from it – invaluable information about a source that is otherwise lost.

Landnámabók is primarily an account of the genealogies and the origins of the first 415 independent settlers.[18] Collectively, the different versions of *Landnámabók* mention 1,500 farm and place-names as well as more than 3,500 people (Jakob Benediktsson, 1993: 374). The material is arranged geographically (a systematic circular survey) and apparently gives a complete picture of the whole country. Men and women are named, along with an account of their homesteads and the boundaries of their settlements, but *Landnámabók* seldom more than hints at how the society may have functioned. The textual transmission of *Landnámabók* does, however, testify to a continuing interest in the settlements among Icelanders of later centuries. There has been a great deal of discussion as to how much one should rely on an account that was written so long after the Settlement and that exists in so many different extant manuscripts. Some of the entries may indeed be questioned, but it is generally considered that names and lines of descent from settlers are probably reliable on the whole. The pedigrees of the settlers themselves are another matter – they are often traced to great men of the dim and distant past. As Whaley (2000: 174) notes, the two works, *Íslendingabók* and *Landnámabók* are to an extent complementary: *Íslendingabók* is concerned with the Icelanders as a nation, and *Landnámabók* with families and individuals.[19]

It should be noted that the archaeological evidence for the dating of the Settlement supports the written sources almost exactly. Archaeologists have examined volcanic tephra (ash) layers found in the turfs used to construct early settlements in Iceland. On the basis of radiocarbon dating, they have

---

[18] There is disagreement on the precise number of settlers mentioned in *Landnámabók*, with scholars relying on different versions of the work. Bogi Th. Melsteð (1916: 47) puts the number at 417 for instance.

[19] Whaley (2000: 174) observes that in the title, *Landnáma* is plural and thus it is an aggregation of local and family histories.

dated the Settlement to 871 A.D plus or minus two years (Dugmore, Church *et al*, 2005: 23–4).[20] Such a conclusion must give us confidence in Ari's chronicles.

The Settlement is also documented in two Norwegian historical texts, both written in Latin. *Historia de antiquitate regum Norwagiensium* was written by Theodoricus monachus in approximately 1180 A.D. While the author of *Historia Norwegiæ* is not known, he is thought to have been active in the last part of the twelfth century (Magerøy, 1965: 9). According to Santini (1993: 284), the text of the *Historia Norwegiæ* is much older than the age of the MS: 'a reference to a volcanic earthquake and eruption as contemporaneous suggests 1211 A.D. as a *terminus a quo*'. Both of these works support the view expressed by Ari in *Íslendingabók* that Iceland was settled by Norwegians in the time of Haraldr *inn hárfagri*. *Historia Norwegiæ* is manifestly Norwegian and states that the settlers had to flee Norway because they had committed murder (*ob reatus homicidiorum patriam fugientes, Historia Norwegiæ*: 92–3).

Apart from the above-mentioned narrative histories there are also various sets of diplomas and charters that are referred to. Reference is made principally to *Diplomatarium Islandicum* and *Diplomatarium Norvegicum* which are scholarly collections of documents, letters, contracts, church inventories and other writings. The evidence of the diplomas adds to the picture of the Icelandic society as rendered by other sources. I use the diplomas therefore as a supplementary source in various contexts. Unlike Sweden and Denmark where diplomas were only written in the vernacular from the fourteenth century onwards, the Icelandic diplomas were written in what became Icelandic from about the year 1200 A.D. (Magerøy, 1993b: 137–8).

1.6.2 *Religious works*

In addition to historical texts, there are a small number of religious works that are of relevance primarily because they were written very early. *Hungrvaka* ('the Appetizer') is an account of the lives of the first five bishops of Skálholt, written between 1198 and 1211 A.D. The text survives in six seventeenth-century transcripts and later copies of these. The primary MS represents three versions: (1) AM 380 4to, AM 379 4to (B); (2) AM 205 fol., AM 375 4to, AM 378 4to (C); (3) AM 110 8vo (D). It is thought that none of these preserves the medieval original (Bibire, 1993: 307).

Religious writings were translated and composed in both Iceland *and* Norway at an early stage. For the purpose of this piece of research, the two principal collections of Old West Norse sermons, Stock. Perg. 4to no. 15 (the 'Stockholm or 'Old Icelandic Homily Book') and AM 619 4to (the 'Old

---

[20] Grönvold *et al* (1995: 149–55) provide a full archaeological analysis of the data.

Norwegian Homily Book'), are relevant because they were both written in approximately 1200 A.D, but in Iceland and Norway independently (or at least so it would seem). Two of the sermons included in these collections are preserved in what is perhaps the oldest Icelandic MS fragment, AM 237a fol., written around 1150 A.D. and itself probably a remnant of a homiliary of considerable size.

Whole and partial sources have been identified for a number of the texts, however, and some of the homilies appear to have a Latin background and are sometimes close translations of Latin homilies, albeit often adapted to a local setting. From the point of view of language and identity, these sermons would be of more interest had they represented original work in the vernacular. A number of the sermons are also thought to be copies of copies. For these reasons, they do not constitute a major source.

1.6.3 Law codes

In *Íslendingabók* (*Íf* Ii, 23), Ari says that at the *alþingi* of 1117 A.D. the legislators took the novel decision to have the laws written down in a book. This is the first certain writing in Iceland that we know about, although it is commonly assumed that a tithe law, introduced on the initiative of Bishop Gizurr Ísleifsson a little before 1100 A.D., was also written down immediately (Orri Vésteinsson, 2000: 11). The name covering all the laws is *Grágás* 'grey goose' – we do not know for sure why it was called such and the name does not occur before the sixteenth century.

Grágás is not a unified corpus of law; the name applies to some 130 codices, fragments and copies made during the centuries. The legal texts must be understood in their fragmentary form: a text transmitted in manuscript fluctuates with alterations, omissions, and additional material added and copied from generation to generation. However, it is considered the main source of Icelandic laws for the period preceding the submission to the Norwegian king. The two principal MS that contain *Grágás* are GkS 1157 fol., usually named *Konungsbók* or Codex Regius, which is kept in the Danish Royal Library, and AM 334 fol., named *Staðarhólsbók*, after a farm in the west of Iceland. The first is believed to have been written about 1260 A.D., the second about 1280 A.D.: both manuscripts are therefore more than a century younger than the original text(s) which we no longer have (Dennis, Foote & Perkins, 1980: 13–14). We do not know who wrote these manuscripts or for whom.

The manuscripts are different in their arrangement and contents: *Staðarhólsbók* lacks a number of sections that are in *Konungsbók* including the sections on assembly procedures, homicide, the Law Council and the Lawspeaker, truce and peace speeches, inheritance, incapable persons, betrothal, duties of communes, tithes and the so-called *baugatal* 'wergild ring list', an atonement payable in killing cases. Certain sections and paragraphs can be found in both codices, others in only one. Despite variations between the known versions of *Grágás*, they show a marked degree of systematic coherence. It is this systematic quality which enables us to use it as one of the most important sources for Icelandic society in its early days. Throughout this work we shall discuss particular parts of *Grágás* as they relate to the topics under consideration, as well as referring to the nature of 'law' in relation to society in more general terms.

Grágás differs in certain respects from the oldest Norwegian laws that we have. As Fix (1993: 235) notes, it is much more detailed, showing less alliteration and fewer picturesque and proverbial expressions than its early continental Scandinavian counterparts.[21] *Grágás* represents the law of the twelfth century basically in the form that was recited by the Lawspeaker. The oldest Norwegian laws stem from the four principal law-provinces of Norway: Frostaþing (chiefly Trøndelag and regions north of there), Gulaþing (west-coast Norway), Eiðsifaþing (south-central Norway) and Borgarþing (the Oslofjord region). These regional laws are compiled in *Norges gamle love* and reference is made in particular to *Gulaþingslög*. The oldest manuscript of the *Gulaþingslög* is DonVar 137 4° (Codex Rantzovianus), dated c. 1250–1300 A.D. Thirteenth-century manuscripts of the laws of the *Frostaþingslög* survive only in fragmentary form, and the earliest complete manuscript of the laws dates from the beginning of the eighteenth century. Manuscripts of the other Norwegian provincial law-books are from the fourteenth century (Boulhosa, 2005: 54–55).

In the 1260s King Magnús of Norway first had the laws of each province revised separately, but none of these revisions is now extant in its regional form. Following the Icelanders' submission to the Norwegian Crown in 1262–64 A.D., King Magnús *lagabætir* (the 'law-mender') then sent a new law-book to Iceland, known as *Járnsíða* ('Iron-sides'), doubtless because iron was a feature of the binding.[22] The text is believed to have been based on the last revision of *Frostaþingslög* (Jacoby, 1986: 224), although some sections were derived from the old native laws of Iceland.

Járnsíða, contained in *Staðarhólsbók*, met with opposition at the *alþingi* of 1271 A.D., chiefly because it often departed from Icelandic legal custom. It was replaced by *Jónsbók* (named after the Lawspeaker Jón Einarsson who brought the law code from Norway to Iceland in 1280 A.D.): a law-book that became over time extremely popular and highly regarded. We do not have the original MS, but some 260 copies are preserved. In fact, the work was read and copied more often than any other in medieval Iceland – and for centuries afterwards too. It was common for children to learn to read from *Jónsbók* (Jónas Kristjánsson, 1988: 367) and they thus came to

---

[21] Erhardt (1977) shows that alliteration in the Icelandic laws is almost non-existent.

[22] Legislative and organisational work characterised Magnús Hákonarson's reign and secured him the name *lagabætir* ('law-mender'). He became king in 1257 A.D., and ruled together with his father until Hákon died in 1263 A.D.

know it almost by heart. For this reason, it is thought to have had much influence on the preservation of the Icelandic language. The ten sections of *Jónsbók* deal with assembly attendance, Church and king, allegiance to the king, sanctuary and peace, marriage and inheritance, land claims, land rents, contracts, nautical law and theft. Although it is only half the size of *Grágás*, the section on inheritance rights is much more detailed. *Jónsbók* was among the first books to be printed in Iceland (Hólar, 1578). Even today, some parts of this medieval law code remain in full force, primarily agricultural rights and the rights over the foreshore.[23]

Since the focus is early Iceland, my interest is predominantly the earliest legal codes. Reference is made on a number of occasions, however, to *Jónsbók* in order to determine how or whether Norwegian legal terminology was used in Iceland after 1262–4 A.D.

1.6.4 *Grammatical Treatises*

The First Grammatical Treatise, written in approximately 1150 A.D., is the only 'grammatical work' in a native (non-Latin) language of the period, and is unique for the time in which it was written. In addition to the First Grammatical Treatise, there are three other so-called grammatical treatises and a Prologue which are transmitted in only one MS, AM 242 fol. (from the second half of the fourteenth century), better known as the Codex Wormianus of Snorri's *Edda*.[24] None of the treatises bore a name and so they were simply named according to their succession in the Codex Wormianus. The Third Grammatical Treatise is the only one with a known author, Óláfr Þórðarson, the famous skald and Snorri Sturluson's nephew. The First Grammatical Treatise is by far the most widely referenced of the four 'treatises' and its author is referred to as the First Grammarian.

The First Grammatical Treatise may be viewed as an early attempt to establish a firm and unambiguous orthographic norm by adapting the Latin alphabet to the actual needs of the Icelandic language. Yet the author went far beyond this practical aim, attaining results in the method of phonological analysis that were extraordinary for the time. In order to explain his proposals he gives a precise description of the sound system as it was in his day, so precise indeed that it has been said that, following his instructions, we can accurately reproduce all the sounds of twelfth-century Icelandic. The First Grammarian identified in a thoroughly scientific manner what would today be called the phonemes of the Icelandic language, using minimal pairs to distinguish

---

[23] This law code and the new laws (*réttarbætr*) enacted in 1294, 1305, 1306 and 1314 A.D. provided the main sources for Icelandic civil legislation over the next four hundred years.

[24] See Section 1.6.5 for a discussion of Snorri's *Edda*. The inclusion of Snorri's *Edda* in the manuscript containing the grammatical treatises points to the fact that the Icelanders used to associate them with this work and consequently with the theory of Old Norse versification; cf. Guðrún Nordal (2001: 19–40).

between sounds and to demonstrate the inadequacy of the Latin alphabet for expressing the sounds of Icelandic. In the words of Haugen (1976: 197), the First Grammatical Treatise 'bears witness not only to the high level of scholastic learning in Iceland, but also to an intense interest in the problems of the native language which has persisted down to the present'. If Ari's history of the Icelanders may be said to have created the 'Icelanders', then the First Grammarian's work must be given credit for having created the 'Icelandic' language – as a specific branch of *dönsk tunga*.

There is disagreement amongst scholars as to the aim of the Second Grammatical Treatise. Its intention might have been to reorganise and rationalise an orthographic practice that, since the introduction of writing into Iceland, had become increasingly inconsistent and confused. Raschellà (1982: 9) concludes that 'the treatise must [...] be considered in all respects a grammatical, or more precisely, an orthographic work', cf. Finnur Jónsson (1898: 327–8). Or it could be considered as a sort of linguistic introduction to the *Háttatal*, the part of Snorri's *Edda* that is concerned with types and structure of metres (see Section 1.6.5). Braunmüller (1983: 43) criticises Raschellà's (1982) interpretation of the Second Grammatical Treatise suggesting that even though there is no direct reference to metre in it, the treatise should be interpreted with reference to Snorri Sturluson's *Háttatal* in the manuscript.

The Third Grammatical Treatise was written in approximately 1250 A.D. and is the most comprehensive of the four. The work is divided into two main sections: the first part is Óláfr's adaptation of Priscian's *Institutiones* and the second is Óláfr's translation of Donatus' book 3 of *Ars maior*, and devoted entirely to the exposition of the principal figures of speech, thoroughly in line with the tenets of classical rhetoric, but fully illustrated by examples from Old Norse poetry. The content of the Fourth Grammatical Treatise is similar to that of the second part of the Third Grammatical Treatise.

1.6.5 *Poetry*

Guðrún Nordal (2001) and Clunies Ross (2005: 141–206) have discussed in detail the relationship between the *grammatica* (the four grammatical treatises), Snorri's *Edda* and skaldic verse in a society that otherwise did not leave much evidence regarding its educational system. According to Guðrún (2001: 42), the fact that that the four grammatical treatises are preserved in manuscripts in conjunction with *Snorra Edda* modifies and even dictates the way we interpret individual versions of the works. It is also likely that the *Háttatal* section of *Snorra Edda* influenced for instance the Third and the Fourth Grammatical Treatises.[25]

---

[25] See Faulkes (1991: x–xxviii): the Fourth Grammatical Treatise quotes from *Háttatal* quite extensively and uses much of its terminology.

Snorra Edda or Snorri Sturluson's *Edda* is sometimes called the Prose or Younger *Edda* to distinguish it from the Poetic or Elder *Edda*, which was formerly known as *Sæmundr's Edda*. *Snorra Edda* is without doubt the most important Old Norse contribution to medieval Scandinavian mythology and poetics. Snorri Sturluson (1174–1241 A.D.) was one of the wealthiest and most prominent Icelanders of his day. His authorship of a history of the kings of Norway, *Heimskringla*, is generally accepted and some regard him as the author of *Egils saga Skalla-Grímssonar*.

Snorra Edda consists, aside from the Prologue, of three main parts: *Gylfaginning* ('the tricking of Gylfi'), *Skáldskaparmál* and *Háttatal*. It was probably composed in stages from c. 1221 A.D onwards (Clunies Ross, 2005: 160). Beginning with an account of how mankind forgot about their creator and began to worship nature, the Prologue places the account of Scandinavian myth in *Gylfaginning* in 'the universal context of Christian cosmography' (Clunies Ross, 1987: 10). *Gylfaginning* is a comprehensive Scandinavian mythography, where Snorri narrates the pagan myths in the form of a dialogue, a contest of wisdom between three of the newly arrived Æsir (etymologised as 'men of Asia', having migrated from Troy) and Gylfi, a king in Sweden, disguised as a beggar and calling himself 'Gangleri'. *Skáldskaparmál*, an *ars poetica*, is an attempt at systematising the poetic language or skaldic diction through its discussion of kennings, or periphrastic descriptions, *heiti* (poetic synonyms) and *fornafn* (a kind of kenning that replaces a proper name). The last part is *Háttatal* ('list of verse forms'): a work that was influenced by an earlier metrical work, *Háttalykill* ('key to verse forms'), a poem consisting of 41 double stanzas, each pair exemplifying a certain metre or formal distinction of a poetic verse.[26]

Háttatal itself consists of a poem, or rather a series of three poems, in 102 stanzas and in a variety of verse forms (although some of the variants are rhetorical rather than metrical). Composed by Snorri himself, it is accompanied by a prose commentary that explains the metres and devices used, such as rhyme and alliteration using Norse (and not Latin) terminology. *Háttatal* is a remarkable achievement of medieval scholarship, and combines analytical description in the prose passages with virtuosic poetic exemplification. *Háttalykill* shows that this development was under way by the middle of the twelfth century (Faulkes, 1991: xviii). Both *Skáldskaparmál* and *Háttatal* are of interest because they were written as guidelines for aspiring skalds, and the function of skaldic verse may provide the link between the emerging textual culture in Iceland in the twelfth century and the strong oral culture that coexisted in the country. The First Grammarian not only alludes openly to skaldic verse in the treatise, but

---

[26] Clunies Ross (2005: 155) believes that *Háttalykill* was composed in Orkney and can be dated to c. 1142 A.D.; Faulkes (1991: xiv) states that *Háttalykill* was written by Hallr Þórarinsson and Earl Rögnvaldr of Orkney in the 1140s.

also supports his elucidation of the orthography of the Icelandic language through the evidence of minimal pairs comparable to those known in the *skothendingar* ('inserted rhyme') and *aðalhendingar* ('full rhyme') of a skaldic stanza (Guðrún Nordal, 2001: 341).

Reference is made both to Eddaic and skaldic verse, albeit sparsely. A distinction can be drawn between the two genres: the authors of the Eddaic lays remain anonymous, their subject material is that of Norse mythology, Germanic heroic legend and didactic lore and they are written in a metre which is simpler than that used in skaldic verse.[27] In contrast to this, the names of both Norwegian and Icelandic skaldic poets are often known; the subject material is that of the poet's own times: skaldic poetry is often encomiastic and dedicated to some ruler or other. As Gade (2000: 71) notes, 'the custom of composing praise poetry in Old Norse society entailed an exchange of favours. The person eulogised would receive underlying fame, and, in return, the skald was rewarded with gifts, high social status and royal protection'. Skaldic verse makes comprehensive use of poetic words and circumlocutions and it is thought that the practitioners were keenly conscious of their mastery of the art. As Hallberg (1962: 11) puts it: 'the authors of skaldic verse often make a virtue of their endeavour to avoid the direct expression, a penchant that sometimes transforms their poems into veritable rebuses'.

It is worth noting that certain genres of poetry in early Iceland were considered to have an illocutionary effect. According to *Grágás* (Ib: 183), a man had no right to compose poetry of defamation or praise on anyone, and a section of the laws is devoted to the punishment for doing so. It would seem that the reason for this is that praising or blaming somebody required social sanction and needed to be measured and appropriate (Clunies Ross, 2005: 232). The fact that there were legal provisions for the composing of poetry in Iceland gives us an impression of a society where vernacular poetry had central status.

1.6.6 *Saga material*

The sagas are the outstanding literary achievement of the Icelanders. In the course of the thirteenth century close to a hundred sagas were composed, and the number of copies and reworkings was many times greater (Stefán Karlsson, 2000: 226). The context of this literary activity was a society which in 1311 A.D. was reckoned to comprise about 3,812 tax-paying households (*DI*, IV: 9–10). Manuscripts were not to be found at all farms, and only the larger among them produced literature themselves.

---

[27] The most common Eddaic metre, *fornyrðislag*, represents a tightening of the Germanic alliterative long line. The earliest attested skaldic metre, *dróttkvætt*, stylises the alliterating and metrical patterns of *fornyrðislag*, but it is also syllable-counting and mora-counting.

The majority of the references to the saga material refer to the so-called *Íslendingasögur* ('the Sagas of Icelanders'), written down in manuscript form in the thirteenth century. These sagas are so called because they refer to the first generations that inhabited Iceland from the Settlement to about 1030 A.D. There exist, however, several other familiar medieval genres also called sagas and occasional reference is made to these: the oldest Icelandic manuscripts containing prose narratives are the stories of the lives of saints translated or adapted from Latin; the Kings' sagas are historical biographies of Scandinavian kings; the Bishops' sagas are clerical biographies; the so-called *fornaldarsögur* are legendary heroic sagas and finally the *Sturlunga saga* describe the conflicts among Icelandic chieftains of the time.

The saga material has given rise to an enormous body of critical literature, but many of the fundamental problems remain unresolved: we do not know for sure when and where the sagas were written or who their authors were; nor can we be certain to what extent their content was factual or fictitious. The sagas' status as historical documents is much disputed. As always, the difficulty is in knowing how far one can claim the witness of the sagas as valid and historical evidence. This is the subject of a long drawn-out debate between saga scholars and it is not the place here to consider these arguments and different points of view in full.[28] These issues are far from resolved and they will undoubtedly continue to be discussed. In Old Icelandic, 'saga' referred to any narrative, historical or non-historical, oral or written. A saga was (and is) what 'is said' (the word saga being derived from the verb *segja*), especially about the past, and whether it represented 'historical truth' or 'artistic truth' was immaterial to the Icelandic mind.

Saga authors will remain nameless forever, but careful study of the sagas does give us some idea of the kind of society that early Iceland was. The reason for focusing on the *Íslendingasögur*, as opposed to the other saga material, is that it is these narratives which depict events that are said to have occurred in the period relevant to the present study, early Iceland. The sagas are not used extensively as 'evidence' in this work, and this is because of the nature of the information which they provide. The events in particular sagas cannot be taken as actual historical truth. The general picture of society provides, however, a truth about the patterns and conditions for social life in Iceland. The sagas are likely to have some basis in Icelandic social reality – such a unique literature could not have come out of nothing.

---

[28] Cf. Andersson (1964: 82–119) for a summary of the views of Sigurður Nordal and the so-called Icelandic school; Clover (1985: 241–45); Vésteinn Ólason (1992, 1998): in Vésteinn's view it was the time following the Icelanders' loss of so-called national independence in which the social energy behind the cultural symbolism of these texts mainly evolved.

The sagas portray the mechanisms of personal and social relationships in the context of a society that is struggling for survival. The saga material thus provides a good impression of the kind of social structures that existed at the local level with kinsmen forming groups in legal conflicts over land and livestock and 'neighbours' forming alliances or fostering feuds. The role of the law as a means of maintaining social order, securing reconciliation and re-establishing peace but also as a means of condoning blood vengeance is clearly important in a number of the *Íslendingasögur*. *Brennu-Njáls saga* contains sections of 'courtroom drama', quasi- or pseudo-legal content, very clearly marked out stylistically within the text. This saga represents a late thirteenth-century Icelander's idea of what legal language should 'sound like' – set in a contrasting context, so that one can measure the language against what is around it: the neutral, unmarked styles of normal saga-narrative.[29]

There are recurrent structural features in all the sagas. These reoccurring patterns give the impression that the saga material represents a very well-defined, coherent narrative type. A saga invariably begins with basic (and often genealogical) information about the main characters of the saga, rendered in a matter-of-fact tone. The main body of the saga is concerned principally with a conflict of some kind or another. The conflict often leads to the death of one of the protagonists, and this is usually avenged by legal procedures, blood vengeance or both. In a number of the sagas the end of the conflict is confirmed by reconciliation between the hostile parties.

The sagas are representations of society and social structures (albeit resolutely individualist and particular), and they are certainly unique. The Icelanders felt a strong imperative to write the sagas, and there was absolutely nothing similar elsewhere, even in Norway where Icelandic saga-production was appreciated (at least by some of the kings). They provide few reflections of linguistic identity, but in conjunction with the law codes they can perhaps provide information on the social identity of the Icelanders. It is reasonable to assume that there was a connection between the unique social aspects of Icelandic society (see Section 4.2.1) and the unique character of the saga literature that it produced. It is much more difficult, however, to know what the exact nature of this relationship was.[30]

---

[29] This could have been of course a parody of legal language and how the legal system worked.

[30] Vésteinn Ólason & Sverrir Tómasson (2006: 2) speculate on the relationship between early Iceland's 'unique' literature and 'unique' social structures: 'the social and ethical order in Iceland held freemen to a stringent code of heroic conduct [...] The heroic tenor of Icelandic society coexisted with a literary culture brought about by the church'.

2

LANGUAGE AND IDENTITY: THEORETICAL CONSIDERATIONS

2.1 INTRODUCTION

The objective of this chapter is to discuss the theoretical considerations relevant to a socio-historical linguistic study on language and identity. The intention is not to formulate a single, clearly defined theoretical framework. The discussion is instead exploratory in nature; it is recognised that there is no one pre-established identity model that can be applied to this particular context. By analysing a number of sociolinguistic theories and identity models, I will attempt to determine which are most applicable to Iceland at the time of the Settlement and thereafter. I will present a variety of theoretical perspectives and principles relating to language change and identity and assess the strengths and weaknesses of each. Not all the models and methods discussed in this chapter will be used directly in my subsequent analysis, but they will act as an aid in understanding and interpreting the issues relevant to the sociolinguistics of early Iceland.

There are a number of problems in applying sociolinguistic theory to distant historical periods. Current models were intended principally for the analysis of synchronic variable speech data, and not historical data which cannot be subjected to empirical testing. Focusing on textual evidence from a period in the distant past where there are no informants, we lack the relevant linguistic (spoken) information. This should, however, not preclude linguistics from socio-historical studies and should not prevent us from attempting to identify plausible sociolinguistic structures in early Iceland. By sociolinguistic structures, I mean the interaction between linguistic variation (if it exists) in a certain speech community and the relevant social structures where these linguistic variants come into contact with one another. Such a study needs to incorporate extra-linguistic evidence, data and theories in order to account for its linguistic facts. A study with this historical dimension inevitably implies a degree of very controlled speculation, but it will be shown that theoretical insights and previous studies are of use in examining the mechanisms of Iceland's sociolinguistic structures.

Most of the theories considered below are concerned with language and its status as a social phenomenon. The notions of identity and group-membership are of particular importance. The chapter begins with a general discussion on socio-historical linguistics and sociolinguistic theory, before considering briefly the causes of language change. In Section 2.3, linguistic norms and language change are discussed. It has been observed that linguistic norms are part of the language change process, and that new linguistic norms tend to emerge as social networks are formed. The focus of the chapter then shifts to dialect contact phenomena such as dialect levelling and koineisation. These topics form the subject matter of Section 2.4.1.

One of the aims of the chapter is to gain a better understanding of the inverse and problematic issue of language development and language isolation. Language and dialect isolation are discussed in Section 2.5. The notion of 'drift' is relevant to Section 2.5 because it serves as an alternative model of language development in the *absence* of contact. The processes of language development, new-dialect formation and identity construction in *tabula rasa* societies remain poorly understood. A number of theoretical perspectives on these issues will be considered in Section 2.6. A socio-historical linguistic analysis of Iceland whose focus is on extra-linguistic factors such as speech community types, social contact models and settlement patterns can contribute to this discussion.[1] It will be shown that accommodation and network models are of special theoretical importance to language and identity, and consideration is given here to how networks formed in early Iceland. Social network theory and language change are the subject matter of Section 2.8.3. Prior to this, a selection of issues relating to place and identity are discussed in Section 2.7.2.

2.2 SOCIO-HISTORICAL LINGUISTICS AND SOCIOLINGUISTIC THEORY

There is at present no all-embracing and complete sociolinguistic theory, and the diversity of social processes researched within sociolinguistics suggests that not only a unified theory does not exist, but that it should not. Although there is an absence of a unified theory, the sub-field of socio-historical linguistics (also known as historical sociolinguistics) is a burgeoning one with a number of recent publications including the forthcoming *Handbook of Historical Sociolinguistics*.[2] Socio-historical linguistics is increasingly concerned with issues ranging from historical dialectology and historical norm-establishment to language contact and language attitudes from a socio-historical perspective. According to Romaine (2005: 1697), 'the main methodological task of socio-historical

---

[1] The term 'speech community' is used and defined in a number of different contexts. Cf. Labov (1972); Hymes (1972: 269–94); Gumperz (1977: 219–30). Here it refers simply to a group of people that communicate, socially interact with one another and share linguistic (and social) norms, see Section 2.3.

[2] Romaine (1982) and Milroy (1992) respectively use these two terms. Nevalainen & Raumolin-Brunberg (1996: 5–7) discuss the usage of these terms.

linguistics is to develop a set of procedures for the reconstruction of language in its social context and to use the findings of sociolinguistics as controls in the process of reconstruction and as a means of informing theories of change'.[3]

The nature of the data means that the field is not restricted to traditional variationist sociolinguistics, but seeks to answer interdisciplinary questions. This contrasts with the majority of sociolinguistic studies whose concern is the present and theoretical, correlative linguistics. The sociolinguistic theories upon which these studies are based are not, however, always suitable for socio-historical linguistic research – the emphasis is typically on linguistic variation within the framework of a quantitative model (cf. Fishman, 1972; Romaine, 1982: 1–14; Romaine & Traugott, 1985; Cameron, 1990: 83; Milroy, 1992).

The most relevant models to this study are those that consider both language *and* society and that combine aspects of both macro- and micro-sociolinguistic theories. The macro-/micro- distinction is well established in all scientific studies of society: macro-social factors are those at the level of large-scale social constructs; micro-social factors are those that pertain to the individual in a social context. With the case of early Iceland, we should be looking at macro-social factors because linguistic information for individuals and small groups is not available for the relevant period.

The table below (Table 1), adapted from Nevalainen & Raumolin-Brunberg (2003: 18), introduces three major paradigms in sociolinguistics, the sociology of language (Fishman, 1972), social dialectology (Weinreich, Labov & Herzog, 1968: 95–188) and interactional sociolinguistics (Gumperz, 1982). These paradigms cannot be defined unambiguously.

It is possible in this study to research questions concerning the sociology of language because our data allow us to study the status and functions of the Norse language and its norms. A small number of the questions relating to social dialectology can also be addressed, with the aid of historical and archaeological data. Interactional sociolinguistics typically requires, however, more information about individual usage and discourse patterns, and for our period that is not available. The *modus operandi* adopted here is therefore one that considers aspects of these various paradigms in a non-discourse context, whilst recognising that certain questions relating to identity go beyond any strict sociolinguistic paradigm.

---

[3] Cf. Milroy (1992: 222) who emphasizes the link between social change and linguistic change, and argues that the primary task of historical sociolinguistics is the establishment of explicit causal links between these two domains. Bergs (2005: 12–13) notes that a socio-historical linguistic analysis may help us understand the present, just as linguistic analyses of the present are used to reconstruct the linguistic past.

Table 1. Three paradigms in sociolinguistics

Paradigm/ Dimension	Sociology of Language	Social Dialectology	Interactional Sociolinguistics
• Object of study	• status and function of languages and language varieties in speech communities	• variation in grammar and phonology • linguistic variation in discourse • speaker attitudes	• interactive construction and organisation of discourse
• Describing	• the norms and patterns of language use in domain-specific conditions	• the linguistic system in relation to external factors	• co-operative rules for organisation of discourse
• Explaining	• differences of and changes in status and function of languages and language varieties	• social dynamics of language varieties in speech communities • language change	• communicative competence: verbal and non-verbal input in goal-orientated interaction

2.3 LANGUAGE CHANGE AND NORMS

As well as using the relevant sociolinguistic models, a socio-historical linguistic study needs to consider some of the difficulties of reconstructing language development in the distant past. Amongst the most important and fundamental questions is the problem of trying to determine the causes and mechanisms which lie behind language change. The sociolinguistic approach to language change adopted here 'embeds' it firmly in the community of speakers: it can only be fully understood with reference to the structure of the society in which the language is used.

In addition to endorsing the 'embedding' approach, it is also recognised that the processes of linguistic change are 'multi-causality' phenomena; that language change can be observed in action and that it follows certain trends.[4] Osgood & Sebeok (1954: 155) (Paul, 1880: 62) discussed the 'conformity hypothesis' at the end of the nineteenth century: the rate of change is slow at first, appearing in the speech of innovators, or more likely young children, becomes relatively rapid as these young people become the agents of differential reinforcement; and tapers off as fewer and fewer older individuals remain to continue the older forms. Both intra-linguistic *and* extra-linguistic solutions have been proposed to the problem of under-standing these trends in language change. The reason for society's preference for a certain linguistic innovation may be system-internal – one of the

---

[4] Cf. Labov (1966); Giles & Powesland (1975); Milroy (1980); Giles & Coupland (1991). Chen (1972: 457–98) speaks of the S-curve model of sound change.

variants may be more economical than the other – but often such preferences are social in origin, reflecting the chance adoption of a particular variant as a symbol of group identity. Extra-linguistic factors may include social relations between the borrowing group and the group it is borrowing from; time scale and intensity of contact; the role of adults and children in language contact as well as the question of whether contact results in language shift or borrowing. Language change has also been shown to be a function of social awareness: 'changes from above' *versus* 'changes from below' (Labov, 1982: 224–26). The primary motivations for language change below the level of conscious awareness of any speaker are local identity and status (Labov, 1963: 273–309).

As indicated, one of the principal difficulties in examining language change in the distant past is that there is a lack of data. In this regard, one has to invoke the Uniformitarian Principle. The Uniformitarian Principle states that the 'knowledge of processes that operated in the past can be inferred by ongoing processes in the present' (Christy, 1983: ix) (cf. Whitney, 1867: 253; Labov, 1994: 22; Farrar & Jones, 2002: 7). Applying, however, linguistic models that are concerned with contemporary societies to tenth-century Iceland is problematic (koineisation and network studies are frequently based on urban communities for instance). One is restricted to these models, but they are concerned with 'different' societies. The Uniformitarian Principle needs to be applied, but not unconditionally. However, the use of the present to explain the past is perhaps more applicable to Icelandic than other languages because Icelandic is a low-contact language. The linguistic present is thus quite literally more like the past than in other languages. In the case of extra-linguistic factors, many important cultural changes have occurred that have arguably altered social factors and their potential impact such as the spread of mass media. These issues are less of a problem for a small society such as Iceland where sociolinguistic structures (in the absence of urbanisation) were largely unchanged until the twentieth century. As Stefán Karlsson (1999: 139) notes: 'The sparse and scattered population of Iceland and the lack of any significant urbanisation until the present century have meant that there have been no influential centres for linguistic innovations'.

Labov (1972: 121) has argued that a key criterion for determining the boundaries of a speech community and its sociolinguistic structures is the existence of a shared system of language norms, as reflected both in overt language attitudes and abstract patterns of linguistic variation associated with different contextual styles.[5] When common values come into existence, are shared, diffused and internalised, they are described as norms. Norms

---

[5] Cf. Haugen (1966: 931) and Mæhlum *et al* (2003: 87) where a norm is defined as a model of social behaviour for a certain group. Norms are maintained with reference to a group that may lie beyond one's normal social networks and may have a certain prestige.

are relevant to this study because they serve to indicate group identity: 'From the point of view of group identity, adherence to the norms is watched closely, much more than would be necessary for the mere functioning of a language as a means of communication' (Bartsch, 1987: 87). It has also been observed that linguistic and cultural norms are in the front line of linguistic change (Coseriu, 1974: 119). One reason for this is that new social and linguistic norms arise as reciprocal accommodation between speakers of mutually intelligible varieties accompanies the emergence of closer-knit networks (Tuten, 2003: 29, 53–4). Tuten (2003: 53) claims that 'new norms can *only* be created as new social networks crystallize' [my italics]. These new social networks are likely to be formed by individuals in a new society in order to meet basic problem-solving needs.

Norms may be abstractions, but they are based on dominant patterns of behaviour and speakers are aware of them. As Milroy (1992: 83) notes, 'there would be little point in having these different norms if they did not carry social meaning, distinguishing between one community and another and carrying a sense of community identity for speakers'. Milroy (1980) shows that the mechanism which allows the conservation of an identity and set of norms is the close-knit social network.

2.3.1 Intra-linguistic versus extra-linguistic explanations of language change

As mentioned above, a fundamental issue in linguistics is the problem of intra-linguistic *versus* extra-linguistic explanations of language change (cf. Milroy, 1993: 220; McMahon, 1994: 13; Lass, 1997: 386; Croft, 2000: 6; Milroy, 2003: 161). It is reasonable to ask whether the dichotomy is valid.[6] Farrar & Jones (2002: 3) note that it is often difficult to distinguish between different types of motivating factors – and even if this were possible, many now debate whether such a distinction is, in fact, a useful one. Milroy (2003: 161) observes for example that the effect of social network structure on the trajectories of linguistic changes is explicable with reference to the local social structure, but also to global psychological constraints. The interrelationship between social and psycholinguistic influences renders problematic a straightforward distinction between so-called 'internal' and 'external' determinants of linguistic change.

The approach that is adopted in this study is that language change, although triggered internally, is dependent on social relations for its spread and is therefore motivated externally. Language change in early Iceland and thereafter can only be understood with reference to the sociolinguistic structures and linguistic norms that emerged at this time.

---

[6] Weinreich (1968); Andersen (1989: 5–29); Milroy (1992); Mæhlum (1999) all address this question.

2.4 LANGUAGE AND DIALECT CONTACT

Linguistic norms in early Iceland came into being in a context of dialect contact and *not* language contact: the distinction between language and dialect contact is therefore fundamental. In accordance with Trudgill (1994: 13), dialect contact is defined as involving mutually intelligible varieties, while language contact is concerned with non-mutually intelligible varieties.[7] It is recognised that mutual intelligibility is a matter of degree, and complications such as whether Swedish and Norwegian have dialect or language status are disregarded here.

As for the notion of a dialect, the most satisfactory definition for our purposes may be simply a language variety which is used in a geographically limited area.[8] Auer, Hinskens & Kerswill (2005: 1) define a dialect as 'a language variety which is used in a geographically limited part of a language area in which it is 'roofed' by a structurally related standard variety'. Norse at the time of the Settlement was probably a dialect continuum: a range of dialects spoken across a large geographical area, differing only slightly between areas that are geographically close, and decreasing in mutual intelligibility as the distances become greater (cf. Mæhlum *et al*, 2003: 18–22).

Dialect contact and language change are fundamental here because it is recognised that language development in a new speech community cannot happen in a social vacuum. The assumption of an idealised, autonomous speech community free from the complicating effects of contact is in fact problematic. As Milroy (2003: 158) states, it is often unrealistic to treat speech communities as isolated from the effects of others. Labov (2001: 19) appears to recognise that a large part of the problem of explaining the diffusion of linguistic change is reduced to a simple calculation. It is purely a matter of who interacts most often with whom – a matter of 'density of communication'.[9] Density of communication is an important, but difficult issue in Settlement Iceland where the data are lacking. It is clear that a settlement pattern of isolated farmsteads suggests less contact than one where there is evidence of villages and more nucleated settlements. The processes of co-ordinating food supplies and agreeing on boundaries and place-names are, however, likely to have required a degree of communication.

---

[7] Weinreich (1968); Thomason & Kaufman (1988); Sebba (1997) and Thomason (2001) discuss 'language contact'.

[8] It is difficult to speak in terms of sociolects in early Iceland.

[9] Cf. Bloomfield's (1933: 476) notion of 'density' which appears to encompass the concepts of accommodation and networks: 'Every speaker is constantly adapting his speech habits to those of his interlocutors [...] The inhabitants of a settlement, village, or town, however, talk much more to each other than to persons who live elsewhere'.

When speaking of the 'density of communication', one is principally concerned with dialect contact: the issue of language contact here is limited to the problem of Norse–Celtic linguistic relations. With regard to dialect contact, Lass (1990: 245–80) makes a useful distinction between intra- and extra-territorial dialect contact. Intra-territorial dialect contact involves relocation of people from different regions to a new area within the same country, and typically occurs as a result of increasing urbanisation. Extra-territorial contact involves the transplantation of dialects to a new setting altogether, most usually as a result of colonialism or emigration. Recent sociolinguistic research has tended to focus on intra-territorial dialect contact. In the case of Iceland in the tenth century, we are, however, clearly concerned with extra-territorial dialect contact.

2.4.1 *Dialect levelling and koineisation*

The issues of dialect levelling and koineisation are especially relevant to this piece of research. According to Hinskens (1996: 12), dialect levelling is a case of language change involving a 'reduction' in inter- and intra-systemic structural variation. On this basis, the levelling of features may occur between users of one and the same dialect as well as between speakers of different dialects. Dialect levelling is understood to be a dialect contact phenomenon that is concerned with the reduction of 'marked' forms when dialects mix. 'Marked' here refers to forms that are unusual or in a minority. Levelling in this sense is closely related to the social psychological mechanism of speech accommodation (Kerswill, 2003: 224). In practice, this tends to mean a decrease in irregularity in morphology and an increase in invariable word forms, as well as the loss of categories such as gender, the loss of case marking, simplified morphophonemics (paradigmatic levelling), and a decrease in the number of phonemes. These are morphosyntactic phenomena that have typological aspects. Markedness is often discussed in terms of 'simplification'. A concrete example of simplification in a dialect levelling context is the loss of distinct suffixes for the first and second persons singular and plural and the failure to adopt the gender distinction in the second person in Bhojpuri (Kerswill, 2002b: 677). The process results in dissimilar varieties growing more similar and often takes place in contexts of migration, urbanisation, formation of new towns and other population movements.

Milroy (2003: 158) notes that in a levelling process there is a tendency for localised norms of the kind supported by a close-knit network structure to disappear. Auer, Hinskens & Kerswill (2005: 11) also discuss dialect levelling and structural homogeneity: 'dialect levelling, the process which reduces variation both within and between dialects, is structural dialect loss' [...] Dialect levelling makes (a) individual dialects more homogenous, and

(b) different dialects more similar and, consequently diasystems more homogenous'.[10] This definition is noteworthy for this study because the dialectal homogeneity of Icelandic became subsequently an identity factor in itself. Jakobson ([1929] 1962: 82) observed that dialects which serve as vehicles of communication in large areas and gravitate towards the role of koine tend to develop simpler systems than dialects that serve purely local purposes. Since one dialect came to serve the whole of Iceland, that might suggest that the dialect that became Icelandic should have a relatively simple phonological system.

Whilst scholars often choose to distinguish between dialect levelling and koineisation, dialect levelling is best considered as the first stage of the koineisation process.[11] Auer, Hinskens & Kerswill (2005: 11) take koineisation to imply simplification and reduction, but this occurs in the levelling process when 'marked' features are reduced. Koineisation is a contact-induced process that leads to quite rapid change. Tuten (2003: 67) puts the timescale for the first stage of koineisation in medieval Spanish from approximately 1291 A.D. to 1374 A.D. It takes typically two to three generations to complete, but is achievable within one. The kind and level of social integration of the new community affects the speed of koineisation.

According to Kerswill (2002b: 669–703), continued immigration seems to have, however, only a minor inhibitory effect on the speed of the koineisation process – as long as, crucially, there is a stable 'core' of speakers who remain after the initial settlement who can act as a focus for newcomers, as in Mufwene's (2001) 'Founder Principle'. Importantly, koine formation requires intimate and prolonged social interaction between speakers.[12] For a koine to form, the speakers must waive their previous allegiances and social divisions to show mutual solidarity. Ross (1997: 236) believes that the koineisation process may be triggered by a radical realignment of a social network (perhaps due to social upheaval).

Koineisation is often discussed in terms of new-dialect formation (Trudgill, 1998: 1–11; 2004: 89–113; Trudgill et al, 2000: 299–318) and Trudgill has argued that the process of new-dialect formation takes place in three stages. On the basis of Trudgill's theory (2004: 89–113), the first stage in the context of levelling of the dialect spoken in Iceland was the initial contact and mixing between adult speakers of different regional and social varieties at assembly points in Norway/British Isles, on the boat journey out, and early on in the new location. According to Trudgill, such a

---

[10] Cf. Bloomfield (1933: 476) who discusses the notion in terms of the 'loaning' of features between dialects, Weinreich (1954: 396), Dillard (1972, quoted in Siegel, 1985: 364: defined in the context of stereotyping of a feature), Mühlhäusler (1977), Thelander (1979), Trudgill (1986: 98) and Hinskens (1996: 5).

[11] Cf. Siegel (1985: 358). Koineisation is also said to lead to a *new*, compromise dialect.

[12] Kerswill (2002b: 669–703) provides a more complete discussion of the necessary conditions for koines to form.

situation gave rise to certain limited types of accommodation by adult speakers in face-to-face interaction.[13] As a consequence, rudimentary dialect levelling took place, most notably of minority, very localised traditional dialect features. Kerswill (2002b: 671) distinguishes between regional and immigrant koines: the original Koine was at first a regional koine, since it did not replace the contributing dialects; on the other hand, a new dialect in a new settlement is an immigrant koine, which once established, becomes the vernacular of the new community. It is immigrant koines that correspond to Trudgill's (1986: 83) 'new dialects'. Siegel (1985: 358) gives the background to the first Koine. The term koine was first used to refer to the form of Attic Greek used as a *lingua franca* during the Hellenistic and Roman periods: this was not a 'new variety' but a compromise dialect.

Accommodation at the first stage of new-dialect formation may also lead to inter-dialect forms – forms which were not actually present in any of the dialects contributing to the mixture, but which arise out of interaction between them. In the second stage, children having many different linguistic models to aim at and no particular reason to select one over another, demonstrate considerable inter-individual and intra-individual variability. Since there is no common peer-group dialect for them to accommodate to, children adopt individual accommodation strategies and the role of adults is more significant than is usually the case. Inter-individual variability is considerable at this stage but is reduced compared to the first stage. There is therefore a degree of levelling. At the third stage, the new dialect appears as a stable, crystallised variety. Trudgill believes a new dialect is formed through a deterministic reduction of the variants.

The majority of dialect levelling studies are concerned with urban, intra-territorial dialect change where the focus is on the rapid development of adolescent norms. Those examining contemporary societies have tended to discuss dialect levelling together with national and standardised languages – neither of which are appropriate in this historical context. Tuten (2003: 94) uses a better parallel – the Castillian koine. This emerged in a similar period (between the ninth and eleventh centuries) in the urban setting of Burgos where there was a convergence of Romance speakers from different regions across the North. Dialect levelling and koineisation research has generally examined linguistic change characterised by high mobility and socio-linguistic heterogeneity which involve social mixing and restructuring. Research has focused on 'new towns' such as Milton Keynes (Kerswill, 1995: 195–207, 1996: 292–300; Williams & Kerswill, 1999; Kerswill & Williams, 2000: 1–13); Telford (Simpson, 1996), and the Norwegian communities of Høyanger, Odda, Røros and Tynset (Omdal, 1977: 7–9; Kerswill, 2002b: 669–703; Kerswill & Trudgill, 2005: 196–220; Røyneland,

---

[13] Trudgill discusses this in the context of the levelling of New Zealand English, not Icelandic.

2005; Solheim, 2006); as well as Butrasek in northern Sweden (Thelander, 1979); the population of the English fens (Britain, 1997a: 15–46); Bhojpuri (Mesthrie, 1992) and Fiji Hindi (Moag, 1977); (Siegel, 1987).

The investigated communities are practically always in a state of social flux, and the continuing transformation of a community's linguistic and social configuration poses considerable problems for research and challenges sociolinguistic analyses. Koineisation studies focus importantly on immigrants *converging* on a new location. However, sustained convergence is unlikely to have taken place in Iceland for the reason that the settlers were so scattered. Convergence is not used here in the sense of Auer, Hinskens & Kerswill (2005: 12) where it refers to 'the similarity between dialects involving the linguistic unification, focusing (*sensu* Le Page & Tabouret-Keller, 1985) and homogenisation of the linguistic repertoire'.

As Trudgill (1989: 229) observes, it is clear that koineisation takes place typically in high-contact situations. Trudgill (1989: 229) notes that high-contact situations lead to simplification (as part of the process of koineisation) whereas low-contact leads to 'complication' such as elaborate phonology and irregular morphology, cf. Andersen (1988: 39–85). In this sense, it would seem plausible that the koineisation process began before the Settlement where the conditions for 'dialect mixing' were in place. It is doubtful whether a prolonged high-contact linguistic environment emerged subsequent to the Settlement.

2.4.2 Markedness in *tabula rasa* dialect-formation

As has been noted, the concept of 'markedness' is often applied to dialect levelling and koineisation. As a notion in dialectology, it dates back to Schirmunski's (1930: 113–22) use of the term *Auffälligkeit* in the context of dialectal features (Auer *et al*, 1998: 164).[14] According to Trudgill (1986: 11–21), the notion of markedness is used to explain why certain features are adopted, and others rejected, in a dialect contact situation.[15]

There are, however, difficulties with the notion of markedness: there are problems of defining what it is exactly and to whom a feature is marked; there are problems of circularity: the very factors that lead speakers to notice and to adopt new features are precisely those that also lead to a feature being avoided.[16] Hinskens (1996: 11) and Trudgill (1986: 59, 125) show how different degrees of markedness explain why accommodation takes place and

---

[14] Cf. Labov (1972) and Kerswill & Williams (2002: 81) who consider markedness to be the property of a linguistic item or feature that makes it in some way perceptually and cognitively prominent.

[15] Trudgill's model is related to Labov's (1972) tripartite distinction between *indicators*, *markers* and *stereotypes*.

[16] Kerswill & Williams (2002: 89) point out that there is no way of predicting which 'marked' features will be adopted and avoided. Instead, we must have recourse to extra-linguistic information.

why it does *not* take place as well as an explanation for why convergence does and does *not* happen. Kerswill & Williams (2002: 105) attempt to define the socio-psychological properties of markedness as linked to internal and extra-linguistic factors – a difficult and complex exercise.

Trudgill (2004: 127) discusses various mechanisms of dialect contact in *tabula rasa* colonial situations. Trudgill (2004: 26) defines *tabula rasa* situations as those in which 'there is no prior-existing population speaking the language in question, either in the location in question or nearby'. According to Trudgill, for markedness to be operative, children need to have their 'own' phonologies so that they can be aware of phonological features different from their own. Although markedness may be a problematic term, it is not clear how dialect levelling can occur without recourse to the notion. There may not have been any pre-established linguistic systems in Iceland at the time of the Settlement, but this should not prevent dialect levelling *per se*. Providing there is sustained dialect contact (peer-to-peer adolescent contact in particular), convergence and a willingness to accommodate, levelling and subsequently koineisation should be able to occur irrespective of a society being *tabula rasa*.

2.5 LANGUAGE AND DIALECT ISOLATION

It is not only the issue of how dialect levelling occurs in a *tabula rasa* situation that is taxing. The larger question of how language change occurs in an environment of relative isolation is in fact an under-researched problem. High-contact language situations have been studied extensively. Trudgill (1989: 231) reminds us for instance that investigations of *lingua francas*, pidgins, creoles and other high-contact language varieties involving adult second-language learning have led us to expect developments such as: change from analytic to synthetic structure, reduction in redundancy and increase in regularity. Much less is known, however, about how a dialect or language develops when there is little contact.[17]

It is worth considering what firstly constitutes 'isolation'. Schilling-Estes (2002: 65) in her study of language isolation lists typical features of isolated communities as: geographic remoteness; dense, multiplex social networks; economic autonomy; historical continuity of the population and limited immigration. 'Isolation' is a relative and not a uni-dimensional notion (we cannot divide the world into 'isolated' *versus* 'non-isolated' communities), and there are very few truly isolated languages or dialects.[18]

---

[17] Samuels (1972: 90) links isolation to linguistic divergence.

[18] Cf. Labov (1994: 9): 'geographical separation naturally and inevitably leads to linguistic separation'; Clifford (1988); Mühlhäusler (1989: 137–72); Trudgill (1989: 236); Eckert (2000: 23, 24); Montgomery (2000: 41–53). A small number of speakers of Amazonian languages are said to have had no contact with the outside world (until recently).

In one of the few studies of language isolation, Schreier (2003) concludes that isolated communities offer 'laboratory conditions' for examining the process of language change and dialect formation. He analyses Tristan da Cunha, an island community in the South Atlantic Ocean that is geographically (and socio-culturally) as isolated as one can possibly get: the next permanent settlement is 2,300 kilometres distant and until 1938 no more than four islanders had ever left the island (Schreier, 2003: 201). The island has a short and well-recorded settlement history (1816 until c. 1850), followed by hyper-isolation until the early 1940s.

Schreier (2003) claims that the complete isolation of the monolingual community of Tristan da Cunha led to the establishment of dense social networks and 'focused' linguistic norms. 'Focusing' refers here to membership identification to a group or community of people: in new societies, it is the process by which the new variety acquires societally shared norms and stability. As for the development of the dialect itself, it has retained certain relic-forms which are well documented in eighteenth- and nineteenth-century English, but equally Tristan da Cunha English (TdCE) has developed independently innovative endemic structures that are not found anywhere else.[19] These forms are powerful testimony to language-inherent innovation. The data that Schreier (2003) presents provide evidence that, given a combination of demographic stability, reduced in-migration, no competition with a superposed, high-prestige standard variety, and continuing insularity and enclave status, dialect stabilisation and focusing may occur quickly and new norms may crystallise within two to three generations.

It should not be assumed, however, that the rapid formation of linguistic norms is characteristic of isolated speech communities, or that it leads to fast rates of language change. The isolation of communities may in fact lead not only to low rates of inter-community contact but also to a lack of opportunities for children and adolescents to mix: an important considera-tion in language development. In certain low-contact situations, the speed of linguistic change may therefore be slow. Trudgill (1989: 234) notes also that slow rates of change may be network related: in relatively small language communities, it is the tight social networks and the absence of dialect contact which are the most significant factors in producing slow rates of change and in producing so-called 'connatural' changes.

Isolated communities are in fact often characterised by tight network structures and high linguistic barriers to entry for non-native speakers. According to Andersen (1988: 39–85) and Trudgill (2002: 707–28), the

---

[19] Cf. Schilling-Estes (2002: 64–85) who shows isolated speech communities in the United States to be linguistically innovative and heterogeneous. This is explained by the absence of levelling pressure that comes with the exposure to heterogeneous usage norms and so speakers are free to retain intra-dialectal variation and carry through internal innovations. See Andersen (1988: 39–85).

changes that occur in high-contact communities are externally induced and are likely to lead to linguistic simplifications of various sorts – for example, reduction of phonological inventories and allophonic variation. The simplification stems from both cognitive and social factors: speakers in high-contact communities come into contact with so many different usage norms that it becomes impossible to assign functions (whether linguistic or social) to all of them, and so formerly meaningful variation is interpreted as free variation. 'Closed' communities with stable networks enable speakers, however, to transmit even the most elaborate norms from one generation to another (Trudgill, 2002: 707–28).

Although Icelandic was never a truly isolated language, it had many of the features that Schilling-Estes (2002: 65) associates with isolation. The limited evidence of dialectal variation may suggest that dialect stabilisation and 'focusing' was rapid. It is also apparent that the rate of language change has been slow in Iceland. It is debatable whether the morphological complexity of Icelandic can be attributed to just its relative geographical isolation; it may be indicative of the tight social networks of a 'closed' speech community. Linguistic features aside, it is also worth noting that contrary to outsiders' perceptions, Icelanders do not generally consider themselves isolated and there is evidence to suggest that they have not done so in the past.[20]

2.5.1 'Drift'

The notion of 'drift' may also be discussed when considering dialect isolation because it is an example of parallel language development in two or more languages or dialects where there is an *absence* of language contact (cf. Sapir, 1921: 147–71; Lakoff, 1972: 172–98). It represents therefore an alternative model of language change. The theory of 'drift' is relevant to this study because one wants to explain the structural similarities that appear at the same time but separately in Icelandic, Faroese and the dialects of south-west Norway in the thirteenth century.

Sapir's (1921: 147–71) argument was that language varieties may resemble one another because, having derived from some common source, they continue to evolve linguistically in similar directions by undergoing similar linguistic changes. In accordance with this theory, there exists therefore an inherent, structural tendency in certain languages to develop in certain ways.

Trudgill (2004: 132) demonstrates the relevance of the notion with examples of 'drift' in colonial Englishes (Australian, New Zealand, Falkland Islands and South African English): this type of 'drift' includes

---

[20] Hastrup (1985: 64) reproduces maps showing Icelanders' conception of the Earth with Iceland prominently placed.

phenomena such as diphthong shift and loss of rhoticity. There are other good examples of 'drift' in the Germanic languages: the Great Vowel Shift in English and High German or *i*-mutation. Lipski (1994: 42) observes also of South American Spanish, that 'some of the shared phonetic traits appear to have arisen independently in several areas'.

2.6 LANGUAGE DEVELOPMENT IN *TABULA RASA* SOCIETIES

A number of the studies that use 'drift' as an explanation of language change in colonial Englishes are in fact also examples of language development in *tabula rasa* societies (cf. Gordon *et al*, 2004; Trudgill, 2004). According to Trudgill (2004: 27), 'we can be confident that colonial dialect mixture situations involving adults speaking many different dialects of the same language will eventually and inevitably lead to the production of a new, unitary dialect'.[21] *Tabula rasa* situations are therefore relevant to new-dialect formation research.

In theory, the process of new-dialect formation is likely to proceed as outlined in Section 2.4.1. The absence of a pre-established linguistic norm in a new society may mean, however, that certain factors are of more relevance to this kind of language development. The lack of competing norms may increase for example the likelihood that the speech of a dominant social group becomes the overall norm (see Section 2.6.3). As linguistic innovators, children and adolescents are also particularly significant in *tabula rasa* situations because there is no pre-established norm to diffuse (Trudgill, 2004: 27, 29). In early Iceland, however, there was a social hierarchy within households and those who established linguistic norms were those that the household most depended upon, i.e. the adults and not the children/adolescents (Sandøy, 1994: 42).[22] In such an environment, new-dialect formation is likely to take longer.

2.6.1 *Language community types (and settlement patterns)*

As well as recognising that the conditions for language development may be different in a *tabula rasa* situation from an urban koineisation process, the approach to dialect formation and norm-establishment in this study puts particular emphasis on two factors: community types and settlement patterns. In Andersen's (1988: 39–85, 1989: 5–29) research on language community types, he develops a model of central and peripheral societies

---

[21] Croft (2000: 73) notes that in such a situation there appears to be a drive to act out of conformity with social norms.

[22] Hazen (2002: 500–25) provides a comprehensive overview of the literature, which demonstrates conclusively that the family and household can be an important factor in the language variation patterns of a speaker.

based on socio-psychological forces on the formation of language in space and time: exocentric (focusing on outside norms) and endocentric (focusing on its own norms) community attitudes (based on socio-psychological forces) and centrifugal and centripetal forces.[23] Andersen stresses the fact that communities may continue to be inward-looking while simultaneously opening up to the outside world; at the same time, comparatively 'closed' communities may be exocentric. Andersen (1988: 73) describes dialect communities from the point of view of their relative geographic location and their attitudes to their own speech and that of other communities.

Open communities have a great deal of inter-dialectal communication, allow variability and are therefore heterogeneous, whereas 'closed' communities have little such communication or none at all, disfavour variability and are therefore more homogenous (Andersen, 1988: 60). Andersen (1988: 73) shows that closed communities provide the ideal context not only for the faithful transmission of elaborate norms of usage, but also for the gradual elaboration of such norms.

Røyneland's (2005: 87) model (based on Andersen, 1988: 60) would suggest that early Iceland was an exocentric, 'closed' (speech) community as it was both rural and peripheral. In theory, such a community favours linguistic homogeneity and the levelling of features between dialect areas. This is likely to be an over-simplification, however, because the model is dependent on the urban/rural dichotomy which had little relevance in tenth-century Iceland.

Even within small-scale societies, different language communities lead to different dialect convergence/divergence outcomes. Sandøy (1994: 42–43; 2001: 127; 2005: 1923–32) differentiates between two sorts of isolated, small communities: the Faroese type, where he claims that, historically, most people lived in villages of about 150 individuals; and the Icelandic type, where the population lived in isolated family units of about ten people.[24] In the Faroe Islands, a small degree of social marking of language could take place within villages, while communities remained very close-knit. This led to linguistic differentiation between, rather than within, villages, perhaps as a marker of local allegiance. According to Höskuldur Þráinsson et al (2004: 339), already in the seventeenth century the minister Lucas Jacobsøn Debes says there is a major difference between the North and the South; Svabo assumes three main dialect areas in his dictionary manuscript dated 1773; Hammershaimb's 1854 dialectal division comprised the southern, northern and Streymoy dialects with the Skopunarfjörður as the main dividing line.

---

[23] Cf. Nichols' (1992: 13–15) distinction between 'spread zones' and 'residual zones'.

[24] Cf. Helgi Þorláksson (1979: 5–12); Björn Þorsteinsson & Guðrún Ása Grímsdóttir (1989: 61–258) who note that only a few clusters of more than one farm can be found in the early period and where even Reykjavík itself had only 300 inhabitants in the year 1800; Magnús Stefánsson (1993: 312) and Orri Vésteinsson (1998: 1–29) believe the Settlement did not comprise just 'isolated' farmsteads controlled by independent farmers.

Höskuldur Þráinsson *et al* (2004: 340) note that today there are phonetic and phonological differences between the dialects as well as morphological differences such as variation in pronominal forms, cf. Vannebo (2005: 1685).

In Iceland, there was neither social stratification nor, for the children or adolescents, any peer groups, a situation which inhibited linguistic differentiation both within a family unit and across the country itself. It is claimed that the Faroese settlement was of a different character than in Iceland, as the fewer but much larger communities represented better conditions for linguistic innovations among young people, and therefore better sociolinguistic conditions for dialectal divergence (Sandøy, 2005: 1929).[25] The dialectal heterogeneity of Faroese may arguably be explained by its settlement pattern and the type of language communities that evolved subsequently, where the mechanics of linguistic interaction may have differed from that of Iceland.

2.6.2 *A deterministic model versus social factors*

The study of community types is helpful when considering dialectal divergence in Faroese, but it is relatively seldom that linguists refer to community types or settlement patterns as explanations of language development. Trudgill (2004: 26) chooses to ignore such factors and makes instead an argument for determinism in linguistic change. He claims that in *tabula rasa* situations, dialect mixture and new-dialect formation are not haphazard processes. Whilst recognising that *tabula rasa* communities are considered exceptional because of the lack of an already established dialect, Trudgill (2004: 125) believes that new-dialect formation is deterministic in the sense that the outcome is predictable from the input. In accordance with this argument, the newly formed 'focused' dialect, which is the third generation outcome of dialect contact and dialect mixture, is characterised, at least at the phonological level, by features which were in a majority in the input. The only exceptions to this are cases where unmarked features are in a large minority and win out over majority features on the grounds of their unmarkedness.

It should be observed, however, that linguistic change in general is not deterministic (cf. Harris & Campbell, 1995: 321). Using linguistic data, Trudgill rejects all social factors such as prestige and stigma and relies heavily on the role of children as explanations for language change: 'we have not found it at all necessary to call on social features such as 'prestige' or 'stigma' as explanatory factors, nor have we had recourse to notions such

---

[25] See Arge (2005: 23): at the first census on the Faroe Islands in 1801, the population was only 5,000. Debes (1995: 34) notes that the *Hundabrævit* from c. 1350 A.D. speaks of approximately 40 settlements. If the population remained stable until 1801, this would imply settlement sizes of approximately 125 people.

as 'identity".[26] Gordon *et al* (2004: 285–6) conclude their comprehensive analysis of the New Zealand English data by saying that they remain open to the idea of social factors, but: 'for the most part, the situation in New Zealand is not clear enough categorically to support or deny speakers' choices and the social factors that influence them in new-dialect formation here'.

According to Hickey (2003: 213–39), there are a number of problems in overlooking social factors in the way that Trudgill does. Hickey argues that the process of new-dialect formation is in fact socially embedded. He promotes a social approach to koineisation and suggests that the distinct prestige patterns attributed to donor dialects have a decisive impact on the future development of new-dialect formation. Schreier (2003: 199) stresses the importance of both social *and* linguistic factors: linguistic contact and new-dialect formation are intricately interwoven processes, and the diachronic and synchronic development of a contact-derived variety depends on a number of linguistic, sociolinguistic, socio-psychological and demographic factors. In Schreier's opinion, it is the combination of all these criteria that ultimately accounts for the linguistic outcome of language/dialect transportation and contact.

2.6.3 *The Founder Principle and prestige*

Both social and linguistic factors have been referred to in discussions in another form of new-dialect/language formation: the development of creoles. With regard to social factors, Mufwene (2001: 26–27) claims that the structural features of creoles have been pre-determined to a large extent by the characteristics of the vernaculars spoken by the population that founded the colonies in which they developed. The implication of the so-called Founder Principle is that the speech of those that found a new society, the founder population, has a disproportionately significant influence on subsequent language development and norm-establishment.[27]

Although prestige is a problematic concept because it is used to discuss aspects of social class, 'standard language' and modern urban societies, and not settlement frontier communities, the notion of the Founder Principle can be applied to early Iceland, even if it is unclear exactly what the implications for the sociolinguistics of the Norse spoken at this time are.

---

[26] Cf. Joseph (1987: 30–31) who believes that as soon as language becomes a variable commodity, the variations are subject to value judgements and assignments of prestige.

[27] Cf. Zelinsky's [1973] (1992) 'Doctrine of First Effective Settlement' on which the Founder Principle is based; Sankoff (1980); Labov's (1994) Pioneer Effect; Poirier (1994: 257): the first group of colonists in America and Canada had a particular influence on the process of linguistic unification; Trudgill (2004: 163–4). Sutton (2008) has shown that the 'founder effect' is demonstrable in parts of Australia where polygamous societies have settled. In a situation where a man has ten to fifteen wives, his dialect can spread to 200 people or more in two generations.

The Founder Principle has been shown to be valid in settler communities which were previously inhabited (Lipski, 1994: 54). Lipski's evidence is from the European colonisation of Latin America whereas Sandve (1976) applies the Founder Principle to language development in the communities of Odda and Tyssedal where the local dialect is based on that of the first inhabitants from eastern Norway.

The effect may arguably be, however, more pronounced in the absence of language contact where there are no pre-existing norms to compete with.Without adequate information on social relations at the time and in a pre-literate society, one is limited in what one can say about social factors such as prestige. The little we know suggests that it is not unreasonable to surmise that there was an elite in early Iceland, but we can only speculate how this was reflected in language.

2.7 IDENTITY: ESSENTIALISM *VERSUS* CONSTRUCTIVISM

The notion of prestige can be subsumed and best accounted for in identity-based explanations. Whilst the term 'prestige' may be vague in its meaning, there would be nothing novel in saying that identity is in fact an abstract and complex concept. The multi-dimensional nature of identity, and its mutations across disciplinary boundaries and theoretical paradigms, makes it difficult too to account for its meaning. It has been defined from a number of different perspectives and discussed in various contexts such as sex, age, occupation, class, religion, nationality, ethnicity etc. The concept of identity is, however, concerned most fundamentally with who we are as individuals and groups, and we can speak therefore in terms of personal and social identities.

There are two schools of thought on identity: essentialism and constructivism. Essentialism is based on the idea that one's identity is permanent, irrevocable and is latent in individuals. A constructivist identity is one that is formed in conjunction with other people and one's surroundings. The latter approach to identity emphasizes the fact that the notion of identity and in particular identity construction is a social phenomenon by definition. A constructivist identity is a dynamic, heterogeneous identity that can and does change over time. The constructivist approach to identity is considered the most appropriate for early Iceland because it implies that an identity is 'formed'; it is constructed and subject to local cultural factors.

2.7.1 *Personal identity and group membership*

A linguistic identity is not only subject to local cultural factors, but is according to Habermas (1984–87) a symbol for the relationship between the self and the others: the self in its entirety is socially, and in particular linguistically constituted. The relationship between the individual, the group and language is undoubtedly complex.[28] Irrespective of how one should define that relationship, the view of the human self as a social construct is widely held and is adhered to in this study. It is reasonable to assume that language and the notion of identity may be particularly significant factors when individuals integrate into new societies.

Whilst the notion of identity can be understood and discussed at many different levels, it is social identity (the identity of the settlers as a group) that concerns us most in this study. 'Social Identity Theory' (Tajfel & Turner, 1986; Abrams & Hogg, 1990) states that an individual has multiple 'social identities'. Social identity is an individual-based perception of what defines the 'us' associated with any internalised group membership. This can be distinguished from the notion of personal identity which refers to self-knowledge that derives from the individual's unique attributes. Social Identity Theory asserts that group membership creates in-group/self-categorisation and enhancement in ways that favour the in-group at the expense of the out-group.

Personal and group identity should not be considered completely independent of one another: one's individual identity can often only be defined at the level of the group. It is reasonable to assume that there were different categories of personal and group identity in Iceland, and that these were formed in the manner explained above. These identities were created most obviously on the basis of the household/farmstead, but also group identities become established at different levels of the complex social structures that the Icelanders developed.[29]

2.7.2 *Place and identity*

Personal identities may be defined at the level of the group and in relation to social structures, but also with reference to a place or specific region. The notion of 'place' can be defined and discussed at a number of different levels such as nation, region, locality, town, village, settlement etc. The sense of belonging to a local place is often a fundamental factor in creating an identity and many sociolinguists believe a pre-requisite to individual identity is the relationship with society: 'to be an individual self, that is, one who is identified within a narrative of past, present and future – requires a community' (Gergen, 2001: 191).

As we have seen, language use indicates fundamentally which social group somebody belongs to, but also where one comes from: dialects and their speakers are typically defined geographically. The settlers to Iceland

---

[28] Bakhtin (1981) claims that the individual has many different social languages.
[29] As discussed in Section 4.2.

had to relate to their new surroundings as physical entities and social constructs. Among the prime markers of this process were the place-names, as well as a range of social and political institutions.[30] The saga material provides also evidence of local identities being formed on the basis of topographical features such as fjords and bays.

In a discussion of place and identity, Giles, Bourhis & Taylor (1977) introduce the notion of 'ethnolinguistic vitality' or the sense of belonging to a place. This is a psychological measure of the degree to which one defines oneself relative to where one comes from. This is a useful concept for the purpose of this study. All the evidence would indicate a high degree of ethnolinguistic vitality in Iceland in modern times at least, and perhaps previously. Ethnolinguistic vitality is probably enhanced in very small, homogenous, mono-dialectal island populations because the parameters for 'belonging' are so clearly defined. This sense of belonging to a location has a historical dimension (Mæhlum, 2002: 77), and the historical continuity of 'places' is something that Icelanders like to emphasize. These 'places' and the settlers' links to them may have led to a reconfiguring of identity models that dated back prior to the Settlement. It is also likely that the emergence of social structures may have reified the notion of place solidarity in Iceland.[31]

2.8 LANGUAGE AND IDENTITY

Irrespective of whether one speaks of place and a personal or group identity, there is a broad consensus amongst linguists, philosophers and psychologists that there is a close relationship between language and identity *per se*. As Saussure ([1915] 1998: 107) noted, the mechanism of a language turns entirely on identities and the problem of identities crops up everywhere. Language ties us as individuals to other individuals and to society, but also gives us the ability to reflect upon our own existence. There is a considerable literature on the subject of language and identity construction, and it is not possible here to review it in its entirety (cf. Mead, 1934; Giles & Smith, 1979: 45–65; Gumperz, 1982; Le Page &

---

[30] Cf. Lefebvre (1991: 44) who comments that the physical boundaries of space are conceptualised according to particular social categories. He speaks in terms of 'social space': the space shaped by human agency and cultural organisation; Giddens (1984: 368). Blomley (1994: 46) focuses on legal space. See Hastrup (1985: 50); Øye (2006: 33–55) for a discussion on the structuring of space in Iceland.

[31] Bortoni-Ricardo's (1985) study of rural life in Brazil identifies the importance of place solidarity in identity construction. A change in social structure associated with rural to urban migration involves a move from an 'insulated' network consisting largely of kinsfolk and neighbours to an 'integrated' urban network where links are less multiplex but are contracted in a wider range of social contexts.

Tabouret-Keller, 1985; Giles & Coupland, 1991; Bourdieu, 1991; Eckert, 1989; 2000; 2003: 3).

For Eckert (2003: 3), the concept of identity, in particular social identity, is the starting-point and is very closely tied to interaction with others: 'a theory of variation as social practice sees speakers as constituting, rather than representing broad social categories, and it sees speakers as constructing, as well as responding to the social meaning of variation'. Labov's (1963: 273–309) study of Martha's Vineyard showed us the social motivation of a sound change and how individuals may go about constructing linguistic identities. Furthermore, it showed that the motivation for the sound change can be understood only in relation to details of local social structure. This is echoed in Milroy's use of the network model to account for the social relations which condition language maintenance and change. Milroy (1992: 202) notes that a 'linguistic change [...] comes about for reasons of marking social identity'.

Trudgill (2004: 157) and Labov (2001: 91) himself claim subsequently that we do not often find correlations between degrees of local identification and the progress of sound change. The example of Martha's Vineyard is therefore considered an exception and there is accordingly seldom recourse to the notion of identity.[32] As Trudgill (2004: 157) notes, it may be the case that identity factors cannot lead to the *development* of new linguistic features, but identity may explain the preservation of existing features. To subscribe to the view that identity factors do not affect language change and simultaneously posit 'accommodation' at the centre of new-dialect formation processes, one would have to maintain that inter-speaker accommodation is wholly sub-conscious. Whilst accommodation through convergence may be below the level of consciousness, it would be difficult to say the same about divergence (the other half of accommodation theory, see Giles & Coupland, 1991), where a group can deliberately employ linguistic differences as a symbolic act of asserting a different identity.

Bourdieu (1991) discusses language and identity with reference to power and social capital. He considers these factors to be omnipresent,[33] whereas Le Page & Tabouret-Keller (1985: 181) consider *all* language activity to be expressions of identity. According to Le Page & Tabouret-Keller's (1985: 181) 'Acts of Identity' theory, 'the individual creates for himself the patterns of his linguistic behaviour so as to resemble those of the group with which from time to time he wishes to be identified, so as to be unlike those from whom he wishes to be distinguished'. The implicit and fundamental

---

[32] Cf. Larsen (1917: 35) who spoke nearly a century ago of the concept of *naboopposition* which claims that speakers of neighbouring dialects often wish their speech to be maximally different.

[33] Bourdieu (1991) regards linguistic identities as expression of symbolic power: the subtleties of language are part of social capital and are major factors in social mobility and identity.

perspective when approaching the problem of language and identity from this angle is that all language activity is considered as expressions of specific 'acts of identity'.

The Acts of Identity model was developed to understand variation in language use and choice in the creole/contact situations of Belize. The authors argue that 'Acts of Identity' are only possible to the extent that: (1) we can identify the desirable group; (2) we have both adequate access to that group, and the ability to analyse their behaviour, i.e. their speech patterns; (3) we have a strong enough motivation to 'join' them, and this motivation is either reinforced or rejected by the group, and (4) we have the ability to modify our own behaviour.

One of the limitations of the model may be that it was often employed in the context of language choice, and not dialect choice. The theory was formulated with reference to multi-lingual, relatively 'diffuse' communities, and not monolingual 'focused' communities. The authors believe, however, that the theory can be used in more homogenous, 'focused' speech communities such as Iceland. If, as Le Page & Tabouret-Keller (1985: 247) claim, 'all linguistic tokens are socially marked', then it should be possible to apply the model to monolingual communities too.[34] The authors speak of 'focusing', as defined in Section 2.5. A 'focused' speech community is to be compared to a 'diffuse' community where the social groups are not easily discerned, many language varieties are spoken, and the norms for language use are either not shared or non-existent.

According to Tabouret-Keller (1989: 179–80), there are a number of agencies which promote focusing: (a) close daily interaction in the community; (b) an external threat or any other danger which leads to a sense of common cause; (c) a powerful model – a leader, a poet, a prestige group, a set of religious scriptures; (d) the mechanisms of an education system. To this list, she adds 'legal institutions'. On the basis of the social structures (the chieftains' power), 'legal' institutions put in place, the sense of group identity on an isolated volcanic island and the evolving relationship with the Norwegian Crown, Iceland would appear to be a speech community that promoted 'focusing' and thus a common cultural identity. A 'focused' speech community would have led to a local (country-wide) 'dialect' identity (cf. Mæhlum, 1992: 123). This 'focused' dialect should be understood as a dialect where there is a measure of uniformity as well as agreement on the social symbolism of the variation that exists (Auer, Hinskens & Kerswill, 2005: 200).

Once dialect levelling had occurred, it is much less clear, however, whether and how Icelanders symbolised their identity by 'acts of identity' if they spent most of their time talking to other Icelanders. In the case of Iceland, it is not obvious therefore how a disparate group of people

---

[34] See Labov (2001: 191-2) for an opposing view to the 'Acts of Identity' model.

could have formed an identity pact to represent themselves indexically as a community through a new way of speaking. That is not the same, however, as saying that language is not important to identity which the work of Eckert (2000) and Milroy (1980) shows beyond doubt.

2.8.1 Accommodation and networks

It is difficult to speak of the development of 'focused' speech communities without mentioning the notions of 'accommodation' and 'social networks'. As well as being influential theories that attempt to explain language variation and change, both 'accommodation' and 'networks' are closely linked to the issue of language and identity, and are central to the new-dialect formation process.

These theories have been widely discussed in the literature and are used to explain language development and change in a wide range of geographical and historical contexts. They will not be described in full here, but reference will be made to the most relevant points.

2.8.2 Accommodation Theory

Both the 'Accommodation Theory' and 'Acts of Identity Theory' have their roots in social psychology. Accommodation Theory is a valuable rapprochement between variationist sociolinguistics and socio-psychological approaches to interaction. While Labovian sociolinguistics associates language use primarily with social structures and social behaviour, research on linguistic accommodation is grounded in theories of 'social action' (how social meaning is produced from interaction).

Accommodation Theory is based on the simple concept that people converge to each other's speech characteristics if and when they want to improve communication effectiveness and/or to boost social attractiveness. There is a tendency to differentiate between short-term accommodation and long-term accommodation in language change. Short-term accommodation becomes long-term accommodation when the accommodation of the innovation becomes an individual speech 'habit'. Speakers linguistically 'move closer' or 'further apart' (in the case of divergence) depending on the relationship the speakers want with one another. The theory was developed in tandem with work on social identity: identity goals are the reflexes of the process of social interaction. According to Trudgill (2004: 28), linguistic convergence is the result of the fact that all human beings operate according to a powerful maxim which Keller (1994: 100) renders as 'talk like others talk'.

It is not known what the mechanics of accommodation were in a thinly populated society and where it took place, but accommodation is universal and there is much empirical evidence for it.[35] There would have been a degree of accommodation at the very local level in Iceland. Otherwise, opportunities for accommodation may have been limited (assembly gatherings etc.) and the stereotypical features of groups one wanted to emulate may not have been established.

2.8.3 Social network theory and language change

A better understanding of the scope for 'accommodation' may be gained from analysing possible social network structures. Social network theory comes to sociolinguistics via anthropology and sociology (Barnes, 1954: 39–58; Granovetter, 1973: 1360–80). According to Milroy (1980: 178), network theory is capable too of universal application and it has in fact been used to analyse the dynamics of various different language communities.[36]

Social networks have been mainly discussed in the context of synchronic language variation, but the theory can be applied to diachronic language change. Few linguistic studies have, however, attempted to apply the model to anything other than modern societies (cf. Lenker, 2000: 225–38; Bax, 2000: 277–89; Bergs, 2005). Milroy (1980) uses social networks – those informal and formal social relationships of which any human society is composed – to analyse patterns of linguistic variation which characterise particular groups within a sociolinguistically complex, urban Belfast community.[37] Her focus is in particular on low-status, non-standard speakers who live in close-knit, working-class communities. The major hypothesis that Milroy validated was that even when sociolinguistic variables were held constant, the closer an individual's network ties are with his local community, the closer his language approximates to localised vernacular norms. Close-knit networks act therefore as norm enforcement mechanisms.[38]

Applying the concept to early Iceland, one might say that this island community was a 'dense' network in the strict sense of the term. In accordance with Milroy (1980: 50), a 'network is said to be relatively dense if a large number of the persons to whom an ego is linked are also linked to each other'. Social networks in Iceland were probably dense and

---

[35] Cf. Coupland's (1984: 49–70) study of a shop assistant's convergence towards her customers in a Cardiff travel agency and Trudgill's (1986) analysis of sociolinguistic interviews in Norwich.

[36] Cf. Gal (1979); Milroy (1980); Bortoni-Ricardo (1985); Eckert (2000). Ross (1997: 209–61) uses social network theory to reconstruct sequences of linguistic and speech community events (SCE's) and sees scope in applying network theory to non-urban settings.

[37] Cf. 'social network' and 'speech community' (Hudson, 1996: 29): a 'community' has a boundary, a 'network' does not; Labov's (1972: 120) definition of 'speech community'; Eckert's (1989; 2000) notion of 'community of practice'.

[38] See Woods (2000: 143) who notes that weak tie networks are more likely to favour change than close-knit communities.

'multiplex', i.e. people were connected to one another in a number of different ways (neighbour, kin etc.). Such dense and multiplex networks typical of closed, stable communities, may lead to conformity in linguistic behaviour and maintenance of group norms.[39] The 'density' of the network is not concerned with the 'amount' of contact between network members. The settlers may have been linked to many others, and in a variety of different ways, but these links are likely to have been tenuous and contracted in a narrow range of social contexts. The settlers to Iceland may have had kin networks spread out across the country, but the contact between these members was infrequent, or even minimal.

Milroy & Milroy (1985: 375–84) attempt to explain Icelandic's conservatism using network theory: linguistic conservatism requires 'strong ties' which are based on compliance with traditional norms.[40] According to them, these strong ties are to be found in the close-knit and extended families that existed in early Iceland. Membership to certain family groups and clans was especially important in times of conflict, such as that which characterised the end of the Commonwealth Period. In short, it was necessary to know who one's relatives were beyond one's immediate family, and it was important for other people to know with whom one was related. The difficulty with this point is that it is known that the *Sturlungaöld* is a period characterised by linguistic change, and yet the close-knit network structures that Milroy & Milroy (1985) describe would not permit that. Milroy & Milroy (1985: 379) state that 'Icelandic society [...] depended in earlier centuries on the strong networks typical of rural life. Hence, despite the difficulties of climate and terrain, social networks proved to be a cohesive force, not only in maintaining social norms, but also in maintaining the norms of language'.

There are different kinds of social networks and Mæhlum (1993: 177ff) makes a useful distinction between so-called 'isolated' and 'integrated' networks. Individuals in an isolated network maintain strong links with the place where they come from originally with a significant bond between their place of origin and where they live now (e.g. 'Chinatowns' in the western world). An 'integrated' network is one whose members are integrated into the new society with little contact with the people from the area where they come from. Individuals in these networks establish norms based on new reference points. Settlement Iceland is likely to have been an 'isolated' network with Icelanders maintaining links with places where they came from. As social structures were established, Iceland became more of an 'integrated' network over time.

---

[39] There appears to be a correlation between social network consistency and language change in Iceland.

[40] Dahlstedt (1958: 22) attempts to explain Icelandic's conservatism in terms of the historical high degree of literacy amongst Icelanders.

It is fair to assume that new societies will create new conditions for network formation as social structures become established. According to Ross (1997: 223), as a community grows, there is an increase in structural heterogeneity, a gradual reduction in network density. The language of the founder community continues to be spoken in new settlements, but innovations occur in local lects. With regard to networks in Iceland, the conundrum is as follows: based on Milroy's (1980) use of the model and the pattern of isolated farmsteads, the network structure of early Iceland suggests that 'local' norms were established and maintained. There is limited evidence of local norms, however. These networks may therefore be enforcing dialectal norms that were established prior to the Settlement.

2.8.4 *Deixis, pronouns and identity*

Analysis of social networks provides us with insights into the dynamics of speech communities. As well as this macro-perspective, there is a need to consider more specifically certain aspects of Norse grammar whose use is analysed subsequently in this study. The usage of deixis and pronouns are briefly mentioned here because in certain contexts they may be considered identity markers, anchoring the location of the speaker to a speech-event (Levinson, 1983: 79).[41]

With regard to deixis, both temporal and spatial relationships can be expressed linguistically by implicitly or explicitly relying on the present position of the speaker and/or the moment of speaking, using expressions such as 'here' and 'now' (Tenbrink, 2007: 21). The usage of a deictic term such as 'here' in a certain context may imply for example that the speaker hopes to identity himself with a certain place. According to Benveniste (1966: 262), deictic words that establish the temporal and spatial location of the speaking 'I' are indispensable for the task of installing subjectivity in a 'here' and 'now'. He claims that personal pronouns cannot achieve the task of installing subjectivity on their own.

Whilst it may be possible to link the usage of deictic terms with a certain identity, linguists and anthropologists recognise more readily the importance of pronouns in anchoring language to specific speakers in specific contexts. By using personal pronouns, language users point to their roles not only as speakers or addressees, but also in their location in time and space and to their relationship to others. Pronouns can be indexical in that they connect utterances to extra-linguistic reality via the ability of linguistic signs to point to aspects of the social context.

---

[41] Lyons (1977: 648) notes that there are two basic ways of referring to objects – by describing or naming them on the one hand, and by locating them on the other.

Pronouns are also often discussed as grammatical expressions of power and solidarity. Brown & Gilman (1960: 253–76) and Mühlhäusler & Harré (1990) have focused on the expression of power asymmetry in pronominal usage in a number of European languages. The authors discuss in particular the use of the two singular pronouns of address in French, German, Italian and Spanish and the dimensions of power and solidarity they encode (so-called T/V systems).[42] Pronominal usage is shown to be a means of conveying in-group membership. Other means of addressing in-group membership include terms of address, use of in-group language or dialect (perhaps in a code-switching situation) (Blom & Gumperz, 1972: 407–34), use of jargon and slang.

Pronominal usage is of particular interest to the extent that it shows group membership and identity. The most relevant pronoun is the indexical first person plural pronoun, making the 'us-them' distinction explicit through deictic pointing. Both 'we' and 'they' can construct, redistribute or change the social values of in-groupness and out-groupness. 'We' in particular opens up a number of referential and pragmatic options such as the inclusive/exclusive distinction (Duszak, 2002: 6). As far as this study is concerned, difficulties arise, however, in determining to what degree pronouns are used to explicitly mark an identity.

2.9 CONCLUSION

One can conclude by saying that it is not possible to identify and discuss a single 'identities' approach to language, with theories and methods of its own. Instead identity tends to be employed as an omnipresent explanatory concept and is discussed using various more or less loosely defined sociolinguistic paradigms. Whilst certain aspects of models and theories are more useful than others, there remains no one applicable model for identity construction and linguistic change in low-contact environments.

The majority of *tabula rasa*, dialect levelling and koineisation studies are concerned with population convergence in a society where there is unambiguous evidence of new-dialect formation. Studies show that new-dialect formation tends to occur in nucleated settlements. It is not yet known how language develops in purely rural communities characterised by population divergence (and not convergence), lack of children-peer groups and pre-established norms. Previous research would seem to suggest that all of these factors would at least lead to a de-acceleration of the new-dialect formation process.

---

[42] Brown & Levinson (1987: 198–206) show that cultural explanations for T/V systems will not do in the face of its widespread distribution across language groups, and they develop an explanation using implicature and social motives in their work.

The notion of 'norms' is useful because it is an effective means of defining a speech community and it can be discussed using networks: new linguistic norms may arise when close-knit networks are established. As well as 'norms', the notion of 'focusing' can be readily applied to this study: 'focusing' is probably the result of norm maintenance over a long period of time, i.e. slow rates of language change. Slow rates of language change and linguistic conservatism may be associated with (a) a period of geographical isolation (following levelling which gives rise to linguistic homogeneity), or (b) local dense, multiplex networks which typically act as norm-enforcers. The emergence of the latter may in turn be explained by a number of factors, among which one may cite: (a) isolation itself, and (b) the settlement pattern of the new society.

Schreier (2003) shows that isolation may lead to the establishment of dense, social networks and focused linguistic forms. Isolation is in this sense a linguistic variable. Although his evidence is restricted to a much smaller and hyper-isolated community, Tristan da Cunha, it shows that isolation itself can plausibly lead to dialect stabilisation and norm crystallisation. There are, however, difficulties with this argument because close-knit networks are often associated with high-contact situations, and there is limited evidence of the network effects of dialect isolation.

A language development model based on settlement patterns and social networks may, however, be able to account for how linguistic norms become established in different environments. Settlement patterns (and information on settler mobility) may provide us with rudimentary information on the density of social networks in *tabula rasa* situations at the very local level. The intricacies of language variation and change may be different in isolated new societies from more 'established' speech communities. The role of the family and the dynamics of the household might be particularly significant in *tabula rasa* situations with a scattered settlement pattern, for instance. Settlement patterns may aid us in determining what the scope and nature of in-group accommodation was: a universal and fundamental ingredient to the levelling and koineisation process and to most models of language change. One theory of language change which is not based on 'accommodation' is the notion of 'drift'; a theory which is endorsed, alongside social factors, in this study.

The problem of accounting for linguistic homogeneity ('one focused dialect') and the absence of norm-conflict (i.e. the 'focusing' process) in a *tabula rasa* situation whose settlement pattern suggests the emergence of local, dense social networks and local norms has to the best of my knowledge not been thus far addressed in any theoretical discussion. Language community models enable us to describe better speech communities and sociolinguistic structures, but they are often too heavily based on a modern urban/rural dichotomy. It is likely that any theoretical model attempting to address the problem would need to consider social factors. Whilst it remains a moot point in the literature, we must allow for the possibility that social factors and speakers' choices (such as the selection of variables to show group membership and identity) play a role in new-dialect formation, language change generally and possibly identity construction.

It is anticipated that any model focusing on norm development and identity construction in a low-contact speech community will need to incorporate the notions of accommodation, social networks and 'Acts of Identity' for which there is considerable cross-linguistic and cross-cultural evidence. In accordance with the findings of language attitudes research by social psychologists (for example Brown & Gilman, 1960: 253–76), the Milroys propose that an integrated model of sociolinguistic structure must take into account the competing ideologies of solidarity and status (Milroy, 1992: 210–213). This study will show that linguistic and place solidarity may be enforced in environments of highly focused dialects with historical norm maintenance, and that they may be important factors in identity construction. Arriving in a new, strange location such as Iceland in the tenth century, it is expected that identity was established along con-structivist lines.

3

NORM-ESTABLISHMENT IN ICELAND

3.1 INTRODUCTION

Chapter 2 addressed a number of the theoretical problems concerned with new-dialect formation and 'focusing' in *tabula rasa* situations. The fundamental problem that will be discussed in this chapter is how is it that the Icelandic language or the Norse dialect spoken in Iceland remained (relatively) homogenous. In discussions of 'dialect', the overall concern in this chapter is phonological as this is the context in in which the discussion thus far has taken place. It is of course recognised that dramatic syntactic changes took place in the development of Icelandic (Eiríkur Rögnvaldsson, 2005), but that is not the focus here. Icelandic is often discussed in the context of linguistic conservatism and sometimes this conservatism is couched in terms of a lack of dialect variation (cf. Hreinn Benediktsson, 1961–62: 72–113; Milroy & Milroy, 1985: 374). These are not the same issues, however: the former is explained frequently by geographical isolation and the literary heritage whereas a range of other factors such as a high degree of internal mobility in Iceland are of more relevance to the latter. As we will see, the explanation is of course much more complex than this, but both factors are relevant to any study of Icelandic. The relative and long-term linguistic homogeneity of Icelandic is what concerns us most here as variation is thought to be some degree 'natural' and 'inevitable'.

Various explanations have been posited attempting to account for the process of norm-establishment in Iceland, but the problem remains not sufficiently well understood. Le Page & Tabouret-Keller (1985: 50) state that communities are typically not characterised by monolingual homo-geneity and Sapir (1921: 160) observes that 'It is exceedingly doubtful if a language will ever continue to be spoken over a wide area without multiplying itself dialectically'. As well as the dialectal variation in mainland Scandinavian languages, we witness dialectal variation in other language-family communities with whom the Norsemen had contact: there were two dialectal areas in Manx (Ball, 2002: 281); there are today several dialectal areas in Scottish Gaelic (*ibid.*: 145–47) and four main dialectal areas in Welsh for example (*ibid.*: 293).

One difficulty is that we are trying to comment on the immediate pre-historic period, i.e. the period immediately before what is historically documented. Our knowledge is therefore not completely secure, let alone our interpretation of what we think we know. In-depth knowledge of synchronic and diachronic language variation from a plethora of sociolinguistic studies gives us, however, firm ground in proceeding on the basis of some assumptions.

The reason for examining this specific question in this piece of research is that the motivation for 'choosing' a particular spoken norm and developing a written norm will tell us about the identity of the settlers. The Icelanders were the only Scandinavians to write continuously and almost exclusively in the vernacular.[1] As for speech, the fact that all Icelanders speak not only the same language, but that there is very little sociolectal and regional variation creates a high degree of linguistic solidarity and a strong communal identity amongst all Icelanders. This is the case now and it would have been thus many centuries earlier. The Icelanders may have had their relatively uniform language since the Settlement unlike some of the other Norse colonies which were more subject to language contact at different periods.

For the purpose of this chapter, I use the term 'norm' in the sense in which Haugen (1966: 922–35) defines it. It refers simply to the 'selected' linguistic variety or pattern representative of a certain community. Norm selection is discussed here because we are concerned with the early stage of language development where in theory a single, widely accepted linguistic norm needed to be chosen to serve a new community.[2] Linguistic norms are often discussed in the context of 'standardisation' or the path that 'underdeveloped' languages must take to become instruments for a modern nation. According to Haugen (1966: 931), this is a process that comprises 'norm selection', 'codification' where the linguistic structure of a language, including phonology, grammar and lexicon is written down and 'norm elaboration' which is defined as a language's maximal variation in function. Standard languages are characterised by a rather complete hierarchisation of their norms, consciously developed, pursued, codified and inculcated; this is not the case here. An attempt was made to codify the *written* norm in Icelandic by standardising the orthography as early as the first half of the twelfth century. Neither the First Grammatical Treatise nor any of the other historical sources give, however, any indication that the problem of norm selection caused any difficulties in early Iceland. The author of the First Grammatical Treatise makes in fact no mention of any variant forms.

As Kristján Árnason (2003b: 247) points out, this is all the more remarkable as 'the phonetic detail and theoretical clarity of the First Grammarian's analysis is considerable, and given his astuteness, it is

---

[1] A small number of documents were written in Latin. Oddr munkr's saga (*Saga Óláfs Tryggvasonar af Oddr Snorrason munk*) of the tenth-century Norwegian king Óláfr Tryggvason survives only in Icelandic translation but was certainly composed in Latin since the text actually quotes one of Oddr's verses in Latin before giving a vernacular version of it (ed. Finnur Jónsson, 1932: 194).

[2] Norm elaboration corresponds to Kloss' (1967: 29–41) *Ausbau*: the concept of *Ausbau* is particularly important in cases where the local spoken varieties across a larger region form a dialect continuum. Cf. Ferguson (1959: 616–30).

expected that he would have been aware of any linguistic variation' present in Icelandic society. The First Grammarian's analysis is based on the language that he heard in Iceland during his lifetime, and yet no mention of variation is made. It is possible, however, that the First Grammarian considered dialectal variation not worthy of mention.

Having discussed the process of dialect levelling and koineisation in Chapter 2, this form of language development is now considered in the context of new-dialect formation in Iceland. It is first useful to know whether levelling occurred prior to or after the Settlement. The factors and conditions that facilitated the process may have varied, depending on whether the process took place in Iceland or elsewhere in the Norse-speaking world. Another important factor for the issue of linguistic identity is the question of which variant was 'selected' to act as a koine. This is a poorly understood issue and various hypotheses are possible: sociolinguistic research shows us that the dominant variety in the levelling process is not always characterised by simplification, and that it is not always the dominant variety that becomes the 'standard'.[3]

As we have seen in Chapter 2, the term koineisation implies sustained dialect contact and entails the levelling of *dialects* and not *language* contact. To discuss the koineisation of early Iceland is therefore to set aside the perennial problem of knowing whether there was *language* contact between for example Norse and Common Gaelic in Iceland.[4] Such a discussion assumes at least that it was not significant enough to play a meaningful role in the development of the language that was spoken in early Iceland.

It is preferable to discuss the relevant linguistic situation in terms of koineisation and dialect levelling and not 'standardisation'. Standardisation suggests that there was an authority overseeing the process, that it was somehow deliberate or that ideologies were implicated, but this is unlikely to have been the case. Milroy (1999: 1) claims that the processes of levelling and standardisation are often confused in discussions of the latter. Cultural models and ideologies, which vary both historically and geographically, are implicated in standardisation, but not in levelling. Standardisation implies also that a learned and accepted form was adopted because it was felt to be 'correct', and this was not the case either. It should be recognised, however, that a 'standard' language may have arisen subsequently out of the koine (Kristján Árnason, 2003b: 245–79).

The approach to this problem is first to comment in Section 3.2 on the information that we have regarding the linguistic situation in Norse prior to

---

[3] See Gilles & Moulin (2003: 312) for developments in Luxembourgish. Leith (1983: 39) notes that it is not always the prestige variant that is chosen as the standard. With regard to English, the East Midland accent was not the dominant variety, but it came to acquire prestige and became the 'standard' amongst the merchants of London.

[4] Jackson (1953: 74) uses the term Common Gaelic for this period. In his view, Scottish Gaelic and Irish Gaelic were a single language until at least the tenth century, and in most respects until the thirteenth century.

the Settlement and the arrival of Christianity in 1000 A.D. The runic evidence will be discussed briefly and the question of what it can tell us about linguistic variation in ninth-century (or earlier) Scandinavia will be addressed. The intention is not here to discuss and chart chronological linguistic change in Norse where the evidence is available – a topic that has been exhausted –, but to focus solely on the more problematic issue of dialect variation and koineisation.[5]

In Section 3.3, the geographic origins and the social background of the settlers will be discussed. It is helpful to have some knowledge of the historical mobility of the Norsemen that settled Iceland, and this information can be gleaned from historical accounts, but also from literature and in particular the saga narratives. This is relevant because if one argues for a pre- (or even post-) Settlement levelled Norse dialect, one needs a linguistic environment in which the levelling could occur. Whilst high degrees of internal mobility alone are not be able to account for such a change, they would clearly facilitate levelling.

Section 3.4 discusses the dialectal features that emerged in the Norse colonies before Section 3.5 tackles the problem of understanding how a relatively levelled dialect was formed in Iceland *or* exported to Iceland. Scholars such as Kuhn (1935: 21–39), Hreinn Benediktsson (1964: 26) and Helgi Guðmundsson (1977: 314–25), all of whom recognise that there must have been dialectal variation in Norway prior to the Settlement, have argued that there are a number of factors explaining how the 'mixture' of Norse dialects was levelled in early Iceland. Alternatively, a koine may have begun to form before the Norsemen settled Iceland. It should also be borne in mind that a levelled dialect prior to the Settlement does not exclude the possibility of subsequent further levelling in Iceland. These views have been discussed in the literature previously, but there is scope now to consider the arguments in more detail and to suggest new solutions.

Section 3.6 addresses some of the issues highlighted in Section 3.5 and is concerned in particular with how a linguistic norm was established in Iceland. Whereas previously the levelling of the dialect has been discussed from a Norse perspective, Section 3.6 focuses solely on the factors specific to the development of linguistic norms in Iceland. In Section 3.7, it is shown that the factors that are commonly thought to have brought about and influenced the relative homogeneity of Icelandic account better for the *maintenance* of the lack of dialect variation over a period of centuries, rather than the *emergence* of a uniform language.

The chapter proceeds on a chronological basis, starting with an analysis of the linguistic situation prior to the Settlement. The focus then turns to

---

[5] Cf. Finnur Jónsson (1901); Noreen (1923); Björn K. Þórólfsson (1925); Seip (1955); Bandle (1956); Haugen (1976); Kristján Árnason (2003b: 245–79) for descriptions of linguistic change in Norse.

the Settlement itself and what we know about the settlers, before addressing the important question of how the language spoken in Iceland itself came to be levelled and how a linguistic norm became established.

3.2. NORSE DIALECTAL VARIATION PRIOR TO THE SETTLEMENT

3.2.1 *The runic evidence*

We begin by examining the earliest attestations of Germanic that date from the second century A.D. and are written in the older form of the runic alphabet (or *fuþark* – so named after the first six characters of the older runic alphabet).[6] The runic corpus comprises approximately 6,000 inscriptions found within the area of present-day Denmark, Norway and Sweden with a small body of inscriptions found elsewhere.[7] Over 70 runic inscriptions have been found in Iceland, but all of them date to post 1200 A.D.[8] The majority of runic inscriptions refer to personal names, place-names and what appear to be statements of ownership of objects. The corpus as a whole is too laconic to provide the raw material for dialect profiles. The runes provide us instead with linguistic information regarding phonology and morphology, and syntax once the longer inscriptions start to appear. In approximately the middle of the eighth century, one gets the reduction from the 24-rune to the 16-rune *fuþark* and the phonological information drops temporarily (Spurkland, 2006b: 27), until the 'dotted runes' are introduced to restore extra distinctions; see Haugen (1973: 83–92). In order to make the *fuþark* fit the phonemic system of Norse (the 16-character *fuþark* fell short with its four vowels instead of nine), the practice of 'dotting' was introduced which was the placing of a dot or a small cross-bar on one of the ambiguous runes to mark a different value.

In order to be able to interpret the runic evidence as a source of dialectal variation, we would require inscriptions dating from approximately the same age which were found in different locations, but that showed variation of the same variable. Instead of providing dialect profiles, runic inscriptions of the syncope period show the results of radical linguistic change such as syncope and mutation.[9] The difficulty is in knowing how these innovations

---

[6] Cf. Kristján Árnason (2003b: 250); Barnes (2005: 174): the Early Runic Language used a 24 character *fuþark* and dates to the period of approximately 200-400 A.D.

[7] See Knirk (1993: 545–52): 75 runic inscriptions have been found in Greenland.

[8] See Knirk (1993: 545–52): Norwegian finds from Bergen and Trondheim sometimes apparently attest to the use of runes by Icelanders who traded in Norway.

[9] See Barnes (2005: 176): syncope (that is, loss) of short, unaccented *a*, *i* and *u* is well attested in seventh-and eighth-century inscriptions, for example in -lAUSZ < *-lausaz* '-less'. Before their loss, these vowels have a tendency to 'mutate' a preceding accented vowel, that is, cause it to adopt one of the features of the unaccented vowel's articulation. For the reason that in most cases the product was a new vowel quality for which there was no pre-existing runic symbol, the effects of mutation do not normally appear in inscriptions.

spread. The linguistic change could have been gradual and a piecemeal affair in early Viking Age Scandinavia where there was no centralised authority. The change could, however, have been sudden. From a purely sociolinguistic or dialectological point of view, sound change is always gradual in some way or other. From a systemic point of view, however, some sound changes can be shown to be sudden: if a system can be in two stable states, between which there is no stable intervening condition, the transition between the two states is likely to be catastrophic. Changes such as the Great Vowel Shift, at least in its upper part, appear to have happened extremely rapidly and this can be dated fairly precisely in the first half of the fifteenth century: see Zachrisson (1913: a crucial text is the *Paston Letters* (1422–1509), because it was written by persons who did not employ a standard spelling-system and who seem to have been trying to represent what they were actually speaking). Other changes (including the lower part of the Great Vowel Shift) took centuries to be completed. One can use the model of push- and pull-chains. A push-chain has to be rapid: displacement from one 'slot' in the system to another will be sudden, as will coalescence. A pull-chain, on the other hand, does not need to be: it simply vacates a slot that can subsequently be filled at a later stage (cf. McMahon, 1994: 29–31; Labov, 1994: 145–54).

For most scholars it is axiomatic that differing runic forms reflect stages of development rather than dialect phenomena (the two need not be mutually exclusive) (cf. Skautrup, 1944: 16, 133–4; Wessén, 1957: 25–9; Torp & Vikør, 1993: 33–5, 44–5; Grønvik, 1987; 1998; 2001). The possibility of regional differences is hardly admitted.[10] There is the added problem, emphasised by Syrett (1994: 31), that in our attempts to interpret the early runic inscriptions we necessarily try to make them conform to our uniform reconstructed Proto-Nordic. The perception of the runic language is that for all that is partially recorded, it has much in common with a typical variation-free reconstructed language.[11]

Arguing against the *communis opinio*, Barnes (2005: 47–66) believes that he has identified particular features suggestive of dialectal variation in the Viking Age, albeit this variation pertains to the division between West Norse and East Norse rather than to variation within West Norse itself.[12] Whilst his evidence may not be substantial, it seems to be unambiguous.

It is true that the runic inscriptions are remarkable for the apparent uniformity of their language, and it is tempting to attribute any 'variation'

---

[10] See Jacobsen & Moltke (1941–2) where Migration and Viking Age language is treated the most systematically.

[11] A distinction should be drawn between synchronic and diachronic variation. Grønvik (1987, 1998) are convincing studies of diachronic variation.

[12] The total coalescence of /z/ with /r/ two to three centuries earlier in Norway and its Atlantic colonies than in Denmark and Sweden; reduplicating verbs; the demonstrative pronoun meaning 'this'.

to rune-smiths' errors or just inconsistencies in runic inscriptions. However, one has to be careful how one discusses the uniformity of the 'runic language'. Whilst the rune-forms are rather uniform, the runic inscriptions themselves are very much not uniform. There seems to be little that is fixed about the representation of some of the vowels, and (at least sometimes) how one represents consonant clusters. There was spelling variety and linguistic variety: digraphic spelling of monophthongs and monographic spelling of diphthongs. There may be a temptation to argue for the possibility of a 'standardised' runic language. One suspects, however, that this is improbable, simply because runic orthography is so obviously not standardised. There is far too much orthographic variation in the earlier inscriptions, for any sort of 'rune-master' standardisation to have taken place. But most of this orthographic variation does not show variation in the language represented, as far as one can tell: it only shows that there was no defined spelling-system (Jacobsen & Moltke, 1941–42).

Whilst it may be incorrect to speak of a 'standardised' runic language, according to some scholars inscriptions of the younger *fuþark* (700–1050 A.D.) show forms very similar in structure to those of the oldest Norwegian and Icelandic texts in the Latin alphabet.[13] It may not be correct to say that the runic inscriptions represent practically the same idiom as the classical Old Icelandic texts. However, it is true that the major sound changes that define Norse had happened by then, and it is arguably the same language in a loose sense.

The runes coexisted with the Roman alphabet, in geographically distinct areas, for two or three centuries and they continued to coexist for four or five more centuries in Norway after Conversion: they were used with different writing materials and usually for different purposes. The Scandinavians learned to write the Roman alphabet directly or indirectly from the English. This is demonstrated, quite apart from the basics of Insular letter forms, by the fact that the letter *þ*, originally borrowed from the runic alphabet, is known in Iceland by its English name *þorn*, whereas the runic character retains its original name, *þurs*. Hreinn Benediktsson (1965: 22–35) claims that the difference between the earliest Icelandic script and Norwegian writing is due mainly to their somewhat different origin. For him, Norwegian writing (especially in the East) is based primarily on English writing whilst the earliest Icelandic script with its distinct Caroline character is much more a direct offshoot of the general medieval Latin writing, adapted directly to the Icelandic vernacular. According to Hreinn, the influence of English writing on the earliest Icelandic script was restricted to the adaption to the vernacular and the creation of a native orthography.

---

[13] Kristján Árnason (2003b: 250) argues that runic inscriptions formed the basis of the Old Icelandic written norm. Spurkland (2006a: 335) has suggested that the language of the Eggja transcription seems to demonstrate more or less the same linguistic structure as we find in the skaldic and Eddaic poems. Cf. Olsen (1941: 60), Grønvik (1985).

Knowledge and use of the runic *fuþark* in Iceland (and likewise in Norway and Sweden) was independent of knowledge and use of the Roman alphabet, and interaction between the runic and Roman writing systems had taken place far earlier in England.

3.2.2 *Runic evidence and the spoken language*

As discussed, the runic inscriptions do not give any indication of a 'standardised' language: there is a great deal of diversity of spelling, which can be explained by attempts to represent actual sounds. The inscriptions of the Early Runic Period (200–400 A.D.) reveal a conservative language whose dialectal provenance has been much discussed. The language of this period has in fact been described as a koine.[14] It is not, however, this period that concerns us. We are more interested in the inscriptions that were carved approximately five hundred years later. Whilst it may be reasonable to assume that the rune-smiths set out to reproduce the sounds of the spoken language, one must be cautious in drawing firm conclusions about the spoken language on the basis of runes carved five hundred years subsequently. Arguments for certain types of speech or a prestige element can be dismissed with relatively few constraints. As with modern languages such as English, a standardised written form can develop in the absence of a spoken language that is standardised in terms of pronunciation at least. Standardisation can in fact be inextricable: Norway shows this with its two standard written languages (Bokmål and Nynorsk) and a rich array of dialects.[15] The various dialects of spoken Norwegian have in fact played an important role in language planning in Norway and have been essential for the development of the two written languages. The question of the relationship between the written and spoken language is relevant because the written norm in Iceland and Norway was very similar, and we need to know what this tells us about the status of the spoken language.

One has to be very careful therefore in analysing the runic evidence from the perspective of dialectal evidence. The earliest certain phonological distinctions between East and West Norse, the monophthongisation of some of the diphthongs, first appear in the corpus of runic inscriptions in the early tenth century.[16] The earliest dialectal feature in Norse that is securely datable is the East Norse monophthongisation of accented *ei* (Gmc. *ai* with *i*-mutation of the first element by the second) to *e*. That is the

---

[14] Makaev (1996 [1965]: 45–6) assumes that the older runic inscriptions of Scandinavia were written in a supra-dialectal, literary koine. Cf. Nielsen (2000: 287).

[15] Faarlund (2003: 311–25) investigates the relationship between a standard language and its dialects in Norway. There has been much written on this subject, cf. Askedal (2005: 1584-1602).

[16] A lot of Germanic languages do monophthongise the diphthong, but in Old English, for instance, the monophthongisation is very early and precedes *i*-mutation, giving *a*: see Bandle (1973: 24–36, 52–56).

first phonological change that distinguishes what was to become Danish and Swedish, from the West Norse dialects which were to give Norwegian, Faroese and Icelandic. There is likely to be variation before that, but not variation that comes through as dialect distinctions in the recorded separate dialects and languages. There is indeed variation within the runic evidence, but not of geographically organised dialectal variation and not before the tenth century. There was a lot of graphic variation nonetheless: it looks as though there were no or few standards for representing the actual sounds of Norse, and the rune-smiths are struggling to show what sounds they are representing. Irrespective of their origin, runes provide little scope for commenting on the establishment of a spoken norm or on dialectal variation for which we are better off referring to our knowledge of community types, sociolinguistic structures and the literature on the universal nature of linguistic variation.

3.3 THE SETTLERS: GEOGRAPHIC ORIGINS AND SOCIAL MOBILITY

3.3.1 *The geographic origins of the settlers*

Having discussed the Norse language prior to the Settlement, we now need to consider the information that we have regarding the settlers. The six extant versions of *Landnámabók* show that the individuals that settled Iceland came from Norway, but also from the British Isles (*Íf* Ii and ii, *Landnámabók*). For more than half a century before Iceland was discovered and settled, Norsemen had maintainted settlements and wielded political power in Shetland, Orkney, the Hebrides, the Isle of Man and coastal regions of Ireland, Scotland and northern England (Jones, 1984: 272). Most historical and archaeological evidence suggests that, after initial periods of conflict, the Norse invaders, most of whom were men, settled and perhaps intermarried with existing populations. Later, when the Settlement commenced, many of these family groups left coastal settlements in the British Isles for a new life in the uncharted territory of Iceland. According to *Landnámabók*, up to one third of the settlers to Iceland came not directly from Norway, but from the British Isles and the Faroe Islands where they had settled. There was therefore considerable so-called external colonisation prior to the Settlement.

Recent genetic research (Agnar Helgason, 2000a: 999–1016; 2000b: 697–717) supports the notion that a disproportionate number of females from the British Isles made up the Icelandic founder population. Agnar's research based on the mitochondrial DNA, the Y-chromosome and blood types of over 400 contemporary Icelanders found that 62 percent of Icelandic women have Irish ancestry, whereas 80 per cent of the male population had a Norse lineage; only 20 percent of males have chromosomes that can be traced back to the British Isles. Of the 48 women whose origin is referred to in *Landámabók*, 16 percent have genealogical ties to the British Isles.[17] This contrasts with the finding that, of the 220 men for whom genealogical information is recorded in the same source, under five per cent have British ancestry. It is known that the founders mentioned in *Landnámabók* represent only a small proportion of the total settlement population. A number of historians have argued that a disproportionate number of the individuals not mentioned in *Landnámabók* originated from the British Isles (Jón Steffensen, 1975; Gísli Sigurðsson, 1988). Thus, for example, numerous slaves were captured by the Vikings in their raids on the coastlines of the British Isles, and many of the slaves were taken to Iceland. The majority of these slaves seem likely to have been female (Clover, 1988: 147-88; Karras, 1988; Sayers, 1994: 129–53). *Landnámabók* is certainly the most comprehensive source for the Settlement, but it is not the only one. The first chapter of *Íslendingabók* (*Íf* Ii, 4–5) is devoted to the Settlement and its perspective is unequivocally Norwegian: *Ísland byggðisk fyrst ýr Norvegi* [...] *En þá varð för manna mikil mjök út hingat ýr Norvegi* 'Iceland was first settled from Norway [...] And then a great many people began to move out here from Norway'. It is to be noted in fact that *Íslendingabók* makes no mention of settlers from the British Isles, and unlike some of the versions of *Landnámabók* was written down much closer in time to the events that concern us.[18]

One is left therefore with the perennial problem of how one puts an accurate figure on the ethnic make-up of the settlement population to Iceland. Since we are interested in the linguistic situation at the time of the Settlement, we need to have information on where in Norway the Norwegian settlers came from as well as estimates on the number of non-Norse speakers. For this degree of detail, one has to rely on *Landnámabók* on the grounds that there is no obvious reason for the information to have been invented. Finnur Jónsson (1921: 5-49) has compiled some of this information and one can summarise it as follows. We know the precise geographic origins of approximately 130 of the Norwegian settlers:[19]

---

[17] See Jón Steffensen (1975) and Sykes (2006: 236–7) who believes that roughly two thirds of the Y-chromosomes (male descent) were Scandinavian while the remaining third were from Ireland and Scotland.

[18] Whilst some scholars believe that *Íslendingabók* is more accurate than *Landnámabók*, it contains far less information regarding the origins of the settlers.

[19] There have been various other attempts at presenting the numbers of settlers from different parts of Norway, see Magerøy (1965: 12–14). Guðmundur Hannesson's (1924–25) figures are based on the number of settlers that came from different Norse colonies and his figures include the settlers' offspring. He concluded that on the basis of *Landnámabók* we know that there were 846 Norwegian settlers of which 385 we do not know the exact origin. He claimed that 126 came from the British Isles. Cf. Munch (1852); Barði Guðmundsson (1959).

Table 2. Geographic origins of the first Norwegian settlers to Iceland

Region of Norway	Number of Settlers
Hålogaland	15
Namdalen	6
Trondheimsfylka	10
Nord- og Sunnmøre	7
Romsdalen	3-4
Fjordane	10-12
Sogn	14-15
Hordaland	25
Rogaland	10
Agder	15
Vestfold	1
Telemark	3
Hallingdal	2-3
Valdres	1
Opplanda	2
Ranrike	2
Total	Approx. 129

This shows that the majority of the Norwegian settlers for whom we have detailed information came from the south-west of Norway where there is a history of rich dialectal variation, with a minority coming from the Trondheim area. One should point out that the sources show that a further 60 settlers or so were definitely Norwegian, but more precise geographic information is not given.

The historical evidence apparently contradicts the genetic evidence. As noted previously, the genetic evidence points to a majority of the female settlers being Irish whereas the historical sources suggest that Common Gaelic speakers may have only accounted for as little as ten percent of the overall settlement population. It is unlikely, however, that the female slaves were counted.

The reason for addressing these questions regarding the origins of the settlers is that one needs the most accurate impression possible of how linguistically diffuse the settlement community in Iceland was. The information that we have regarding the Settlement may at first glance lead us to believe that the linguistic community of early Iceland was rather heterogenous with the settlers coming from different parts of Norway and the British Isles.

3.3.2 *Social background and mobility of the settlers*

As well as the settlers' geographic origins, any study of the Norse dialect of early Iceland would benefit from knowledge regarding the settlers' social background. This information helps us to draw conclusions regarding the issue of sociolinguistic variation. *Landnámabók* shows us that a small number of the settlers that came from the external colonies, such as the British Isles, were primary settlers and thus heads of households.[20] This is significant because these heads of households (some of whom were female) had considerable linguistic authority, especially over the young girls brought into the household to marry the sons. It is also the speech of these primary settlers that was most prone to prior linguistic interference because they had settled previously in the British Isles (and the Faroe Islands).

There are a few insights into social divisions that were present in Icelandic society at the end of the ninth century. There are several different and partly independent criteria for social status: (1) birth: genealogies, more particularly those in the sagas, show the importance of genealogical origin. Genetic status can be independent of other sorts of status. Vífill, a slave belonging to Auðr *in djúpúðga* in *Eiríks saga rauða* happens to be of noble birth but had been seized in warfare; Auðr recognises his inherent genetic status, grants him land, and he becomes the grandfather of the heroine of the saga. Similarly, in *Laxdæla saga*, Melkorka is a slave, bought by Höskuldr, who turns out to be the kidnapped daughter of an Irish king; she becomes the grandmother of the hero of the saga, Kjartan son of Óláfr pái, Höskuldr's bastard son; (2) wealth: it was often inherited. It was often mentioned, and sometimes allowed a partial equivalence with political power. This was not always the case, however: the figure of the wealthy but cowardly or incompetent man is another frequent literary type; (3) political power. It is not based upon wealth, but upon the threat or actuality of force, which can be sublimated into the legal process. *Sturlunga saga* depicts the reality of such underlying military violence in thirteenth-century Iceland; (4) ethical authority: it is almost always associated with Christianity and is not usually heritable. Such divisions would have existed and one can be confident that the settlers included Norsemen of high birth as well as slaves. The best sources for details on social division are the sagas. The saga-picture reflects what thirteenth-century saga writers and audiences recognised in their own society, past and present.

The saga evidence shows that there was a degree of hierarchy in Icelandic society, but also that there was quite a high degree of social mobility (vertically). From our perspective, the second point is in fact more important. The social strata that existed in Icelandic society were not set in stone, and Icelandic society was very willing to accommodate the 'self made-man'. One witnesses in *Bandamanna saga* the ironic use of the 'local lad makes good' figure (Oddr Ófeigsson). *Eyrbyggja saga* uses the

[20] By 'primary settlers' I mean settlers mentioned in *Landnámabók* who distributed land to his or her clients, such as Helgi *inn magri* and Auðr *in djúpúðga*. These two settlers appear to be of particular significance because they are two of only four settlers who are also mentioned in *Íslendingabók*.

'unpromising youth motif': Snorri *goði* appears as a very unheroic figure in his youth, but outwits those of apparently far greater personal and genetic status to dominate the saga. But although the saga does not introduce him as such, he also has as fine a pedigree as anyone around – but the saga lets the reader work that out for himself. Auðunn *inn vestfirzki* is a clear example of a person without birth-status who by personal integrity or sheer cleverness achieves high status, often at the expense of those with more traditional status.

As a *terra nova* and a colony, there were fewer social constraints in Iceland than in Norway. There was not much social distance between different sectors of the population: there was no aristocracy and institutional power (the Church, for example) was weak. Speakers did not have preconceived notions about identity-marking functions and did not automatically belong to a particular sociolinguistic group. According to the sagas, any Icelandic peasant was able, and had the right, to compose and perform skaldic poetry, which in Norway after Conversion was an aristocratic pursuit. We are told at the beginning of *Hreiðars þáttr* (*Íf* X: 247) that Hreiðar was barely intelligent enough to care for himself (*hann var ljótr maðr ok varla sjálfbjargi fyrir vits sökum*) and yet towards the end of the tale, he composes poetry to the king. A very esoteric and apparently prestigious style of speech was therefore accessible to individuals from any part of society.

If this frontier society was a socially rather homogenous community or a community where social divisions could easily be crossed as indicated above, koineisation would have occurred faster than if there had been considerable social divisions. There was a community of core speakers in Settlement Iceland, perhaps the most influential members of society and potential koineisers, but they were scattered around the island. The levelled Norse dialect or mixture of dialects had been spoken in the country for only a short period of time before the population stabilised.

3.3.3 The status of Norse and Common Gaelic at the time of the Settlement

Looking beyond Iceland and its putative social divisions, it is clear that Norse became the superstrate, dominant language in the period c. 800–1050 A.D. which saw the arrival of the Scandinavian settlers in places as far apart as Normandy, England, Ireland, Greenland and the North American continent. The linguistic situation was different in Iceland and the Faroe Islands because these islands were still largely unsettled and language contact was therefore much less of an issue. As one is only left in Iceland with an assortment of lexical remnants, place-names and personal names from Common Gaelic, it is probable that the Common Gaelic language was a substrate. This would fit with the socio-historical information that we have regarding the Irish emigrants as slaves in Iceland.[21] One notes that for all his knowledge of linguistic matters, the First Grammarian only mentions Irish in the sense of the Irish pronunciation of Latin.[22]

It is often believed that some of these Celtic immigrants were independent settlers and wives of Norwegian settlers whilst a number were slaves. Most of these slaves were soon freed, and some of their descendants came to occupy an important place in Icelandic society. Gísli Sigurðsson (1988: 25) notes that a number of literary historians have argued that the Celtic influence was essential in the development of Icelandic literature, in particular poetry.

Irrespective of their status, the most likely scenario is that the female settlers with Celtic origins were Norse speakers by the time of the Settlement: Common Gaelic speakers integrated into Norse-speaking communities in the British Isles well before the Settlement.

3.4 DIALECT FEATURES IN ICELAND, THE FAROE ISLANDS AND SOUTH-WEST NORWAY

There were no real spoken linguistic boundaries in Scandinavia at this time. It is difficult therefore to know for sure what were the linguistic features of the dialect(s) taken originally to Iceland.[23] There are few linguistic innovations that appear in Old Icelandic before they do in the relevant West Norwegian dialects. We are thus mainly concerned with features that were either 'exported' to Iceland or that developed in parallel in different parts of the Norse-speaking world.[24]

In order to speak of dialect features, we must turn instead to the phonological structural similarities that appear in Icelandic, Faroese and the dialects of south-west Norway subsequent to the Settlement in the thirteenth century. These include the following developments in post-vocalic clusters involving sonorants: *rl* > *dl*: *karl* [kadl]; *rn* > *dn*: *korn* [kodn]; *ll* > *dl*: *kalla* [kadla]; *nn* > *dn* (post-long vowel only): *steinn* [steidn] (cf. *finna* [fina]). Sandøy (1994: 44–45) has suggested that some of

<hr>

[21] See *Íf* V (*Laxdæla saga*) for textual references to slaves in Iceland. Cf. the small number of Norse words in the English language, and yet Norse was the court and administrative language of the Scandinavian rulers of England before it disappeared in the eleventh century. See Baugh (1959: 83–6) for the Common Gaelic influence on Old English.

[22] Hreinn Benediktsson (1972: 235) where the Irish are in fact referred to as *Skotar*.

[23] There are relatively few linguistic boundaries in Scandinavia today; there is instead a pattern of dialectal isoglosses. Seip (1955: 31) discusses the emergence of dialectal variation in Scandinavia on the basis of different written languages, but it is very unclear what the evidence is for that.

[24] Cf. Celander (1906: 41, 57); Indrebø (1951: 124, 140); Kuhn (1955: 21); Chapman (1962); Kjartan G. Ottósson (2003: 117) for a discussion of a range of sound changes that may have been taken to Iceland, or alternatively may have developed in parallel.

these features may be explained in structural terms. The *ll* > *dl* development only occurs in geminates and the same cluster has been palatalised in dialects of northern Norway and certain Swedish and Danish dialects. This indicates that the cluster is unstable and that it may undergo the same change in different areas without contact. It is also claimed that the *rl* and *rn* consonant clusters, which have almost the same distribution, are universally unstable and are susceptible to phonological change, undergoing assimilation or palatalisation in certain Norwegian dialects. It is more difficult to see the structural motivation for the *nn* > *dn* phonological shift. Similar developments of stops before post-vocalic consonants can be found in Norwegian dialects, chiefly in western Norway, in particular in the area of Gula.[25]

Sandøy (1994: 45; 2001: 130) has claimed that these changes date back to the thirteenth century because they are not found in earlier written texts. There is a pun in *Eyrbyggja saga* (*Íf* IV: 100) that requires one of these sound changes. 'Nú er örnin gamli floginn á æzlit...' It refers to Arnkell, the first element of whose name is the 'eagle' word *örn*, gen. sg. *arnar*. The second element is ketill 'pot' reduced to low stress to *-kell*, but *karl* means '(wretched) old man'. The *rl* and *ll* groups must have coalesced phonetically for Arnkell to be referred to as 'the *old* eagle'. *Eyrbyggja saga* is usually considered to date to the third-quarter of the thirteenth century.

It is reasonable to ask therefore how Icelandic can have the same structural, phonological tendencies as Faroese and the dialects of south-west Norway, if the language (dialect) spoken in Iceland was the result of dialect mixing. If they date back earlier to the Settlement, it is surprising that these *unstable* consonant clusters could have survived the levelling process. These changes are often attributed to 'drift', and the question of whether they can be explained by social contact or 'drift' has been much discussed.[26]

In addition to these widely-discussed consonant clusters, one needs to mention pre-aspiration. Pre-aspiration, the period of aspiration preceding the closure of a voiceless obstruent as in 'de^{h}ta' (*detta*) 'to fall, to drop' and 'k^{h}e^{h}pa' (*keppa*) 'to compete, to strive for', is another phonological feature found in Icelandic and Faroese, but also in south-western Norway around the modern town of Stavanger. The difficulty is to know what the centre of

---

[25] Cf. Chapman (1962: 63–71) and Lockwood (1955/57: 18–20): the same applies to Faroese. One also notes that a number of the first settlers came from Gula and that the first Icelandic legal code was also based on the precedent of the Gula region; Jóhannes L. L. Jóhannsson (1924: 83) discusses the sound changes that might have been taken from Norway to Iceland, such as *rr, nn* > *dn* and *rl, ll* > *dl*.

[26] Cf. Björn K. Þórólfsson (1925); Hreinn Benediktsson (1961–62); Chapman (1962); Kjartan G. Ottósson (2003: 111–52). Icelandic develops in its own way from about 1400 A.D. which is the period when contact with Norway drops off (due to the plague). Social contact is relevant to a degree, but is unlikely to have been sustained long enough to explain all the phonological similarities.

origin of this particular feature was. Pre-aspiration is also found in Scottish Gaelic and so the inevitable question that arises is whether this can be attributed to a Celtic influence dating back to the Settlement. Pre-aspiration is more widespread than is sometimes recognised.

Pétur Helgason (2002: 213–28) has produced a comprehensive study of Nordic pre-aspiration and found it to be present in the Norwegian dialects of Jæren, Gudbrandsdalen, Trøndelag and Senja, as well as in a number of Swedish dialects, Saami, Icelandic and Faroese (cf. Gunnar Ólafur Hansson, 1997: 158–64). It may be that pre-aspiration was geographically more widespread in Scandinavia at earlier stages than it later turned out to be. In the light of recent research, one should not focus too much, however, on the factor of pre-aspiration since Andersen (2002: 15–34) has shown that it may in fact rise spontaneously.

Chapman (1962: 85) claimed that pre-aspiration was 'an example of a feature taken to Iceland by the original settlers'. It is tempting to imagine a scenario whereby the Norsemen settle in Orkney, Shetland, the Hebrides etc., taking the pre-aspiration feature with them, and then Norwegians and Norsemen living in the British Isles (some of whom are pre-aspirators) settle Iceland. Irrespective of how and when this feature developed, it would seem that pre-aspiration is a relatively stable variable that survived levelling.

According to Chapman's (1962: 78) highly controversial and widely criticised monograph, these discussed sound changes are Norwegian innovations which spread to Icelandic (and Faroese) through 'socio-culturally determined channels' (cf. Sandøy, 1994: 43–5). Hreinn Bene-diktsson (1963: 152–62) and Ulvestad (1964: 601–04) express doubt on a number of Chapman's conclusions on chronological grounds. The fact that the changes which Chapman discusses have occurred in related idioms such as Icelandic, the West Norwegian dialects and Faroese shows they can partly be seen as the result of some phonological structural tendency. Phonological features such as pre-aspiration may be best explained by the fact that they were simply part of the phonological system of the dialect spoken in West Norway which had been diffused (in the geographical sense) prior to the Settlement and that this levelled dialect was the idiom that was taken to both the Faroe Islands and Iceland.

With regard to the argument between 'drift' and 'social contact' as an explanation for language change, one should not exaggerate the isolation of Iceland and underestimate the scope for social contact between the various Norse colonies. If the saga evidence is to be trusted, it would seem that the wealthy and powerful travelled frequently between Iceland and Norway, albeit the journey was dangerous and there are reports of drownings (see *Íf* V, *Laxdæla saga*: 41, 224). Human beings are socially organised; they are not able to survive in complete isolation and the archaeological and saga evidence would point to high degrees of contact between Iceland, Norway and the British Isles. Magerøy (1993a: 33–57) observes that there was a relatively high degree of contact with Norway and England: 1100–1160 A.D.: eight references to Icelandic ship-owners; 1160–1200 A.D.: 16 references to Norwegian ship-owners. In 1118 A.D. alone, 35 ships came to Iceland which, based on our knowledge of ships at the time, amounts to approximately one thousand people. Unlike the Faroese, the Icelanders did not own their own ships post 1200 A.D. According to Debes (1995: 118), the Faroese continued to actively trade with Iceland and Norway in the medieval period, but it is not clear what the evidence is for that.

Looking back over this section, one can say that on the basis of the historical evidence, approximately 40 per cent of the settlers to Iceland came from western Norway, a further 40 per cent came from other parts of Norway (the Trondheim area in particular), with the remaining settlers coming from the British Isles. High degrees of social mobility amongst the settlers from Norway and the British Isles to Iceland meant that sociolinguistic barriers, if they existed at all, could be crossed. Through the existence of skaldic poetry, we know that the spoken language of early Iceland showed register variation and that the higher registers were available to all speakers. There are a number of phonological similarities and common innovations to be found in Icelandic, Faroese and some of the West Norwegian dialects. This comparative evidence seems to tally with the idea that the language which the Icelandic community adopted was that of the West Norwegian settlers, some of whom had connections in the Scottish Isles and the Faroe Islands and came to Iceland via these places. It is possible that these dialects came to share these features through very high degrees of contact between their speakers after the Settlement, but it is surely more likely that the settlers had in essence the same idiom from the outset.

3.5 ICELAND AS A 'NEW SOCIETY'

3.5.1 *Features of 'new societies'*

Irrespective of what the features of the dialect(s) taken to Iceland may have been, a linguistic norm would have emerged in a 'new society'. One of the key challenges of this chapter is therefore to understand better how a linguistic norm developed in a speech community such as Iceland where there was scant language (not dialect) contact. We know little about the formulation of a spoken norm in Iceland because the lack of historical language contact and thus apparent absence of substratal or superstratal effects does not leave us much linguistic evidence to look at. However, in order to address the problem of language development in this specific context, one can look at other so-called new societies. These new societies have linguistically something in common.

In new societies around the world such as New England, New Zealand and Iceland, there appears to be for example some evidence of linguistic conservatism that is not evident whence the settlers came.[27] An example of this would be the phonological (but not lexical) conservatism of American English which has retained the rhoticity of the English settlers. However, it is by no means true that all new societies are characterised by linguistic conservatism: one might contrast New Zealand with Australia, for instance. New Zealand English has not undergone the considerable restructuring of the vowel system and the loss of unaccented vowels that Australian English has. It is true that in certain respects, New Zealand may seem to be a close analogue to Iceland. New Zealand English shows for instance very little dialectal variation; its relationship with Britain is not that different from the medieval Icelandic relationship with Norway; there was a degree of external colonisation with approximately ten per cent of the settlers coming from settlements in Australia (cf. the settlers to the Faroe Islands who went subsequently to Iceland for example); and the apparent dialect levelling over a short period of time led to a high degree of linguistic homogeneity. By 'external colonisation' here, I mean Iceland was settled partly by groups of people living in other Norse colonies such as the Hebrides or the Faroe Islands, but which came originally from Norway.

There are, however, a number of major differences between these two types of new society such as different settlement patterns. Gordon *et al* (2004: 250) note that the settlement of New Zealand soon led to nucleated settlements and urban centres (gold-mining settlements in particular), as well as rural dispersal. Trudgill *et al* (2000: 305) observe that new-dialect formation took place in nucleated settlements where there was a density of speakers from different backgrounds.

Other differences were the background of the settlers and social bonds between the settlers (perhaps the most significant difference between the Australia and Iceland case: convicts *versus* a potential elite); the nature and duration of the journey to the 'new society';[28] much steadier and more continuous immigration in the case of New Zealand; the evidence of early social stratification in the towns; and the presence of a small Maori-speaking population meant that New Zealand was not a *tabula rasa* in the way that Iceland was.

---

[27] Cf. Tomasson (1980); Trudgill (1986). The Origins of New Zealand English (ONZE) Project, directed by Elizabeth Gordon at the University of Canterbury, New Zealand has enabled a great deal to be inferred about the processes leading to the formation of New Zealand English.

[28] Trudgill (2004: 90) observes that the voyage to New Zealand lasted from four to six months (cf. Norway to Iceland – approximately eight days). Levelling could therefore have taken place 'at sea' in the case of Australian/New Zealand English. Trudgill (2004: 91) notes that rudimentary dialect levelling of features on the way to New Zealand can be inferred from the ONZE Project data.

The process of initial language development in Iceland was different for another reason too: the numbers of women and children. As discussed in Chapter 2, an important factor for language development is the number of women and children. In Iceland, according to *Landnámabók*, out of the first 415 settlers, only eleven were women. The apparent virtual absence of non-slave women and probably children (for whom precise figures are unavailable) suggests that there was therefore at the *very beginning* at least a lack of linguistic innovators: female speakers and adolescents are often considered the most innovative speakers (in contemporary societies at least). Also, the nature of the Settlement resulted in children's language acquisition being 'controlled' by parents and grandparents with the children and adolescents lacking a stable peer-group variety. The male-female disequilibrium is unlikely to have lasted for any length of time. It is not just language development, however, that was unusual in Iceland, but also the outcome of relative linguistic homogeneity which lasted for over a thousand years.[29]

3.6 LANGUAGE DEVELOPMENT IN EARLY ICELAND

In accordance with sociolinguistic theory and our knowledge of language communities around the world, the relative (but not absolute) absence of dialectal variation in Icelandic is an anomaly. This issue concerns us because it seems to have always have been the linguistic status quo in Iceland. It is an oddity that few, if any demonstrably old dialect distinctions, seem to be reflected in the subsequent dialects and ultimately distinct Scandinavian languages that develop from the tenth century onwards. If early dialect distinctions had developed, they had subsequently been lost or suppressed. According to Stefán Karlsson (1999: 140), 'There is evidence in the written sources for quite a number of linguistic innovations which seemed to establish themselves [...], only to disappear at a later date. [...] we have been unable to define with any certainty the dialect-areas in which they manifested themselves'. Björn K. Þórólfsson (1925: xvii–xix, xxxiii) mentions alleged dialectal variation in the fifteenth and sixteenth centuries in Iceland. However, it is difficult to draw dialect-maps on the basis of such fragmentary evidence.[30]

In some instances, dialect distinctions may have appeared as a phonological feature arose in one geographic area, but they do not appear to have spread and have been subsequently lost. The lack of dialectal variation may be linked to the historically strong attempt to 'normalise' the Icelandic language

---

[29] There is now evidence of limited dialectal variation in urban speech in Australian, New Zealand and Canadian English (Trudgill, 1986: 146). It appears that in certain cases, such as American English, it takes several hundred years for dialectal distinctions to start to appear.

[30] One exception is the pronunciation of *hv* and not *kv* in some pockets in the south of Iceland.

through the schooling system, albeit this particular development occurred later. One notes, however, that some changes such as the coalescence of *i* and *y* and the Quantity Shift – where every stressed syllable was long but the degree of stress could be amplified by drawing out the pronunciation of a long vowel – seem to have taken place without resistance whereas others (for example *flámæli*) were strongly resisted sociolinguistically.[31] *flámæli* or 'slack-jawed speech' is a vowel merger where the affected speakers make little or no distinction between *i* and *e* or between *u* and *ö*.

There is some evidence for some divergence in the language of the Vestfirðir in the Old Icelandic period.[32] According to Bandle (1956: 125), the sound change *lf, rf > lb, rb* appears in 1200 A.D. and is common in fourteenth- and fifteenth-century diplomas, but is restricted to the western part of north Iceland (the area west of Akureyri) and the north part of west Iceland (i.e. the Vestfirðir). It is possible that this anomaly died out with the spread of standardised Icelandic through the schooling system and now the broadcast media. The other modern (phonological) dialectal features of different regions of Iceland cannot be shown to go back to the medieval period.

The problem is to explain how a scenario of (relative) linguistic homogeneity in Iceland was maintained. According to Auer, Hinskens & Kerswill (2005: 1), this requires dialect convergence and focusing (*sensu* Le Page & Tabouret-Keller, 1985). Using Trudgill's (2004: 83–99) model of new-dialect formation, the Icelandic idiom came about via mixing, levelling, unmarking (elimination of linguistically marked variants), inter-dialect development (compromise forms), reallocation (the reallocation of input variability in the mix to either a social marking or a phonological function) and focusing (acquisition of norms and stability).

It cannot be overemphasized that we do not have any direct evidence regarding the status of the spoken dialect(s) in Iceland in the earliest period. Icealndic runes aside, the earliest linguistic evidence that we have is manuscriptal. The emergence of manuscripts in the vernacular in Iceland is over 200 years after the Settlement. Hægstad (1909) has shown that 'local' scribal norms were established in Norway. As in most manuscript traditions, Old Icelandic and Old Norwegian was characterised by variance in spelling rather than standardisation and uniformity. According to Hagland (2002: 1015–18), the heterogeneity displayed in the corpus of manuscripts does in effect reflect variation based on dialectal differences in the spoken language as

---

[31] See Kristján Árnason (1980a) for a discussion of the Quantity Shift in Icelandic which refers to the phonological change by which Icelandic lost distinctive vowel length and evolved stressed syllables of equal weight. In modern Icelandic, stressed vowels are either long or followed by two consonants, whereas Old Icelandic had unpredictable vowel length: stressed syllables could contain either long or short vowels, followed by zero to two consonants.

[32] Bandle (1956: 125): the sound change *lf, rf > lb, rb* appears in 1200 A.D. and is common in fourteenth- and fifteenth-century diplomas, but is restricted to the western part of north Iceland and the north part of west Iceland.

well as random orthographic inconsistencies.[33] The written norm of Old Icelandic was similar to local forms in Norway. Hægstad (1909) thinks that the similarities between the earliest Icelandic and Norwegian indicates that the language in Norway (Gulaþing) received the greater number of its special characteristics in its phonetics, grammar and vocabulary, in short its basic form, before 900 A.D., and that it is this special form of Norse which the settlers took with them at the time of the Settlement.

3.6.1 *The 'mixture theory'*

In response to the problem of how linguistic homogeneity came about in Iceland, Hreinn Benediktsson (1964: 26) and Helgi Guðmundsson (1977: 314-25) have argued in favour of the 'mixture theory'. The 'mixture theory' states that the language that was taken to Iceland was a mixture of different dialects that was spoken in different parts of Norway and the British Isles.

The theory does not state clearly whether all the dialects were Norse dialects only, or whether the 'mixture' comprised English dialects too. Bandle (1967: 504–38) claims to have found traces of original dialect mixture in the terminology used in connection with domestic animals in the West Norse dialects. It can be shown that these dialectal lexical variants are geographically defined, but they do not appear to be going back to the old language. It is also the case that the lexicon is extremely susceptible to contact-induced change. As the name suggests, the theory claims that since the migrants came from different regions of Norway and the British Isles to Iceland, a mixture of dialects were spoken. According to this theory, the notion that the settlers spoke different dialects is based principally on linguistic atlases of western Norway compiled approximately 100 years ago. As we have seen, the different versions of *Landnámabók* tell us that the settlers came from western Norway, but also from other parts of Norway and the British Isles. These areas of Norway such as Sogn, Hardanger and Hordaland, where the majority of the settlers came from, show rich dialectal variation today (Sandøy, 1985). One can infer from the current levelling of rural dialects in Norway that dialectal differences were even greater between the relevant regions at a time when there was no urbanisation (cf. Papazian, 1997: 161–90; Røyneland, 2005).

One thousand years ago in the absence of any roads and railways, there would have been less contact between people living in these different mountainous parts of Norway than there is today. If linguistic interaction between Norwegians was limited, there would have been rich dialectal

---

[33] Scribal errors can often be identified since they tend to render the text non-sensical, and, if poetic, non-metrical. They may be paleographically explicable: if a scribe consistently represents *e* by i-mutation of *a* as *æ*, but *e* of origin as *e*, then that is not scribal error. One does not know the sounds the scribe was making, but one knows that the distinction must be linguistic.

variation amongst the settlers as the 'mixture theorists' believe. It is right to assume dialectal variation in Norway in the early period, but even then these communities would not have been static. The impression that one has from historical and literary texts is that there was a degree of contact between Norsemen up and down the Norwegian coast (*Íf* II, *Egils saga Skalla-Grímssonar*: 7–12). It is actually a mistake to think of Norway as a 'country' in this particular historical context: it was the 'North Way', the sea-route from the waters north of Denmark up way into the Arctic.

Dialect levelling can be seen as a gradual process; even if it occurred prior to the Settlement, this does not preclude it from continuing after the Settlement. The levelling could have certainly begun in Norway, and then continued in the Norse colonies: the Faroe Islands were settled prior to Iceland, but its settlers, some of whom went on to Iceland subsequently, came originally from Norway and the British Isles.[34] This created a high degree of linguistic and cultural continuity.

3.6.2 *Dialect levelling in early Iceland*

If the dialect levelling took place in Iceland as the 'mixture theorists' claim, one would require in this new society a settlement pattern that supported the process.[35] However, the settlement pattern of isolated farmsteads is not at all conducive to levelling. Jón Viðar Sigurðsson (2006: 57) notes that 31 per cent of the original 415 settlers went to the Vestfirðingafjórðungur (West Quarter) which was more than went to any other Quarter and according to Orri Vésteinsson (2000: 11) is mainly a 'fjord environment'. Jón Viðar infers from this that the original settlers were dependent on fishing and hunting since this part of Iceland is the worst for crop-growing and cattle-herding. Initially, at least, there was minimal contact amongst a ship-owning elite and Orri's analysis shows that such environments do not support social interaction.

The Settlement comprised typically groups of up to ten people from a region of Norway and the British Isles settling in Iceland (Ólafur Lárusson, 1944: 16). There is no reason to believe that these numbers are too small for a dialect to survive, or that these dialects quickly gave way to common features. Hreinn Benediktsson (1961–62: 103) claims that the settlement

---

[34] See *Íf* XXV (*Færeyinga saga*: 3, 9–10: Einar and Snæúlfr come from the Hebrides to the Faroe Islands) and Unnr *in djúpúðga* (*Íf* V, *Laxdæla saga*: 7–8) who moves from Orkney to the Faroe Islands to Iceland. *Íf* XXXIV (*Orkneyinga saga*: 7–8) and *Íf* IV (*Eyrbyggja saga*: 3–4) tell of how Vikings used to raid over the summer and use Shetland and Orkney as their winter base. There are many accounts in the sagas of Norsemen spending time in the Northern Isles and the Hebrides before settling in Iceland (see *Íf* IV, *Eyrbyggja saga*: 11, for example).

[35] Schulte's (2002: 886) argument that dialect levelling must have occurred in Old Icelandic because it was 'a direct off-shoot of its non-homogenous parent language Norwegian' is unclear.

pattern explains the dialect levelling process. He asserts rightly that Norwegians from different parts of Norway did not necessarily stay together in Iceland, and that dialect divisions and boundaries were not therefore taken to Iceland. In the absence of a high degree of and sustained contact between these groups of speakers, this alone will not explain the levelling process for the *whole* of Iceland. The scattered settlement of different dialect speakers might lead to the establishment of local norms or in an environment of very little contact even encourage dialect splitting, as the Mæhlum (1997) study and Fortescue's (1997: 111–22) research on Greenland shows. Sutton (2008) has shown that there is no theoretical minimum number of speakers for a language or dialect to survive (providing it is more than one). The evidence from Cape York Peninsula, Australia shows that very large numbers of languages with as few as 20 speakers can survive.

The number of settlers is relative to geographic position (isolation, physical and other boundaries etc.), and also to conscious and deliberate extensions of community (in the legal communities represented by the þing, for instance). The survival of dialectal features is therefore relative: what works in one instance might not in another set of circumstances. Mæhlum's (1997: 204–5) research in northern Norway for example shows that low population density contributes to a slow koineisation process. In her case study of isolated farmsteads in northern Norway, linguistic norms are local (perhaps based on an individual valley) and linguistic uniformity is shown to be slow in forming. If the Norse dialect taken to Iceland had not levelled beforehand, this study implies strongly the maintenance of dialectal difference in early Iceland.

As discussed in Chapter 2, the dialect levelling process begins with speakers 'accommodating' to one another. There is the question therefore of which group of people are most likely to have adapted to others' speech in early Iceland. Studies have shown that the most innovative speakers are adolescents (Eckert, 2000). As mentioned previously, it is difficult to find plausible contexts for the movement of large numbers of adolescents between farmsteads and isolated communities dotted around Iceland. Single individuals entering established speech communities does not lead to mixing, a prerequisite for levelling. Mixing requires disruption of established speech communities and the creation of a new norm. It should also be borne in mind that although children and adolescents are key to language change, our perception of these categories may be cultural-specific. In societies such as medieval Iceland where a person is an adult aged 12, the effect will be different from that of a modern urban society. Men and women aged 14 will not need to rebel against their parents, and deliberately create an innovative argot: they are likely to be parents themselves.

If the movement of adolescents cannot account for levelling, one may consider marriage as an explanation. Intermarriage may be seen as a key to the problem of explaining dialect levelling in early Iceland. Marriage was necessary in order to produce a legitimate heir, but it was mainly *local*.[36] Icelanders married somebody of equivalent status (*jafnræði*); only those of high status, wealth or power had to look beyond their district.[37] Despite this local focus, however, the objective of marriage was often to forge family alliances and therefore it may have had some consequences for social networks and communities. Kuhn (1935: 29–30) claims that the *alþingi* ('General Assembly') was an important factor in the levelling process, but the *alþingi* only met for two weeks a year and certainly did not provide a context for *sustained* contact.

It is also worth noting that whilst the initial settlement pattern was scattered, nucleated villages or urban settlements are not necessary for communities to exist: the individual Icelandic district, *sveit*, or even the legally defined *hreppr*, forms a well-defined community. A local *þing* served to show the existence of local communities, and they served plausibly as marriage-markets (as the saga evidence suggests), and places for hiring servants (some of whom took part in bringing up children). They also dealt with conflicts that arose concerning land claims. These social structures show that human cooperation did not take place in a vacuum. There was certainly contact, but it was principally based on local 'cooperative clusters' and thus one should expect local norms to have established.[38] I would therefore argue that certain kinds of larger communities did exist in early Iceland, but it is nonetheless unclear how these communities facilitated the dialect levelling process.

3.6.3 *The basis for koineisation*

As we discovered in Chapter 2, dialect levelling is the first part of the overall koineisation process. It is difficult to determine how and where dialect levelling occurred in Iceland, and to know what the basis for the putative koineisation was.[39] One must therefore put the postulated linguistic happenings into an historical and social context. There have been previous attempts at doing this. On the basis of the distribution of a number of modern dialect forms, in particular diphthongal variants of the words for 'here' and 'is', Hesselman (1936: 143) posited the existence of a type of

---

[36] Sandøy (1994: 41) claims the opposite but does not quote his sources: 'det var vanlig å ha giftarmål over store avstandar' ('long-distance marriage was common').

[37] *Grágás* (Ib: 29, 241): the term refers to both social prestige and wealth. See *Íf* XII (*Brennu-Njáls saga*) and *Sturlunga saga* (*Íslendinga saga*) for instances of local marriage, and for the meeting of potential marriage partners at assemblies (the saga evidence indicates that women attended the *alþingi* – *Íf* V, *Laxdæla saga*: 63-66); *Íf* XVI (*Ísleifs þáttr byskups*: 336) for a case of travelling a long distance to propose.

[38] See Birgir T. R. Solvason (1993: 97–125) for a discussion of 'cooperative clusters' and the evolution of social structures in the Commonwealth Period from a socio-economic perspective.

[39] Sveinn Bergsveinsson (1955: 55) believes that the preposition *um(b)* was subject to dialect levelling in Norway and that this was completed before the literary period began.

Viking Age Scandinavian speech originating in the trading centre Hedeby but radiating out from the Birka-Uppsala area of Sweden. In conformity with its dual origin, he termed the type of speech both Birkasvenska and Hedeby-nordiska.[40]

Looking for a place where linguistic mixing may have occurred, Hedeby is an obvious starting-point, at least during its rather brief existence. It was located between Scandinavia and the Frankish empire, between Norse and Low German, near to Wendish and with direct access to the Baltic, and not that far from south-easternmost West Norse, with direct links up to the equally transient trading town of Kaupang.[41] We know from Anglo-Saxon sources that English merchants also traded at Hedeby, and beyond into the Baltic.[42] Whilst Hedeby is a plausible location for mixing to take place, it could just as easily imply a polyglot trading population where multiple languages were spoken and understood, rather than an urban koine.

The trading centres and in particular the Viking communities in the British Isles and the Faroe Islands in the decades preceding the Settlement created a suitable context for dialect levelling. The difficulty may be to link the koine in the British Isles with the Settlement. There was a noticeable drop in Viking activity in the British Isles and Francia during the 870s and 880s A.D. This coincides with the Settlement and it is likely that the settlers that came from the British Isles and the Faroe Islands to Iceland had lived in established communities there for some years previously.

The Viking raiders took their increasingly levelled dialect with them to Iceland, whether they travelled from Norway or the British Isles. There is the occasional indication that the places in Norway whence the settlers to Iceland came were the same as those of the Viking raiders: 'Here Beorhtric took King Offa's daughter Eadburh. And in his days came first three ships of Northmen from Hörðaland (*Hereða lande*); and then the reeve rode there and wanted to compel them to go to the king's town because he did not know what they were; and then they killed him. These were the first ships of the Danish men (*Deniscra manna*) which sought out (*gesohton*) the land of the English race'. The F-version is slightly briefer but has identical content; the A-version omits the crucial point that they were from Hörðaland (Swanton, 1996: 55) (the Anglo-Saxon Chronicle for 787 A.D. (E-version)). Having gained experience across Europe, the Great Army arrived in Britain in late 865 A.D.[43] If one wanted a specific point of social mixing, at least of

---

[40] For reviews of this theory, see Laur (1983: 9–25) who rejects the theory; Nielsen (1984: 17–25) and Peterson (1992: 95) who examine the runic evidence; Lagman (1990: 62).

[41] Cf. Benedictow (2003: 237–49); Andersson (2003: 312–42): Kaupang was founded in the late eighth century. Ribe, Hedeby, Birka and Kaupang may have had a total of 3,000–5,000 inhabitants.

[42] See Bately (1980: 16): the account of Wulfstan's voyage to Estonia via Hedeby (*Hæðum*) given in the Alfredian translation of the Orosius.

[43] Sawyer (2003: 111): within five years the army had conquered two kingdoms, Northumbria and East Anglia, and dismembered a third, Mercia.

males, probably from a very wide catchment-area of Scandinavia, one would not need to look very much further.

However, this would only account for a small number of the settlers to Iceland. The roots of the koine lie in the considerable, if undocumented, social upheaval in mainland Scandinavia in the immediate pre-Viking period (sixth to eighth centuries), which is shown by archaeological evidence. Significant population movement and abandonment of unculti-vable land (for which there is much evidence), leads to population-mixture, and ultimately dialect levelling. According to Näsman & Lund (1988); Myhre (2003: 83–90), the causes of the crisis were sought in external factors such as poorer climate, migrations and changes in trade routes, soil exhaustion, overpopulation and societal collapse. Archaeological evidence shows that there was a sudden and catastrophic change in settlement patterns: settlement-sites which had been in use since the Bronze Age were abruptly abandoned in the seventh and eighth centuries. The reason for this is that there were changes in climate and subsequently farming practices at this time. The overwhelming expansion of the Scandinavian people during the Viking Age is linked with the considerable social upheaval during the seventh and eighth centuries. *Landnámabók* (*Íf* Ii, 52) gives accounts of Norsemen such as Geimundr heljarskinn who left Rogaland on a Viking expedition and returned subsequently, just to discover that King Harald had taken over the district and driven the farmers from the estates. This period of internal turmoil coincides with that of a sudden and considerable linguistic change that distinguishes Norse from earlier North Germanic.[44] Social upheaval of this kind can be associated with linguistic change: population movement away from abandoned farm-sites permits levelling of local variation.

Considerable social change, largely attested in the archaeological record, just preceding the beginnings of the Viking Age had disrupted social and geographical structures across most of Scandinavia. Old Icelandic devel-oped from a unitary language, which strongly suggests a degree of levelling of any previous diversity on arrival (if not before). The reason for this is that there are likely to have been more early dialect distinctions in Norse than the runic record shows as dialectal homogeneity is not the norm in a mountainous country like Norway. There is an argument for koineisation at the beginning of the Viking Age at the end of the eighth century. The Viking settlements in the British Isles such as Orkney where there is evidence of an early Norse literary culture, acted as dialect melting pots and

---

[44] Spurkland (2006a: 333–45): the most comprehensive changes in the spoken language in this period are the innovations summed up under the terms vowel mutation – umlaut – and syncope. Mæhlum (1999: 96; 99) and Indrebø (1951: 53) link correlates such as social upheaval and population movement to language change. Jespersen (1954: 261) claims that the Viking Age witnessed the greatest linguistic changes for the reason that the men were absent and women had other things to attend to than their children's linguistic education.

were thus conducive to dialect levelling, prior to the Settlement.[45] Anecdotal saga evidence shows clearly that the Norsemen settled in large households which were Norse speaking, even though some of their members were not Norse speakers. The Norse that they spoke did not necessarily correspond to any single location in Scandinavia, but their speech would have had the discernible features of West Norse. The linguistic context described here is therefore one of dialect mixing in Norway and Denmark, before a process of levelling that continued in the British Isles, the Faroe Islands and ultimately in Iceland itself. The Norse colonisation laid the linguistic foundations for a dialect continuum. All the scenarios that have been described would have been characterised by linguistic instability and one can look therefore for quite rapid change.

One could argue that the Settlement itself could cause dialect levelling, unless people from the same place in Scandinavia went to the same part of Iceland. There is a small amount of evidence to support this: the various families settling Breiðafjörður, according to *Laxdæla saga* and *Eyrbyggja saga* were largely from the same ultimate geographic origin, even though they came by different routes (*Íf* II, *Eyrbyggja saga* and V, *Laxdæla saga*). In practice, however, the sagas do not really give us sufficient hard evidence for deciding this question of specific place of origin.

3.7 ESTABLISHMENT OF A LINGUISTIC NORM IN ICELAND

3.7.1 *Pre-and post-Settlement linguistic norms*

Now that we have identified an historical context in which dialect levelling took place, we need to consider further the question of how a norm became established. We are therefore concerned here with the *elaboration* and not the origins of the norm. Kristján Árnason (2003b: 245–79) argues too that a linguistic norm was established prior to the Settlement. He points out that there lies a paradox in the 'mixture theory': 'if the written standard in Iceland was an Icelandic mixture of Norwegian dialects [...], we would have to assume that the Norwegians adopted the new Icelandic norm, i.e. that the language was transported back across the Atlantic in the mixed and then standardised norm' (Kristján, 2003b: 249).

As we have seen, it is probable that a spoken norm was established prior to the Settlement, and that a written standard was developed subsequently as has occurred in modern Norway. It might not be the case, however, that a *particular* spoken norm was adopted as a basis for the written standard. Nynorsk is for instance based on a cluster of west Norwegian dialects. We

---

[45] The story of the Hjaðningavíg is said in *Skáldskaparmál* to have taken place in Háey in the Orkneyjar, therefore Hoy.

do know that literacy and the written language came with Christianity to Iceland and that the Latin alphabet was adapted to the phonology of Icelandic as the First Grammarian tells us. The First Grammarian uses a theory of writing which recognises the independence of separate languages: he invokes the models of Hebrew, Greek and Latin, different languages which each had a different alphabet. The question of whether Christianity came to Iceland from Norway, England or both is not usually adequately answered, but it seems, as we saw earlier in this chapter, that the Scandinavian Christians learned to write the Roman alphabet from English models. Some specifically English letter-forms or graphemes come through: <æ>, <ð>, insular <f>, probably <œ> from English <oe> used for the [ö]-sound, <y> used for the [ü] sound (Hreinn Benediktsson, 1965: 35). Similarly, English seems to have provided much of the Christian vocabulary of Norse: words such as *sál*, *kross* and *kirkja* are derived from or through English. There is also good evidence for knowledge of Old English in early Christian Scandinavia. There is a set of legendary genealogies, quoted by Snorri Sturluson in the Prologue to *Snorra Edda* and preserved more fully in *Hauksbók*, which are clearly derived from the Anglo-Saxon Chronicle, probably from the genealogy of King Alfred's father. The Icelanders who wrote them are aware of the bilingualism involved, because they give examples of 'X, whom we call Y', where X represents the English form of the name, and Y the Norse form. There is also a translation of one of Ælfric's homilies (*De falsis diis*) in the Norwegian Homily Book. It is perfectly plausible, however, that a written standard was established independently in Norway. As we will now come on to see, it is also best to consider the koineisation of the spoken language and the 'standardisation' of the written language as separate phenomena.

3.7.2 *Spoken norms and 'standardised' written languages*

The corollary of Kristján's (2003b: 245–79) argument appears to be that one needs to have a spoken norm in order to have a standardised written language. The relationship between the spoken word and the written word was more blurred and complex than is hinted at here. The development of the written language was influenced by a variety of factors other than speech. People may have set out to write what they speak, but they can only do so with the tools they have: the writing conventions they have learned, and which were probably developed for quite different languages.[46] According to Barnes (2005: 187), the language of the Icelandic and Norwegian manuscripts tends to reflect several factors: the practices of the

---

[46] Höskuldur Þráinsson *et al* (2004: 340): Svabo invented an orthography for Faroese that was phonetic and gave valuable information about his pronunciation. Although Svabo was writing in the eighteenth century, this is evidence that grammarians tried to write what they spoke.

scriptorium in which a scribe had learnt to write or in which he worked, or both; the language of the exemplar from which he was copying (most manuscripts we have are copies of older originals); and – to a lesser extent – his own forms of speech. Superimposed on this mix are, according to Barnes, the various traditions of writing that developed in secular or ecclesiastical centres. In Norway, for example, norms for Trondheim, Bergen and Oslo have been identified; as the court and chancellery moved from Trondheim to Bergen and finally around 1300 A.D. to Oslo, a type of written language developed that contained elements of all three.

It would seem that very few manuscripts are the product of more than one or two scribes working at any one time. Whilst scriptoria may have existed in Iceland, there were not organised scriptoria in the way in which they appear on the Continent or in England, where large-scale manufacture of books was possible, and where 'house-styles' developed. The evidence for scriptoria in Iceland in the middle ages is indirect. It comes primarily from instances where more than one hand can be identified in a single manuscript (preferably interchanging in such a way that the scribes were contemporaries working together) and the same hands can, in addition, be identified in other manuscripts (cf. Lönnroth, 1964: 1–97; Stefán Karlsson, 1999: 138–58; on scribes at Helgafell and Möðruvellir monasteries, see Stefán Karlsson, 1967; 1970a: 347–49; 1970b: 120–40; 1982: 320–22).

It is difficult to see, as Barnes does, any standardisation of scribal practice emerging from scriptoria in Iceland,[47] let alone the development of specific separate 'chancery hands' used for legal documents, and comparably specific legal linguistic usage, as happened in England.[48] There might not have been standardisation in the sense of a specific scriptorium standardising upon a given set of scribal conventions. The local variation that is assumed to underlie and precede standardisation, might itself not have developed. By the thirteenth century, it is clear, however, that written Icelandic had established itself as a gold standard, to which Icelanders have always returned. The same claim could not be made for Norway.

3.7.3 *The establishment of a norm: skaldic poetry (and the laws)*

Kristján Árnason (2003b: 250-54) claims that the recital of laws and poetry is the correct linguistic context for the development of a norm, i.e. the Icelandic standard was based on the speech of an elite and the influence of poetry and the laws led to the development of a written standard. The

---

[47] This does not mean that individual Icelandic scribes could not be linguistically aware. *Flateyjarbók*, for instance, may well have been written for presentation to a Norwegian king: it is a much-enlarged cycle of the sagas of the kings of Norway, highly decorated and very expensively and carefully produced: a luxury manuscript.
[48] Anglo-Norman survives as a legal language for legal records very late and long after it was any sort of spoken language.

earliest texts committed to writing in Iceland and Norway were the laws and poetry. Both of these forms have long pre-literate oral histories and in the case of the laws at least we have concrete evidence that they were memorised from the period from about 930 A.D. until 1117–18 A.D. (*Íf* Ii, *Íslendingabók*: 12). Oral transmission of the law by the Lawspeakers had prevailed for some considerable time at all the legal gatherings and these legal texts were codified in basically the same norm in the twelfth century, perhaps a bit earlier in Norway. Later forms of literature (genealogies in particular) were also spoken forms originally and were memorised and passed down from generation to generation before being written down.

The arguments put forward in Kristján's (2003b: 245–79) paper regarding the role of poetry and the laws are very plausible, but require some qualification. Kristján is concerned firstly with high-level registers, obviously so in the case of poetry, but also that of the laws. One would have to argue (probably rightly) for some unusual social systems to permit these to control other registers of the language.[49] *A priori* one could make a case for the linguistic norm to be based on legal language, and this could be given sociolinguistic backing given the function of legal assemblies for social interaction. The difficulty with this is that the actual norm(s) that we see outside the law are dissimilar to legal language in vocabulary, syntax and style. The contrast between legal and non-legal language is evident in *Brennu-Njáls saga* and to an extent in *Grettis saga Ásmundarsonar*.

Turning to the poets, one might say that even if these unusual social systems were in place, the evidence shows that the poets were only guardians of the poetic corpus. One might expect the poets to have controlled, at least in part, the study of Norwegian royal history because of the importance that the historians gave to skaldic poetry (cf. Guðrún Nordal (2001: 23) who claims that *grammatica* was the most important discipline in school and that the poetry of the revered court skalds took a seat next to the honoured poets of classical Latin literature). Part of their training was to memorise the existing known corpus of skaldic poetry. In due course, when training their successors, they passed on the poetic corpus. One could argue that *Skáldskaparmál* in *Snorra Edda* gives us a written representation of that process. Most instances of kennings are unique. Given the limited range of things for which kennings were used, the range of kenning-types and the very considerable size of the known corpus, this is noteworthy. The only possible explanation is that skaldic poets deliberately avoided any repetition of any actual kenning that had ever been used before. In order to avoid repeating kennings, they had to know all the previously used kennings. It is a big step to extend this 'guardianship' of the

---

[49] It is unlikely that such arguments can apply equally at all periods: there are dramatic changes in both poetry and law during the thirteenth and fourteenth centuries, which must have affected performance, and so changed their impact on the spoken language.

poetic corpus to guardianship of the entire language. The strongest evidence for this might be the passage in the First Grammatical Treatise: *Skalld erv hofvndar allrar rynni eða máálsgreinar sem smíðar eða lögmenn laga* (Hreinn Benediktsson, 1972: 224–6). Hreinn translates *rynni eða máálsgreinar* as '(matters touching the art of) writing or the distinctions (made in) discourse', whereas Haugen (1972a: 20) translates it simply as 'writing or speaking'. The latter translation seems far too loose: I would take it to mean that the poets have authority over 'grammatical enquiry and points of metre'. It is probably 'authority' in a poetic context, however, as the passage is followed by a piece of verse and a discussion of metre and syllables.

It is unlikely that they controlled the use of Icelandic more widely simply because Icelandic prose developed so differently from the poetry. It is easiest therefore to see them as completely separate literary and linguistic developments. Having said that, skaldic poetry did constitute a solid, immovable and largely immutable 'lump of language' in the middle of Icelandic – a 'lump of language' which (because of internal rhyme and alliteration) also preserved phonological features. The parallel with the law is interesting in this regard. One can compare the end of skaldic poetry during the fourteenth century with the end of the Commonwealth law code, and the introduction of royal law-books, with the king as the source of legal authority, from 1271 A.D. onwards. Skaldic poetry came to an end for sound linguistic reasons: the metres of skaldic poetry, derived from the quantitative patterns of the language itself, ceased to be viable at the Quantity Shift, where quantity became a property of (accented) syllables, not of segments. There was a fundamental shift with the laws too: the primarily oral law of *Grágás* (written, but where the written text was notionally at least a record of oral pronouncement) shifts to the concept of the written text being fundamental. The orality of *Grágás*, coupled with the notion of the immutability of the law (where a deviation of wording could invalidate a law-suit) set up the law as again a more or less immutable 'lump of language' in the middle of society, which had to be reproduced accurately at most levels above the phonological. Given the size of the poetic corpus, the inherent conservatism of poetry acted as an anchor on the language, rather than as a catalyst for it to act as a language-wide benchmark.

Very high registers such as skaldic poetry are usually archaic, both in the case of languages with strong written traditions, and in the case of those with strong and highly formalised oral traditions, where preservation of those traditions is prestigious (for whatever reasons), and so controls prestige forms of the language. The language of skaldic poetry is very far removed from that of prose, let alone from what we might recover from the spoken language. One might envisage a model for Norse where there are some high registers which are in some respects different from 'usual' language, and archaic. It is difficult to see how such an archaic language could have had an overriding influence on the spoken norm of *all* society.

Aside from the register issue, Kristján relies on evidence from the Third Grammatical Treatise. As evidence of poetic texts providing the norm for the spoken language, Kristján (2003b: 263) quotes the following passage from the Third Grammatical Treatise: *Barbarismus er kallaðr einn lastafullr hlutr máls-greinar í alþyðingri ræða, en sá er í skáldskap kallaðr metaplasmus* (Óláfr Þórðarson: *Málhljóða- og málskrúðsrit*, 1927: 40). The passage is translated as '*Barbarismus* is called a sinful part of popular speech, but it is called *metaplasmus* in poetry'. I would deduce simply that something can be objectionable in normal speech, but an ornament in poetry. An alternative translation of the passage might be: '*Barbarismus* is called a fault of diction in normal speech, but it is called *metaplasmus* in poetry'.

My reading of the Third Grammatical Treatise is that it is a rhetorical treatise, not a grammatical or phonological handbook.[50] The Third Grammatical Treatise reproduces the rhetorical classification system of the Latin grammarians, but instead of Vergil it quotes skaldic poets. It would be difficult to claim that these treatises show how to pronounce, decline or conjugate words. The sort of rhetorical devices which they discuss are mostly far removed from normal speech: they are 'artificial' and 'unnatural'.

Whilst recognising that the role of poetry and in particular the language of the assemblies and Lawspeakers undoubtedly played a role in the development of the early language, these factors alone may not explain the establishment of a spoken norm. The other difficulty might be that if the Norse dialect had levelled prior to the Settlement and the basis for the development of a norm was the poetic and legal texts, then one would expect to find a culture that centred on poetry in Norway. This appears to have been, however, largely an Icelandic phenomenon although the first skaldic poets were Norwegian. It was the Icelanders that had a disproportionately large number of prominent poets: this was much more a feature of Icelandic than Norwegian society.

3.7.4 *The establishment of a norm: the role of the sagas*

The role of poetry has been discussed in the context of the norm-establishment process, but little mention has been made of the saga material in this regard. Even if the saga material did not contribute to the dialect levelling process, it was a factor in ensuring a degree of linguistic homogeneity and conservatism in the longer term. As the sagas were

---

[50] Guðrún Nordal (2001: 37) believes that skaldic verse had a strong position in the Icelandic curriculum.

written at a later date, they are only therefore a relevant factor in the context of the longer-term homogeneity and conservatism of the language where, as Kuhn (1935: 30) points out, they played a major role. Whilst they were not immutable, the sagas constituted a corpus representing the language that identified Icelanders to themselves – increasingly so as the centuries passed – and they are one of the reasons why modern Icelandic has retained its ancient language so nearly unchanged. They were written texts intended for oral performance.

It is clear already by the thirteenth century that the sagas have obtained high status and were highly valued. Kings commissioned Icelanders to write their sagas: Sverrir is the best example. Copies were made in order to be presented to kings. The kings themselves valued them: Hákon Hákonarson, dying in the Bishop's Palace, Kirkwall in 1263 A.D., when he no longer had the strength and concentration to listen to Latin saints' lives, had the sagas of the kings read to him, from the beginning up to *Sverris saga*, his own grandfather's saga – and then he died. Importantly, the Icelanders read them to each other and went on reading them to each other for the next seven centuries and the purists of the early nineteenth century simply (and successfully) aimed to restore the 'language of the sagas'. The language of the sagas was arguably more representative of the whole language than other registers. Instead of being representative of the whole language, the poetic, legal and religious works would probably have been distinct registers with their separate lexicons, just as they are today.

The norm was probably also *elaborated* and *accepted* through early Christian writing. Turville-Petre (1953: 109–42) notes that translators of religious literature in the 12th century had striven for linguistic purity which suggests perhaps that some degree of linguistic purism had been present in Iceland from the early period onwards.

In discussions of norm-establishment, one needs to be particularly careful not to rely too heavily on the so-called 'standardisation' of the spoken language based on a written norm. There are a number of factors such as poetry, legal texts and sagas which explain how linguistic norms have developed in Iceland. The sagas, in particular, have moulded the language in the longer term and created a linguistic benchmark.

3.8 THE HOMOGENEITY OF ICELANDIC

3.8.1 *Background*

Once the dialect was levelled, the language spoken in Iceland was to be characterised by minimal dialectal variation for the ensuing period. As for the structure of the language, it is also true that whilst the other Scandinavian dialects or languages have changed considerably in their grammar, Icelandic's morphology is almost entirely intact and the syntax of the modern language does not differ greatly from that of the language of the Vikings.[51]

The roots of the homogeneity of Icelandic lie in several factors such as a high degree of literacy at a very early period, the significant literary output and circulation of literature, the circular movement pattern and the social structures that were established shortly after the Settlement.[52] Helgi Guðmundsson (1977: 315–25) has discussed at length a number of the possible factors that may explain the lack of dialectal variation in Icelandic (cf. Hesselman, 1948: 13; Stefán Karlsson, 2004: 64–66). One could argue that these and other factors were responsible for what must have been a rather rapid levelling of the Norse dialects that came to Iceland. However, it is more likely that the dialect that came to Iceland had already been levelled and it was these same factors that ensured the language remained uniform throughout the Settlement Period and beyond.

3.8.2 *Factors explaining the homogeneity of Icelandic*

As has been previously discussed, the Icelandic settlement pattern itself does not support country-wide dialect levelling. The settlers were Norsemen from different parts of Norway and the British Isles and they settled around the periphery of the country in isolated farmsteads. Such a settlement pattern would not support a model where the language is uniform and almost dialect-free. Instead, in the absence of nucleated settlements, it is more likely to preserve dialectal distinctions.[53] It would have required a very high degree of internal mobility for linguistic homogeneity to have been achieved in a short period of time. This is especially true for Iceland since there are numerous natural barriers to communication, impassable rivers, mountain ridges, glaciers and volcanoes even within the inhabited areas – barriers which one would *a priori* have expected to produce a much more extensive dialect splitting. Communication must have been especially difficult in the winter months.

---

[51] Cf. Faroese, the most 'conservative' Scandinavian language after Icelandic, which has undergone morphological simplification and case reduction with the loss of the distinction between nominative and accusative case endings in the plural; the genitive tends to be replaced by prepositional phrases (Braunmüller, 2001: 75). There has been considerable morphological and syntactic change in the relevant Norwegian dialects (Sandøy, 1994: 39). The phonology of Icelandic has also, however, changed considerably over the last one thousand years.

[52] Dahlstedt (1958: 5–33) discusses the significance of a high degree of literacy.

[53] Cf. Trudgill (1986: 128): the Falkland Islands were settled by only 2,000 people in the mid-nineteenth century with some of them living to this day in isolated, scattered settlements. A consequence of these factors and its geographical isolation is that many of the settlements, particularly on West Falkland retained dialects of English (in the view of Sudbury (2001: 63), immigration from the UK after the 1982 conflict has changed this situation dramatically).

Due to the inaccessibility of the Interior, movement around the country then and now is circular. This is not dissimilar to the situation in Australia. One major difference would be, however, that Iceland (unlike Australia) was essentially a community of isolated farmsteads for a period of about one thousand years. Travelling round the edge of the country prevented the formation of isolated regions (perhaps with the exception of the West Fjords), but also rather obviously led to a circular (or perhaps semi-circular) movement of people. This *contributed* to the maintenance of the norm, and thus the homogeneity of the language. There is clear evidence in the sagas and the law codes of labourers travelling at set times of the year (*fardagar*) (*Grágás*, Ia: 128; *Íf* VI, *Gísla saga Súrssonar*: 34). Movement became therefore systematised. Within the main industries of fishing and agriculture, there have always been seasonal fluctuations in employment in different parts of the country. It is also apparent from *Grágás* that vagrants were itinerant, moving from one farmstead to another.[54] More significantly, there was contact between settlers along the coast: the majority of the population lived in close proximity to the sea and some ships were available.

There are various other explanations for high degrees of movement around the country such as the predilection for livestock farming over crop farming (conditioned by the climate) and the migrations and resettlement as a result of major plagues.[55] All these (and other) factors led to a high degree of internal mobility and thus prevented the isolation underlying dialect splitting.

It has also been argued by Helgi (1977: 321–22) that the minimal social stratification contributed to minimal linguistic variation. It is often alleged that there was minimal social stratification in Iceland and this notion is perpetuated even in Iceland today. Our knowledge of the working of the assemblies with its chieftains may contradict that view and there is some evidence from *Landnámabók* that some of the families that moved to Iceland were powerful. However, we do not know enough about linguistic variation based on social factors at the time.

Overall, the factors relating to internal mobility and the need for people to move around the country are compelling arguments for the maintenance of a norm. These conditions did not bring about the levelling itself, but they ensured that the language remained relatively homogenous. The homogeneity and conservatism of modern Icelandic is due to other factors too such as Iceland's relative geographical isolation, the attempts to rid the language of any foreign influences and the schooling system. The external factors discussed in Helgi's paper explain better how the language of

---

[54] See *Grágás* (Ia: 229); (Ib: 14): the fact that a number of laws were formulated against them suggests that they may have comprised quite a large group.
[55] Stefán Karlsson (1999: 140) notes that the clergy often changed residence, as did members of the wealthiest families who commonly entered into marriages, inherited farms and settled down in places far from where they were born.

Iceland remained homogenous over a period of centuries rather than accounting for the koineisation of the dialect itself. For levelling to take place, one needs sustained and long-term inter-dialectal contact and the convergence of people on one place and not just high degrees of internal mobility.

3.9 CONCLUSION

This chapter has looked at the question of variation in Norse and subsequently Old Icelandic from a number of different perspectives. I began by examining the runic evidence and it was shown that variation first appears in the tenth century. This evidence is not a reliable source, however, for geographically organised dialectal variation.

The earliest manuscripts from Iceland and Norway show a written language that is very similar. The phonological similarities between the dialects of Iceland, the Faroe Islands and western Norway suggest either a high degree of contact between these speakers after the Settlement or 'drift'. Accounts of perilous journeys, shipwrecks and drownings in *Landnámabók* and the sagas suggest that frequent and regular contact between significant numbers of Norsemen in their respective colonies were difficult to maintain, even if archaeological and saga evidence point to high degrees of contact.[56]

A settlement pattern of small groups of settlers principally from Norway, living in isolated farmsteads around the perimeter of Iceland does not in itself account for the dialect levelling process.[57] The distribution of settlers could only explain the levelling process if the communities dotted around the country were too small to sustain dialect differences, i.e. in order to survive these small groups merged with larger communities and levelling took place. Evidence from other parts of the world has shown, however, that linguistic and dialectal differences can be sustained even if the community has very few speakers. Factors such as intermarriage do not explain levelling on a national scale either, but it may have been a contributing factor to local levelling of dialectal differences.

The lack of historical evidence for dialectal variation in Iceland shows that a norm had been established at an early period. Poetry, legal texts and subsequently the saga tradition facilitated the concretisation of this norm in Iceland. The formation of the written standard in Norway (and England) and the levelling of the Norse dialect spoken in western Norway and parts of the British Isles can be considered independent processes.

---

[56] See *Landnámabók* [Hermann Pálsson & Edwards, 1972: 70–71, 76, 126]; *Íf* Ii (81); *Íf* XXV (*Færeyinga saga*: 107).

[57] *Landnámabók* tells the story of individuals. There are very few accounts of settlers travelling in groups larger than four.

There are a number of different contexts in which the Norse koine came about. None of the explanations are entirely adequate, however: the link between a Hedeby-centred dialect levelling and the settlement of Iceland is too tenuous; a Viking conquest induced koineisation would only account for the dialect levelling of young male speakers travelling from the British Isles to Iceland. Social upheaval (of which there is much evidence) led to dramatic movements of population in mainland Scandinavia. These developments provided a suitable context for dialect levelling to have taken place. It is clear that the dialect taken to Iceland became and remained homogenous for the longer term. A variety of factors such as Iceland's geographical isolation and the respect for the older forms in Icelandic literature ensured that the conservatism of Iceland was preserved whilst the language(s) of the regions whence the settlers came underwent considerable change.

The koineisation of the Norse dialect taken to Iceland is a significant factor to be taken into account in a discussion of the linguistic identity of the settlers. It led to a convergence of linguistic norms and thus formed the basis for a new linguistic identity. Once the levelled (or levelling) dialect had been taken to Iceland, it was shaped further by the language of the sagas and other prominent oral forms such as skaldic poetry and the laws. The establishment of a significant Icelandic prose and poetic corpus thus played its role in the emergence of an Icelandic identity. At the same time, the speech community characterised by a single, levelled dialect with 'focused' linguistic norms created an environment of linguistic solidarity.

4

SOCIAL STRUCTURES IN THE LEXICON

4.1 INTRODUCTION

Having discussed in some detail the complex problem of norm-establishment in early Iceland, we now turn our attention in the subsequent two chapters to the issue of identity. Identity has thus far been largely discussed in the context of how a single, levelled dialect with focused linguistic norms may have led to a Norse (or even Icelandic) communal linguistic identity. The aim of this chapter is not to discuss further norm 'focusing', but to show instead how language reflected changing social and individual identities in Iceland by analysing terminology that describes social structures. The approach in this chapter is lexical, but it is not the intention to provide the most comprehensive analysis possible of the lexical data. A number of these terms have been discussed by Maurer (1906–10), but thus far the data have not been used for the purposes of analysing issues relating to identity. I will restrict my comments to those terms that are most relevant to this particular study.

The data to be analysed cover a number of social structures, some perhaps more familiar to readers than others. All of the items have been chosen because they describe social structures that are somehow representative of early Icelandic or conceivably West Norse culture.

The chapter begins with a discussion of what may have been peculiar about an Icelandic social identity, which in accordance with Chapter 1 is defined as an individual's perception of what defines the 'us' associated with any group membership. It is argued that the social identity of the early settlers was inextricably linked with the *landnám* ('Settlement'). As a new society that knew its origins and documented its settlement in unprecedented detail, the Icelanders could see their history with considerable unity.[1] The same could not be said of their ancestors in Norway or the British Isles. The land-taking laid the foundations for the Icelanders as a nation, and already in the construction and organisation of the new society they may have developed a consciousness of themselves as a distinct people. Meulengracht Sørensen (2000: 27) notes that the country's most important common institutions were inscribed in texts by means of the written word.

---

[1] See Tomasson (1980: 14): when there is knowledge of the origins of the society and when there is celebration of its founding, there is a tendency for national institutions to assume a particularly prominent position in society. This may have been the case for the *alþingi* ('General Assembly') at Þingvellir.

Literacy (and perhaps the introduction of Christianity in the year 999/1000 A.D.) is likely to have facilitated the creation of a new historical consciousness in a new society. This is evident from early texts such as the First Grammatical Treatise and *Landnámabók*. As a textualisation of a landscape, *Landnámabók* gave a permanent meaning to the Icelanders' perception of their land.[2]

In this chapter it is suggested that the *landnám* itself triggered a new form of social organisation, and subsequently identity, and that the settlers used their freedom to develop a new and different society, operating within the constraints imposed by the thin and scattered population. In this new society, the Icelanders may have seen themselves as a distinct people with the Settlement being perceived as a new beginning following the break-up of kin groups and communities. The *landnám* was a significant experience and rupture that left the settlers feeling the need to remember the time before through genealogies, myths and poetry.

The two key defining features of Icelandic social structures were innovation and archaism.[3] This is reflected in structures such as the *alþingi* ('General Assembly') and the oligarchic *goðar* ('chieftains'): both unique constructs, but modelled probably on older institutions. The general characteristics of these Icelandic social and legal structures are explained in more detail in Section 4.2.2, before a more in-depth analysis is made of them in Section 4.3.

In addition to social identity, consideration is given in Section 4.4 to the issue of individual identity. A changing individual identity is discussed with reference to kinship and *landnám*. The *landnám* process is likely to have had ramifications for the individual as well as the social identity of the early Icelanders. The catalysts for these changes may have been two-fold: the disappearance of *óðal* ('allodium'), the notion of inalienable, ancestral land, and the individualistic nature of the land-taking. The cause and effect of these processes are complex and opaque, and only some of the issues are explored in Section 4.4.2. No discussion of Icelandic kinship and individual identity would be complete without mentioning the role of genealogies. The importance of genealogical knowledge in Icelandic society is beyond doubt, but it is not evident how one should interpret all this material in the light of an Icelandic identity. This is the subject matter of Section 4.4.3. A comprehensive analysis of Icelandic kinship terminology is not given here, but mention is made of kinship terms that were specific to Iceland in Section 4.4.4.

---

[2] Bruhn (1999: 155–202) uses the term *textualisation* for the double process which consists of a society's adoption of writing as a social usage, and as a consequence of that, understanding and construing social life.

[3] These two features are likely to be found in many societies.

4.2 SOCIAL IDENTITY AND ICELANDIC SOCIAL STRUCTURES

4.2.1 *Emerging social structures and identities*

It is not the intention in this chapter to *describe* Icelandic social structures; descriptions are available elsewhere (cf. Jón Jóhannesson, 1974; Jón Viðar Sigurðsson, 1999; Gunnar Karlsson, 2000; Byock, 2001). The objective is rather to attempt to explain why these emerging social structures and identities should be perceived as specifically Icelandic.

We can begin by reminding ourselves what was unique about the Icelandic social structures in the early period of the island's history. Firstly, Iceland was unique in the sense that certain social structures that were found elsewhere were obviously absent in Iceland. There was no kingship or any other single leader in Iceland, no courtly culture, no *óðal*-system of land-ownership, no trading centres or army and no urban bourgeoisie. Town-foundation in Northern Europe is related to the existence of social and ecclesiastical superstructures. Towns can develop spontaneously, but for the most part they are specifically founded, and specifically maintained, for both military (garrison) and economic purposes (provision of local services; taxation of a controlled market and of the hinterland that supplies it). These foundations tend to be royal, noble and/or episcopal. When such royal, noble or episcopal support is removed, towns can decline or even vanish. The lack of nobility and townships were therefore two factors that were inter-linked and both ostensibly absent in Iceland.

The absence of aristocratic social structures in Iceland is surprising because these social structures had become established in the other Norse island communities: the Orkney earldom first controlled Orkney and perhaps Shetland, before turning its ambitions to the Scottish mainland and the Hebrides.[4] There was also no executive or collective exercise of power in Iceland, but instead an innovative system of self-governing farmers or householders that lasted for nearly 400 years. The early Icelanders established complex and sophisticated social structures *ab initio* in a relatively short period of time and in the absence of any coercive state institutions. The founding principle of these social structures was a decentralised distribution of power and a corresponding emphasis on the integrity of the individual.

The oddity of Iceland's status as a community which lacked not only a king but also a centralised state of any sort, registered both abroad and at home. Adam of Bremen wrote in 1080 A.D. that the Icelanders regarded their bishop as king, and accepted his scriptural pronouncements as law; or (in a scholium) that 'they have no king, except the law' (*Apud illos non est*

---

[4] The main source for this history is *Orkneyinga saga* (*Íf* XXXIV).

rex, nisi tantum lex, Schmeidler, 1917: 273).[5] The Icelanders did not just replicate the social model that they knew. Ari in *Íslendingabók* (*Íf* Ii, 7) tells how Úlfljótr's law code was based on the Norwegian *Gulaþingslög*, but was also the first departure from Norwegian law: *en þau váru flest sett at því sem þá váru Golaþingslög* [...] *hvar við skyldi auka eða af nema eða annan veg setja* 'they were for the most part modelled on how the laws of Gulaþing were at the time [...] where things should be added, or removed, or set up differently'. Whilst recognising their ancestry, there appears to be some evidence of a concerted effort by the settlers to create a different society, or at least establish a legal system and social institutions in a different manner.

It is worth considering why the settlers chose to develop these particular social structures. The emergence of Icelandic social structures may be attributed to factors such as new patterns of social liability that may have developed in response to the scattered population. As is explained in Section 4.4.2, the scattered population, individualistic land-taking and new principles of land-transfer led to a dissociation or decoupling of kinship and locality. It is not suggested that kinship became a less important part of the fabric of Icelandic society, but it seems that a communal system developed alongside it. This new social liability may have motivated the creation of *hreppar* ('communes') whose main purpose was to aid the poor and the needy. The shift in social liability may have contributed to the creation of the *búar* ('neighbours') system too. The *hreppr* and *búakviðr* were not exactly democratic social structures. Their creation contributed, however, to a system of checks and balances, distributing power between the chieftains, by establishing smaller, local networks of judicial power.

It is unlikely that any change in social liability could be attributed solely to the introduction of Christianity. The Conversion is conveyed as a peaceable political act, not as a religious act. It appears above all as an affirmation of the need for nationally agreed laws: '*Þat er upphaf laga várra*', *sagði hann*, '*at menn skulu allir vera kristnir hér á landi ok trúa á einn guð...*' 'This is the foundation of our laws', he said, 'that all men in this land are to be Christian and believe in one God...' (*Íf* XII, *Brennu-Njáls saga*: 272). In the literary sources the change in religion is not represented as a radical change. Ari tells us for instance that it was permitted to sacrifice to the heathen gods, to expose newborn babies and to eat horse meat.[6] In consideration of the fact that *Íslendingabók* was approved by the bishops, this information bears witness to a considerable tolerance, not only in the

---

[5] This seems to show that the Icelandic system was not only considered 'different', but perhaps incomprehensible to others. See Sigurður Nordal (1942: 132).

[6] See *Íf* Ii (17): the concessions that Ari mentions are usually interpreted as provisional economic measures (Jón Steffensen, 1966–69: 196–97; Jón Jóhannesson, 1974: 136–37). Sveinbjörn Rafnsson (1979: 167–74) has attempted, however, to relate them to clauses in medieval penitentials.

period after the change in religion, but also in the Icelandic scholarly environment in Ari's own time.

As for the individual settlers, by breaking away from society (in Norway, the British Isles or elsewhere), they showed themselves to be independent. This group of people became more than just settlers, but progenitors of the Icelandic people. Every aspect of the *landnám* was recorded, ensuring that the Settlement became part of the collective memory of all Icelanders. Turville-Petre (1978–9: 7–23) observes that there was a conceptualisation of history through periodisation in Iceland. This is most evident in Ari's account of the history of Iceland (*Íslendingabók*) which is broken down into set periods. Long lists of historical events formed frequently the basis of historical accounts (cf. genealogies and the *lögsögumannatal* ('the list of Lawspeakers')).

In the Þórðarbók version of the *Landnámabók*, the Icelanders themselves couch their identity in terms of the *landnám*. It is argued that the Settlement provides the truth of Icelandic ancestry and a means of proving that Icelanders are not descended from slaves.[7] This suggests perhaps a subsequent preoccupation with identity. It is also clear from *Landnámabók* that the origins of Icelandicness were tied to the land, explicit in the title *Landnámabók*, and that this became an important feature of the Icelandic identity (Hastrup, 1990: 80).

4.2.2 *Characteristics of Icelandic social structures: role of the law*

Alongside their relationship to the land, the identity of the Icelanders was partly based on emerging social structures. It is therefore worthwhile considering how identity and social structures are linked in new societies. It has been suggested by the sociologist Tomasson (1980: 12–13) that law tends to assume a central role in new societies, a more prominent role than in the country where the settlers came from.[8] Tomasson compares seventeenth-century New England to tenth-century Iceland. Law gained a commanding role in New England, settled by overseas migrants from the country where the doctrine of fundamental law had been most fully developed. Tomasson claims that new societies are characterised by the lessened influence of kin, and that in response law develops over kinship as a source of authority. It is certainly true that law (and not government) was central to Icelandic society and that this fact is reflected in the terminology

---

[7] See Hermann Pálsson & Edwards (1972: 6): this passage seems to suggest that Iceland's beginnings were stimulated by foreign misconceptions. It is also remarked that all civilised societies should wish to know the origins of their own society. Cf. Torfi Tulinius (2000: 258).

[8] Cf. Toynbee (1962: 99–100) where migration resulting in the breakdown of kinship is seen as the explanation for the early development of an English legal polity. Cf. Bryce (1901: 287): 'In no other literature is fiction or history, by whichever name we describe the Sagas, so permeated by legal lore'.

describing legal attachment. It is less clear that this was due to a change in kinship-ties. One could argue, however, that the significance of law may have been linked (initially at least) to the issue of *landnám*. It is perhaps no coincidence that the first laws were cited in the year 930 A.D. when the land was declared *albyggt* ('fully settled') and that a legal framework was required to manage the settlers' claims and rights to the land: *Svá hafa ok spakir menn sagt, at á sex tegum vetra yrði Ísland albyggt, svá at eigi væri meirr síðan* 'Wise men have also said that Iceland was fully settled in 60 years, so that no further settlement was made after that' (*Íf* Ii, *Íslendingabók*: 9). Orri Vésteinsson (2000: 11) takes this to mean that all the land had been 'claimed' at this point, but not necessarily 'utilised'. This interpretation seems eminently plausible: the 'utilisation' of land is likely to have been a longer process, as he claims.

There are various reasons for believing that law was fundamental to Icelandic culture and identity. Looking at the very earliest texts, one is reminded of Ari's account of the Conversion with the Christians and the Heathens declaring themselves 'out of law with the other'. The Lawspeaker, Þorgeirr, warns that if the Icelanders tear apart the law they tear apart the peace – law was the unifying factor. It is clear from Ari's *Íslendingabók* that an important feature of self-definition for the early Icelanders was that they should all have one law and that this Icelandic law was a means of differentiating themselves from others: *hvárir ýr lögum við aðra* 'each side was *out of law* with the other' (*Íf* Ii, 16); *es vér slítum í sundr login, at vér monum slíta ok friðinn* 'if we tear apart the law, we tear apart the peace' (*Íf* Ii, 17); *ok sagði, at hónum þótti þá komit hag manna í ónýtt efni, ef menn skyldi eigi hafa allir lög ein á landi hér* 'and said that he thought people's affairs had come to a bad pass, if they were not all to have the same law in the country' (*Íf* Ii, 17). Much later at the end of the Commonwealth Period, the Icelanders agreed to the *Gizurarsáttmáli* (the agreement that effected the union between Iceland and Norway in 1262–64 A.D.) on the basis that they could enjoy peace and Icelandic laws (*íslenzkum lögum ok friði*).[9]

One of the reasons why the First Grammarian established an Icelandic alphabet was so that the Icelanders could write and read laws. The First Grammarian lists the genres of Icelandic letters as laws, genealogies (*áttvísi*), interpretation of religious texts and the learned works of Ari: *til þess at hægra verði at rita ok lesa sem nv tiðiz ok a þessv landi, beði lög ok ááttvísi* 'in order that it might be easier, as is now customary in this country as well, to write and read laws and genealogies' (Hreinn Benediktsson, 1972: 208). A similar list of written genres of vernacular prose is found in *Hungrvaka* ('Appetizer'). The genres then current are described as laws,

---

[9] *DI* (I: 620): it is significant that here at the time of the submission to the Norwegian Crown, the laws are referred to as *íslenzk lög* and not *vár lög*, as had been the case previously; cf. Sigurður Nordal (1942: 121–22) and Jón Viðar Sigurðsson (1999: 153) for a discussion of this point. The adjective *íslenzk* was able to act as an identity marker at this stage.

sagas and historical lore (*mannfræði*): *Þat berr ok annat til þessa rits at teygja til þess unga menn at kynnisk várt mál at ráða, þat er á norrænu er ritat, lög, eða sögur eða mannfræði* 'And secondly, this writing is intended to allure young men to whom our speech is known to read that which is written in the Norse: laws, or stories or historical lore' (*Íf* XVI, *Hungrvaka*: 3).

It is easy therefore to make the case for law being the basis for social organisation in Iceland. More specifically, a distinguishing feature in early Iceland was the importance of being 'attached to the law'. There was an emphasis on explicit legal identification not witnessed in other Norse colonies. It became a legal requirement to attach oneself to a legal household. This attachment implied a special relationship between the householder and the person to whom he gave lodging. Members of a householder's immediate family were automatically attached to his household; others joined it by agreement, as workers or in other capacities. A man's household attachment would determine what his legal duties were, where he should be summoned, which assembly group he belonged to.[10]

The distinction between those who were attached to the law and those who were not applied to the whole of society and led to basic social distinctions between individuals. In accordance with the Social Identity Theory discussed in Chapter 2, this created in-group and out-group identities. The most obvious out-group were the thralls because they were not bound by the laws of the free men. Slaves had to be 'led into the law' in a process that is called *í lög leiða* ('manumission'): a phrase that is peculiar to Iceland (*Grágás*, Ia: 192).[11] Elsewhere, as in Norway, the manumission process was referred to as either *gefa frelsi* or *gera frelsisöl sitt*: both phrases imply the 'giving of freedom' as opposed to the 'leading into the law'.[12] In-group/out-group social identities were defined in early Iceland in 'legal' terms: in-groups were people attached to a household and considered *lögfastr* ('legally domiciled') (*Grágás,* Ia: 153, 154, 162),[13] and to be living in a *lögheimili* ('legal domicile') (*Grágás*, Ia: 4, 16, 20, 52, 122, 131, 132). As well as being the lodging of a priest serving the district, a *lögheimili* referred to a person's legal residence that decided various matters of legal importance. A domicile may also have been described as a *heimilisfang* and its residents were considered to be *heimilisfastr*, once again emphasizing

---

[10] *Grágás* (Ia: 128–39); §22 of *þingskapa-þáttr* (*Konungsbók*) is devoted to the procedures for enquiring about the nature of an individual's attachment to an assembly (*at spyria at þingfesti manna*); see also Jón Jóhannesson (1974: 354–57). Birgir T. R. Solvason (1993: 97–125) notes that in order for anyone to settle in a new community, he was required to provide references. These references served as some form of status identity.

[11] Note the parallel with *ættleiðing* (*Jónsbók*, 1970: 87); *NgL* (I: 31).

[12] Maurer (1906: 104–5): the phrase *gera frelsisöl sitt* is found only in *Gulaþingslög* and *Frostuþingslög*. *at gefa frelsi* is a term that is used in the Icelandic legal codes too (*Grágás*, Ia: 191–92, 224, 227–28).

[13] Cf. usage in *Jónsbók* (1970: 133, 142–44, 154–56, 172, 185) where the adjectival use is absent: *at lögfesta* is used as a verb in the sense of 'to make something legally your own'. The sense of 'legally domiciled' appears to be exclusive to the Commonwealth Period.

the notion of 'attachment'. *Grágás* (Ia: 41, 139). All of these terms (and others) have a degree of exclusivity in the laws of early Iceland, and are either absent or do not have the same *legal* sense elsewhere in the Norse legal corpus. There emerged therefore in early Iceland quickly a sense of what defined the 'us', its basis being the law, and in particular 'legal attachment'.

4.2.3 *The significance of assembly-attachment*

This overriding sense of legal attachment is fundamental to an early Icelandic social identity and it set the Icelandic laws apart from other laws in Scandinavia. To understand more fully how a social identity was formed, we need to consider, however, assembly-attachment as well as legal attachment. As for the 'assembly', one should firstly note that the *þing* ('assembly') functioned differently in Iceland from elsewhere: it was not simply a gathering of people who came to hear law-suits and discuss new laws; instead one had to align oneself to a householder and *via* him to a chieftain (*DFP*, I: 240). Unlike elsewhere, there was a unique requirement to have a formal and *legal* (*í lögum við*) attachment to an assembly. To be part of a household (*bú*), one had to be part of an assembly group which was expressed by the phrase *i þingi* (*með*): *Maðr scal segiaz iþing með Goða þeim er hann vill. scolo þeir nefna ser vatta baþir hann oc Goðinn* ... 'A man may say he is joining the assembly group of what chieftain he pleases. Both he and the chieftain are to name witnesses' (*Grágás*, Ia: 137). The assembly to which a chieftain belonged dictated the assembly-attachment and attendance of the men who were his supporters; they belonged to his 'assembly-third' (*þriðjungr*): *Ef annaR þeirra hefir til. eN annaR eigi. þa er sa skyldr til. at fa honvm er til hefir* [...] *er hann er i þriðiungi með* 'If one of them has a man available and the other not, the one who is required to provide him [...] whose assembly-third he belongs' (*Grágás*, Ia: 50). According to *DFP* (I: 240), everyone had to be (probably) *i þingi* (*með*) and thus belong to a chieftain's assembly group, 'householders independently and others through their householders, but it was a matter of contract: a man said publicly that he was joining the assembly group of a given chieftain, and if the chieftain concurred, his assembly- 'attachment' was fixed' *Grágás* (Ia: 136–42).

This assembly-attachment was known as *þingfesti* and the term was employed to denote a legal domicile in a *þing*-district in *Grágás*.[14] A person's status as *þingfastr* was an important means of identification in a society that was preoccupied with the notion of legal identity and identification. The abundance (and frequency of use) of such terminology

---

[14] *Grágás* (Ia: 40–43, 118): the procedures for a confiscation court (*ferans dom*) state that the prosecutor must first determine the residence (*heimilis fangi*) and assembly-attachment (*þing festi*) of the defendant. Both terms appear to be absent from *Jónsbók*.

denoting 'domicile' is likely to be significant. It represents one of the major ways in which an individual was legally defined and shows perhaps not just the focus on legal identity, but on *local* legal identity. It shows a geographical definition, largely relative to the local *þing* and to related practices such as the summoning of 'neighbours'. A person's local legal identity was relevant for various aspects of life such as *hoftollr* ('temple toll'), *þingfararkaup* ('assembly-attendance dues'), *hreppr*-obligations, and above all the tithing-system.[15] Effectively all 'taxation' was domicile-related, whether or not it was also related to the system of assemblies. More importantly, the terminology regarding legal domicile and assembly-attachment shows that language reflected a changing social identity for the Icelanders as social structures became established in this new society.

To summarise, one may say that the uniqueness of early Iceland could in part be explained by the fact that it was a new society which was quick to establish social structures. Amidst exceptional circumstances, the settlers created a different society for themselves and thus became custodians of their own culture. The settlers must have been self-conscious of their *kingless* Iceland at a time when Norway and England were becoming kingdoms with increasingly centralised power. Their new social identity was reified in the wealth of vernacular literature written across a range of genres (Meulengracht Sørensen, 2000: 10). The early development of social structures has been unusually well chronicled in this literature: literacy pre-dated a centralised 'government' in Iceland.

The basis for this single culture that united the scattered settlers was law. The law had become an important social dimension under which one had to be attached. The language of the historical and legal texts of the period reflects a growing emphasis on the socio-legal identity of the settlers. These texts view Iceland as an independent entity, a kingdom without a king. They portray also a land with a pervasive legal culture, a country united by one law, an Iceland where even the *siðaskipti* (literally 'change of customs'), the conversion to Christianity, is described as a legal and political act. The term *siðaskipti* appears to trivialise the Conversion (note that the term *kristnitaka* might be used to refer to the Conversion in Icelandic, and *siðaskipti* often refers to the Reformation). One gets the impression that the legal act of 1000 A.D. (or possibly 999 A.D.) was simply exchanging one formulation of the legal oath for another. In fact, individuals might not have had to do much more than give acceptance to one set of religiously defining narratives in place of another. The change of heart might already long since have taken place. The term might have been formed by analogy with *landsskipti* ('division of the land') (*Íf* IX, *Valla-Ljóts saga*: 241).

---

[15] See Gjerset (1925: 44): the *þingfararkaup* was a tax of ten *alnar vaðmál* assessed by the *goði* on all the *þingmenn* who did not attend the *alþingi*. The *hoftollr* was a collection for maintaining the temple and defraying the expenses connected with public worship.

4.3 Specific Icelandic social structures

4.3.1 *hreppr* (*'commune'*)

Now that we have described the kind of social identity that began to emerge in early Iceland, we can focus more specifically on Icelandic social structures. The particular social structures discussed here have been chosen because they may provide evidence of group identities in early Iceland. We begin with *hreppar* whose establishment was probably indicative of a new form of social organisation that was taking place in Iceland. The commune was defined and its responsibilities laid out in the law: *Loghreppar scolo vera alanðe her. EN þat er löghreppr er xx. bændr ero i eða fleire* (*Grágás*, Ib: 171) 'There shall be established communes here in the country, and an established commune is one in which there are 20 householders or more'. In order to be on a 'commune list' one had to be a householder who paid *þingfararkaup* ('assembly-attendance dues'). In each commune five land-owners were selected to prosecute all those who failed to meet their *hreppr*-obligations. These obligations included: *scipta tiundom* [...] *oc matgiofom. eða sia eiða at monnom* (*Grágás* Ib: 171) 'allocate food gifts and tithes and declare oaths'. There was an obligation to feed and board those people who became destitute *there* in the commune (within its defined boundaries), but men had no right to board vagrants from *outside* the commune.[16] The clarity of the legal definition of the *hreppr* shows that it was a well-defined legal community where an in-group identity was favoured at the expense of the out-group.

The remit of the *hreppr* was to look after the needy and the destitute, providing they were considered legally within the *hreppr*'s boundaries. The *hreppr* appears at first glance to be a Christian institution with a clearly defined, albeit non-all inclusive, sense of social responsibility. However, it may be too simplistic to believe that care for the poor had to be Christian or that the *hreppr* was in any way indicative of a Christian identity; it is equally possible that an older pre-Christian institution acquired new functions later. One important point in favour of this second view is that the *hreppr* does not, in Iceland, seem to overlap with the parish: the two systems seem unrelated.[17]

One might argue that there appears to have been a shift away from kindred responsibility to the *hreppr* in certain contexts: it was the *hreppr* that bore the responsibility for children of outlaws, the *hreppr* that compensated a farmer for loss by fire or disease among his beasts.[18] There is the sense of creating a community with an element of mutual maintenance

---

[16] *Grágás* (Ib: 171): criterion to be on the 'commune list'; boarding of vagrants outside the commune; *ibid.* (Ib: 172): *hreppr*-obligations.

[17] *KLNM* VII (18–22): the *hreppr* received a quarter of the tithe (from the parish) for the maintenance of the poor.

[18] *Grágás* (Ib: 23): responsibility for children of outlaws; *Grágás* (II: 260–61): another role of the *hreppr* was to insure against plague (*fallsótt*) and damage to buildings by fire.

and insurance against unwanted people or actions. However, one should not take the notion of a shift in social responsibility too far: the opening section of the *ómaga-bálkr* section of the laws ('dependants section') details kin maintenance obligations, *Svá er mælt at sina omaga ahver maðr fram at föra alande her* 'It is so prescribed that every man here in the country has to maintain his own dependants' (*Grágás*, Ib: 3). The *ómaga-bálkr* bears witness to a deep-rooted sense that people who cannot sustain themselves are a menace to society.[19] It seems clear that one of the results of the introduction of the *hreppar* was to divide society into those who could provide for themselves and those who could not. The formation of the *hreppar* created communities of in-group/out-group identities and contexts in which social networks could form. The *hreppr* was geographical in jurisdiction, while the *þing* was not. Once a farm had joined a given *hreppr*, its affiliation could not be changed. The farmer, on the other hand, could change his alliance to another chieftain and therefore another *þing*, whenever he wanted.

With the exception of two references in *Hákonarbók*,[20] the term *hreppr* does not appear in the corpus of Norwegian laws and it has a *legal* significance only in Iceland,[21] although cognates of the term are to be found elsewhere. The term gave rise to a number of Icelandic *hreppr*-compounds; this new legal and socio-legal terminology applied to all Icelanders and must therefore have reflected a notion of an all-embracing Icelandic social identity.

4.3.2 *búar* ('neighbours')

The notion of 'neighbour' also became important in early Icelandic society and had implications for identity and social network formation. Both the system of *búar* and *hreppar* are evidence of an incipient system of social networks, giving us some indication of the form of early social groupings in Iceland and the kind of ties that were established between individuals. These forms of social and judicial organisation were not known in the same form elsewhere in the Norse-speaking world.

It is perhaps unlikely that *búi* ('neighbour') should be a term that was widely used in Iceland given that the country was previously unoccupied and that the settlements were fairly scattered. Equally, one could argue the reverse, however: the fewer neighbours one has, the more important they

---

[19] See Orri Vésteinsson (2000: 81): this is an extremely detailed piece of legislation which has few parallels.

[20] *NgL* (I: 293, 294): it is used in the phrase *innan heraðs ok utan hreps* 'within the district and outside the commune'.

[21] Its use is not restricted to the Commonwealth Period. See *Jónsbók* (1970: 109–10); *KLNM* VII (18): the term refers to a settlement (*byggð*) in certain Norwegian dialects and a part of the parish in certain Swedish dialects.

become. The term *búi* had a wider meaning than in modern Icelandic where it refers to somebody who lives in the vicinity. In *Grágás*, it invariably connotes 'juror' instead.

The term is used throughout *Grágás* in this very specific sense – five or nine *búar* form the back-bone of early Icelandic law. The *búi* often has to estimate the value of something or somebody in the event of damage to property (in the widest sense) or death or injury to an individual. It is not entirely clear how important the *búa quiðir* ('panel verdicts') were in the overall implementation of justice, and the name implies that the focus of their role may have been principally oath-taking.

The *term* (not the concept) with this particular legal sense appears to be specific to the Commonwealth Period. At least it does not occur at all in *Jónsbók*, whose content is admittedly slightly different.[22] The term appears infrequently in the sagas but there it is used very much in the sense of 'somebody who lives in the vicinity' (*Íf* IV, *Eyrbyggja saga*: 34; V, *Laxdæla saga*: 20). There existed no similar jury-based system in Norway. The word *búi* occurs just twice in the Norwegian legal corpus and the sense is 'somebody who lives nearby or in the same house' *NgL* (I: 255). Overwhelmingly, the word used in the Norwegian regional laws to denote 'neighbour' was *granni*. It seems that a *granni* tended to refer to a 'neighbour' in the modern sense, but more frequently a co-habitant.

One may note that the *granni* term appears in *Jónsbók* but not *Grágás* which is perhaps evidence of a Norwegian influence (*Jónsbók*, 1970: 134, 181, 191, 282). Even so, the term does not connote 'neighbour' in the Norwegian sense, i.e. somebody living in the vicinity. Instead, it is used in a purely juridical sense and its meaning is similar to that of *búi* in *Grágás*. The main difference is that there are no references to 'panel verdicts' and the number of *grannar* summoned is invariably six and never five or nine (*Jónsbók*, 1970: 160). This is evidence of Icelandic conceptual continuity using the Norwegian term. One is almost tempted to suggest that the Icelandic system was tampered with under Norwegian influence.

If it comprised more than oath-taking, the role of the *búa quiðr* implies that justice was to a degree meted out at a local level and that it was inclusive – almost a community effort in a stateless society. Any notion of statehood at the time is likely to have been based on the single person of the monarch. The priority at this time is more likely to have been social stability than a system of democratic justice. The laws (excluding *kristinna laga þáttr*) are not concerned with ethically-based judgement or guilt at all. Instead, they are concerned with maintaining social stability, and in particular commuting feud into something less destructive. In order to ensure such stability one had to ensure that the most powerful participant won. It was justice and equity, local power, authority, wealth, both of the

---

[22] There is no *vígslóði* ('manslaughter') section in *Jónsbók* for instance.

individual and his family, that counted most importantly. Judging it by our own modern standards, it may seem surprising to see neighbours acting as jurors in a small-scale society. The point may be, however, that the *búar* knew things immediately and personally. They were not there to witness the truth, but to witness, above all, the juridical oath which was the essential legal act: *at hlyða til eiðspiallz* 'to hear oath-taking' (*Grágás*, Ia: 54). The legal act would enter the communal memory of the local community, and this was essential in a pre-literate society. Once it was witnessed, it was accepted by that society, as though the witnessing constituted that social acceptance. The point of the exercise was not justice as one may recognise the concept in a Judaeo-Christian tradition. If this interpretation of *búar* is correct, it would imply that relatively dense social networks formed. A large number of persons to whom the ego was linked were connected with each other in order for information to have been known and exchanged. Social structures such as *búar* give us an insight into the kind of social contact models that may have been established in order to ensure social stability.

The fact that the Icelanders placed an unprecedented jury system at the *centre* of their legal procedures suggests that the Icelanders chose to move to a different manner of socio-legal representation. The role of the *búar* in early Icelandic society may thus help us to understand how Icelanders acquired, and possibly also how they saw, their separate identity. Early Iceland was self-governing and communal and it seems as if it wished to present itself as such. The notion of *búar* shows also that despite its scattered settlement, communities were formed in Iceland. As these were based on socio-legal ties, they must have created local socio-legal identities.

4.3.3 *alþingi* (*'General Assembly'*) and *lögrétta* (*'Law Council'*)

The establishment of the *alþingi* ('General Assembly') became ultimately a symbol of an Icelandic identity. The parliament of the Icelandic Commonwealth was invested with the supreme legislative and judicial power. It consisted of the *lögrétta* ('Law Council'), *fjórðungsdómr* and *fimtardómr* ('Quarter Court and Fifth Court'), *goðar* ('chieftains'), *lögsögumaðr* ('Lawspeaker') and the *lögberg* ('Law-rock') (Jón Jóhannesson, 1974: 35–49). All of these terms were used to describe socio-legal institutions that were in essence Icelandic, or at least it was the Icelanders that gave them formal expression. Magnús Stefánsson (2003: 206) claims that there was a *lögrétta* in Orkney, and that Orkney, with Caithness, was divided into *fjórðungar* ('Quarters'), but the evidence for the *lögrétta* is late medieval and it is not clear what the evidence is for *fjórðungar* in Orkney. *alþingi* is referred to in the Norwegian laws (*NgL* V: 70), but not in the sense of a national assembly. Magnús claims here that the same term was used in the Icelandic sense in the Faroe Islands. *Færeyinga saga* (*Íf* XXV: 10) mentions an assembly on Straumsey, but it is not clear if it acted as a national assembly, and the saga reference, at least, is not to an *alþingi*. The *alþingi* was held annually at mid-summer, during the fortnight which included the summer solstice, at Þingvellir, a site still sacred in Icelandic national consciousness. The celebrations for the fiftieth anniversary of the republic in 1994 were held at the *alþingi* and attended by 60,000 people – nearly one quarter of the population. In a speech to the nation, the President of Iceland, Vigdís Finnbogadóttir, described Þingvellir as the *fjöregg* ('egg of life') of the Icelandic people. Furthermore, it was suggested that Þingvellir was what set Icelanders apart from others – its spiritual beauty accessible *only* to Icelanders.

As a national centre the *alþingi* was the first Icelandic social structure to be based on a conception of national boundaries. This distinguished it from the other *þing* in Iceland and the local *þing* in Norway and elsewhere.[23] One is hesitant to use the word 'national' in this very early context, but the *alþingi* embraced all Icelanders who had a right to attend (*eiga þingreítt*).[24] The word 'nation' is not unduly anachronistic if one conceptualises a 'nation' as a self-identifying people: that is exactly what the *alþingi* constituted. It was obviously an assembly, but not more than that – no permanent edifices were connected with it. It was cult, legislature, court of law, market, trading place and social gathering all in one. The assemblies, and in particular the *alþingi*, had cult functions. The astronomical solstices and equinoxes seem to have had religious significance; the *alþingi* was hallowed at its opening by the *allsherjargoði*, '*goði* of the entire host' (see *Íf* Ii, *Landnámabók*: 46 and Gunnar Karlsson, 2004: 213–66), and legal acts were invariably ratified by religious oaths, making them also cult acts. These cult associations were translated into Christian terms at Conversion. A church was built at the *þing*-site, at one end of a processional way leading to the Lawspeaker's mound, where law and judgement were pronounced.

Iceland lacked urban centres (at least until the twentieth century), but one must not forget the existence of the *alþingi* for a fortnight each summer. Informal and formal social relationships were established at the *alþingi*, and this led to the formation of dense and multiplex social networks whereby assembly-goers formed links with one another in a number of different ways. People of different *þriðjungar* ('assembly thirds'), *hreppar* and *buar quiðar* met, and to a degree linguistic accommodation and network formation is likely to have ensued. Had prestige varieties existed in early Iceland at the time, they would have been present at such gatherings.

There is an argument to be made for this gathering of people not being an innovation, but also (and almost certainly intentionally and knowingly) an archaism: a successful attempt to recreate a system of governance that had

---

[23] *Íf* Ii (8) mentions regional assemblies in Iceland (Kjalarnes) that predated *Íslendingabók*.
[24] See Maurer (1909: 327): the *alþingi* was a public meeting open to all free people. Cf. Gjerset (1925: 45) and *Grágás* (Ia: 149, 150, 175).

operated before the arrival of centralised kingship.[25] The reference is here to the annual gathering of the Old Saxons that endured until about 784 A.D. The parallels between the annual gathering of the Old Saxons described in the *Vita Lebuini* and the Icelandic *alþingi* are very close indeed.

The constitution did not, perhaps, develop *ex nihilo* either, but it was devised for purposes consciously shared and supported by most of the men of power in early medieval Iceland. Early Icelandic social structures such as the *alþingi* give us an insight into the nature and type of social contact between the Icelanders. With the establishment of assemblies, individuals are likely to have formed new reference points. Thus, Iceland shifted from an 'isolated' to an 'integrated' network model. Irrespective of whether the *alþingi* was or was not based on a distant precedent, it and Þingvellir became an important part of Icelandic identity for the next thousand years.[26]

Like the *alþingi*, the *lögrétta* represented a social and physical space (the fixed place where the body met) as well as the ultimate legal authority comprising the men acting in the 36 full and ancient chieftaincies (*goðorð*). There is good reason to believe that this institution is also an Icelandic innovation, with nothing directly comparable found elsewhere in the Norse colonies. It is also evident that the *lögrétta* remained part of the Icelandic legal system after the submission to the Norwegian Crown because it is attested in *Jónsbók*. The *lögrétta* had a number of duties which are outlined in the *lögréttu-þáttr* ('Law Council Section' (of *Grágás*)). The *lögrétta* in Iceland (not elsewhere) elected the *lögsögumaðr* ('Lawspeaker') for a period of three years, decided on laws and licences (*ráða logom oc lófum*); each member of the Law Council appointed (*scipa*) two men to advise him (*ráða með ser*); framed laws and made new laws (*rétta lög sin oc gera ny mæli*) (*ibid.*) and granted (*leyfa*) licences for mitigation of penalty and all licences for settlements for which special permission was required (*Jónsbók*, 1970: 8–10) (cf. Ólafur Lárusson, 1958: 131).

4.3.4 *goðar ('chieftains')*

Looking for potential speakers of a prestige variety, one can begin with the *goðar* ('chieftains'). Debates at the *þing* were conducted by chieftains with the title *goði* (pl. *goðar*). In the beginning there were 36 *goðar*, while the number was later increased to 48 (cf. Sigurður Nordal, 1942: 126–28; Barði Guðmundsson, 1959: 49–55). These men were responsible for the 'government' of the country and they had clearly defined public obligations. Their power was not defined in the law on a territorial basis, apart from the fact

---

[25] The Icelanders might have been opposed to the new ideas of centralised monarchy, in a land sufficiently far removed across the Atlantic from the threat of monarchic military power.

[26] The two are no longer co-terminous as the parliament (still called *alþingi*) has been based in Reykjavík since the year 1845.

Table 3. Phraseology of the *goðar* ('chieftains')

Phrase	Meaning	Occurrence
dom nefna	'to nominate a court'	*Grágás* (Ia: 98)
bioða til sacar søkianda oc at rengia þa menn or domi	'to invite the prosecutor of a case and to reject men from court'	*Grágás* (Ia: 98)
ráða hve nær domr scal ut fara	'to decide when the court is to adjourn'	*Grágás* (Ia: 99)
eiga þing saman	'to hold an assembly together'	*Grágás* (Ia: 96)
veria lyrite	'to put under veto'	*Grágás* (II: 21, 104, 125)
coma til þings ondverðz	'to come to the beginning of the assembly'	*Grágás* (Ia: 97)
þing hælga enn fyrsta aptan	'to inaugurate the assembly on the first evening'	*Grágás* (Ia: 97)
queða aþingmöre hver ero	'to state what the assembly boundaries are'	*Grágás* (Ia: 97)
queða a hue þing heitir	'to state what the assembly is called'	*Grágás* (Ia: 97)
nefna vatta	'to name witnesses'	*Grágás* (Ia: 137)
fa bvðar rúm	'to provide booth space'	*Grágás* (Ia: 44)
luta með ser	'to draw lots'	*Grágás* (Ia: 50)
selia goðorð	'to sell a chieftaincy'	*Grágás* (Ia: 141)

that three *goðar* belonged to each local *þing*. The office of the *goði* was his *goðorð*, a peculiar mixture of public office and private property. The *goðorð* was not defined by boundaries; it was rather a political centre of many powers, a social rather than a geographical space.[27] The *goðorð* was heritable and transferable: it could be lent, given or even sold, just like property other than land, but it was not taxable (according to *Grágás* Ia: 141).

The *goðar* had a number of responsibilities and duties and these are listed in the *þingskapa-þáttr* ('Assembly Procedures Section') of *Grágás* (Ia: 96–101, in particular). These are described using the modal verb *scolo* (*skyldr at*) ('to be obliged to, to need (to)') plus the infinitive throughout. Table 3 lists the relevant phrases.

The phrases listed above represent only notions that are couched in terms of an obligation or duty. Some of them are attributable exclusively to the *goðar*. It is only the *goðar* for instance who have the power of veto (*verja lýriti*) and provide booth space (*fa buðar rúm*). It is not, however, necessary to be a chieftain to name witnesses (*nefna vatta*). These phrases give an impression of the power and 'social capital' that the *goðar* enjoyed. If the *goðar* represented a powerful model, it is likely (in accordance at least with the Acts of Identity Theory discussed in Chapter 2), that this would have been a contributing factor in promoting 'focusing', and thus ultimately a common cultural identity.

The origin of this Icelandic office has been much debated, but it must not be forgotten that the *goðar* are exclusive to the Commonwealth Period (cf.

---

[27] See Hastrup (1985: 118). The term *goðorð* means literally the words of *goði* – it refers both to the terrain or power of a *goði* (his sphere of influence) and his speech.

Ólafur Lárusson, 1960: 8–12; Jón Jóhannesson, 1969: 46, 49). They were a unique construct, but one that may have had a pre-monarchic Germanic basis. Monarchy was a late introduction into the Germanic world. The king seems etymologically to have been the head of a kindred, a clan (cf. Scottish clans and clan-chiefs). In Norwegian history, the term *king* was applied to individuals of very local authority: *Þá váru fylkiskonungar í Nóregi, er þessi saga gerðisk* 'There were regional 'kings' (chiefs) in Norway at the time of this saga' (*Íf* XXVI, *Heimskringla* I: 3; VIII, *Vatnsdæla saga*: 3). Thus, kingship was extremely localised, but also divisible and transferable, and thus bore a resemblance to the Icelandic *goðorð.*

The portrait of this archaic institution and its constitutional and legal functions, put forward in *Íslendingabók, Landnámabók* and *Grágás* is essentially that given by Icelandic scholarly historians of the early twelfth century, while the Icelanders' system of governance was apparently still functioning more or less effectively. It may represent an over-rationalised and idealised understanding, but it is not likely to be unrealistic. It is also a self-portrait: the scholar-historians who put it together, where their identities are known, were themselves *goðar*. Ari Þorgilsson, for instance, held a half-share of the Helgafell *goðorð* on Snæfellsnes: *Ari sterki bjó á Stað á Snæfellsnesi. Hann var goðorðsmaður og er líklegt að hann hafi erft a.m.k. hluta Þórsnesingsagoðorðs eftir föður sinn og afa, en gera má ráð fyrir að Ari fróði hafi erft hluta goðorðsins eftir afa sinn* 'Ari the Strong lived at Stad in Snæfellsnes. He was a chieftain and as might be expected he had inherited a share of the Þórsnesing chieftaincy from his father and grandfather, and we should assume that Ari the Wise inherited a share of his chieftaincy from his father' (*Íf* Ii, vi).

It is probably not a retrospective creation of the violent and at times almost anarchic *Sturlungaöld* of the earlier part of the thirteenth century, when the system of checks and balances inherent in the constitution were breaking down. The author of *Hungrvaka* observed that on the death of Bishop Gizurr (1118 A.D.) peace crumbled, and whatever one says about the *Sturlungaöld*, it is notable for its *ófriðr*, its lack of peace: *En fráfall Gizurar byskups bendi til ættar um öll óhægendi á Íslandi af óáran [...] en eptir þat ófriðr ok lögleysur...* 'And the death of bishop Gizur led to all kinds of difficulties in Iceland [...] and after that to unrest and lawlessness' (*Íf* XVI, *Hungrvaka*: 21). Nor was it a nostalgically romanticised invention of the post-Commonwealth Period, after Icelandic submission to the Norwegian Crown in 1262–4 A.D., when the *goðar* of each Quarter collectively transferred their own authority to the Norwegian king.

It seems that the archaism of the Icelandic system is a deliberate attempt to look back to pre-monarchic Germanic societies as a means of establishing roots. The result was a collective identity by origin, not geographical but social and legal. The Icelanders took these archaic constructs and moulded them in an innovative manner, leading thus to a social identity by creative distinction from other societies.

Summing up, one should observe that the social identity of the Icelanders in the early period of their history was reflected through archaic and innovative institutions. Whilst some of these constructs may have been based on (much) earlier forms, they are always distinctively Icelandic. The settlers may have modelled their institutions on archaic forms in order to secure roots to their ancestors as part of a collective memory, but the fact that they made them innovative must be significant too. There were reasons for choosing to develop a *different* society. It may be that by using the model of the pre-Germanic kingless society, they thought they would be able to circumvent the social problems of kingship in Norway – often considered the rationale for leaving Norway in the first place.

Some of these social structures appear to have been motivated by new priorities and social responsibilities. The introduction of *hreppar* and the mechanics of the juridical system suggest that social stability was the main concern of the era. In a wholly new landscape, actual and metaphorical, there was little personal or social security. Until the institutions were set up that created stability, or at least contained and constrained the violence of feud, let alone protected to some extent against the extremities of climate or famine, individuals or individual families were without any physical, economic or legal protection.[28]

All of these social structures and the terminology describing them show how Icelanders acquired, and how they perceived their identity. Significantly, a number of the historical and legal texts represent the reality of the time. Texts such as *Íslendingabók*, *Landnámabók* and the First Grammatical Treatise appeal for a recognition of distinctiveness and a separate identity at different levels, socio-legal, cultural and linguistic. These social structures also show how the 'new society' of early Iceland created conditions for social network formation, and thus linguistic norm-development. With the exception of the *alþingi*, the decentralised and local social structures based on voluntary cooperation show how local 'cooperative clusters' formed. There is good evidence for the formation of local communities, but not for the development of local linguistic norms.

4.4 INDIVIDUAL IDENTITY AND ICELANDIC KINSHIP STRUCTURES

4.4.1 *landnám ('Settlement') and kinship structures*

In addition to the emergence of a social identity for early Icelanders, we need to consider issues of individual identity. As we will see, the absence of

---

[28] One could also set it in a wider context, of the violent social upheavals of the Viking Age 'back home', and of the fundamental changes being introduced by the new monarchies.

certain social structures in Iceland is likely to have had consequences for individual identities too. The process of integrating into a new society affects our perception of who we are as individuals as well as groups.

It should be clear from the previous discussion that the *landnám* led to a society that was different from Norway or the British Isles. The process of the *landnám* may also have led to changes in kin-organisation. The reason for this is that the Settlement was individualistic in nature; the settlers were scattered and brought seldom more of their kindred than their immediate family (*Íf* Ii and ii, *Landnámabók*). It is debatable if this triggered any erosion in kinship solidarity. Phillpotts (1913: 255) considers kindred solidarity to be a less important social bond in Iceland than in other parts of Scandinavia; Hastrup (1985: 74) claims that 'an individualistic view of property (expressed in individual land-takings) should develop kindreds rather than maintain a principle of unilineal descent groups geared to common ownership of the means of production'. The argument is very unclear: kindreds as groups of persons who have a single relative in common appear to have always existed in both Icelandic and Norwegian societies, and it is not obvious how their emergence can be linked to land-ownership. Evidence from the laws (such as *ómaga-bálkr*), genealogies and the sagas show kinship to be still important even if grouping patterns were different from before the Settlement.[29]

The settlers' kinship ties were permanently *disrupted*, but it is not clear to what degree the migrants were cut off from their past. There are many reports of Icelanders in Norway and of Norwegians in Iceland in the sagas.[30] In *Egils saga Skalla-Grímssonar* for instance, Egill Skallagrímsson claimed and successfully acquired for his wife her inheritance in Norway (*Íf* II, *Egils saga Skalla-Grímssonar*: 148–73).

In instances where kinship organisation had been disrupted, there were new 'localisations'. New communities formed in new localities, and kinship ties were established again: *Með henni kómu út margir göfgir menn...* 'With her came many noblemen...' (*Íf* IV, *Eiríks saga rauða*: 196). Certain saga evidence shows that *major* figures such as Auðr *in djúpúðga* took local social structures (*ómagur* 'dependants' and *vinir* 'friends') with them when they moved, and this saga evidence reflects earlier accounts of the Settlement in *Landnámabók*.

There has always been a high degree of internal geographical and social mobility in Iceland. As we have seen, there was the temporary mobility of the *alþingi*. People from all parts of the country, at least from the upper

---

[29] Vestergaard (1988: 180) envisages a degeneration of kinship organisation in Iceland with the disappearance of minimal *ætt* (three-generational patrilineage). Icelandic kinship was more a matter of bilateral, genealogical networks of relations centring on individuals than corporate groups. Cf. *Grágás* (Ia: 218–27): calculation of genealogical distance for the basis of inheritance – the basis for Vestergaard's argument.

[30] See also *Grágás* (Ib: 195–97): provisions in the law for the rights of Icelanders in Norway.

levels of the social system, got together once a year. This enabled the establishment of links of *vinfengi* ('friendship'), fosterage and also marriage. There was also the Church as a vehicle of social and physical mobility: the Church included some of the culturally most influential individuals, even if after the Reformation women were excluded.

4.4.2 *Kinship and land-transfer*

In order to speak of social structures and individual identity, we need to discuss kinship and land-transfer in early Iceland. Before the migration to Iceland, the system of land-ownership in Norway had been that of *óðal* land. This was a principle of land tenure which kept property in the family, as it defined a particular relationship between a kin group and a piece of land. The *óðal* system of land-ownership represented the totality of rights and concepts connected with non-transferable, non-saleable ancestral property. The term *óðal* implied not only 'family estate', but also 'patrimony', 'birth place' and 'fatherland'. *óðal* was defined legally as an unbroken succession from father to son. It was the opposite to *útjarðir* ('out-lands') and *lausa-fé* ('movables') which descended to the daughter (*NgL* I: 91, 237).[31] The *óðal* was inalienable within a family, so that even when parted with, the possessor still retained a title or convenant (*landbrigð, máldagi á landi*).

Given that Iceland was *terra nova* at the time of Settlement, there could be (by definition) no *óðal* system of land-ownership as there were no local ancestors. This may have marked a clear break between Iceland and Norway and meant that the settlers identified with their land in a different way. *óðal* was allegedly being appropriated by the new kings of Haraldr *inn hárfagri*'s dynasty in Norway, at the time when the settlers were abandoning the concept in Iceland. Even if the Icelanders give this as a reason for their emigration, they did not take the institution with them. As we observed in Chapter 2, the relationship to a place is often fundamental in creating an identity. The absence of the *óðal* system and the individualistic nature of the *landnám* process are likely to have led to a relative (not absolute) dislocation of kinship and locality. Thereafter one has two social systems in operation: locality and kinship, whereas previously these had been co-terminous.

The implications of the disappearance of *óðal* in Iceland have been misunderstood. Hastrup (1985: 74) notes that 'the disappearance of common ownership of land is connected with the emergence of the cognatic kindred', i.e. a group of persons who have a single relative in common and

---

[31] Vestergaard (1988: 178): the precise definition of *óðal* varies. According *to Frostuþingslög* XII (4) (*NgL* I: 237), land would be *óðal* to a man if three patrilineal ancestors had owned it; in *Gulaþingslög* (266) (*NgL* I: 87) the criterion is five generations of individual ownership in a patriline.

for whom descent is through male or female. To use the term 'common ownership' is as tendentious as it is misleadingly anachronistic and appears to be creating the romantic illusion of a pre-monarchic Marxist idyll: *óðal* as understood in medieval Scandinavia was certainly not 'common land'. As for 'emergence of cognatic kindred', it should be stressed that cognatic kinship had always been significant to Germanic kinship-structures.[32] The important point is specifically that the *óðal* had to be inherited down the male line, but movable property could always come into and leave the family by marriage.

Icelandic society does not seem to have substantially altered the balance between agnatic and cognatic kinship (i.e. the balance between relationship by male link exclusively and descent through the male *or* the female): it was just that the concept of inalienable, agnatically inherited land was abandoned. Any Icelandic estate could be bought, sold or granted with legal and personal freedom. The *óðal* system implies certainly patrilineal inheritance. That is unlikely to have changed: at the time of the Settlement the kin system appears to have been patrilineal; the implications of the phrase *at leiða í ætt* ('to adopt') are that one was becoming a member of the paternal *ætt* (*Jónsbók*, 1970: 87). It appears that it was the ability to transfer land that changed, both within the *ætt* and beyond it, leading of course to far greater mobility (change of legal domicile had to take place at legal times of the year, *fardagar*). Kinship and land-transfer were actually two aspects of the same matter in Norse. *óðal* signifies what pertains to somebody as part of inherent qualities, properties in the double sense of that word. *ætt* signifies those who belong together, and to whom particular properties, such as land and personal qualities belong. Thus *óðal* and *ætt* are that which belongs to them and those that belong together respectively, in both cases by virtue of descent: a fundamental relationship that was modified in early Iceland and thus created a difference from other Norse colonies.

In a country which regarded its own history in terms of land-taking, a basic change in the way the settlers related to that land was significant for an individual's identity and led to a reconfiguring of identity models. However, one aspect of the identity model that was not reconfigured is that of the genealogies through which the settlers maintained or established links with the places where they came from. Let us therefore now turn to these genealogies and their role in identity construction.

4.4.3 *Genealogies and identity*

Whole chapters of the sagas are devoted to genealogies and use them as their primary means of identifying individuals (*Íf* II, *Egils saga*

---

[32] It had always been important who married whom, and all the Germanic peoples employed the practice of dowry-giving.

Skalla-Grímssonar: 3–6; IV, *Eyrbyggja saga*: 3; VI, *Gísla saga Súrssonar*: 3–6; XII, *Brennu-Njáls saga*: 6). The reader of a saga is typically introduced at the beginning of the narrative to the main characters, their ancestors and where they came from: both kinship and to a lesser degree locality are represented.

Genealogies form the basis of Icelandic historiography and have been an important part of the identity of the Icelanders since the time of the Settlement. As a collective and systematised origin legend for every locality in inhabited land, *Landnámabók* establishes in precise details who the Icelanders are. In both the sagas and *Landnámabók*, kinship relationships derived from Norway were remembered and recorded – possibly even reconstructed if they had not already existed. The interminable saga genealogies that introduce the main characters go almost invariably back to Norway, or back to 'standard' genealogies which in their turn go back to Norway. These written texts were obviously considered very important, and are given pride of place in the larger texts in which they survive; there is good evidence that in at least some instances they are older than the sagas that preserve them. The strong impression given by the *texts* is that there was a clear concern to define, express and preserve kinship information across the entire country. That might indicate some degree of anxiety that such information could be lost, but it also shows the importance of that information.

Iceland never had nobility or a king and yet genealogy was and remains a favourite occupation of the Icelanders and not the Norwegians, although genealogy was popular in certain rural communities in Norway until relatively recently. Unlike Norway, there was in Iceland no legal advantage to have been gained from demonstrating that you had aristocratic relatives. However, the Icelanders memorised the genealogies as they did the laws, and nearly all our direct evidence for Norwegian genealogies comes from or through these Icelandic sources.[33] The Icelandic genealogies stress both the Icelanders' common origin with that of the Norwegians and their own divergence from it at the specific point of Settlement. The Icelanders no longer saw themselves as Norwegians, and the relationship with Norway was largely couched in terms of the past rather than the present. It was not simply a matter of residence: any notion of 'nationality' was a matter of personal allegiance and subordination to the person of the monarch – a quasi-feudal relationship to the monarch. Icelanders found it also important to trace their ancestors back to 'legendary history'. These ancestors may have served as defining archetypes, but archetypes which the Icelanders ultimately rejected. These archetypes were part of a well-defined

---

[33] Ólafur Briem (1968: 499–509): the eddaic poem *Hyndluljóð* where the goddess Freyja's favourite Óttarr needs to learn and memorise his genealogy after he has wagered his inheritance on his pedigree. The proper enumeration of kinship was required in certain procedures in the Icelandic legal system (*Grágás*, Ia: 48).

period of Viking adventures that took place around Scandinavia and the British Isles and whose participants were known for their strength and endurance. The characters of the *fornöld* were not the complex and ambiguous figures of 'history', but emblematic figures expressing simple primary values of heroic endeavour. The Icelanders did not, for the most part, live in a heroic age, but they remembered one – the so-called Viking Age – and valued the memory, just as they valued but rejected their Norwegian past. All these factors were part of their identity, or, one might say their identity-crisis. There was and is in Iceland a clear need to search for roots, but also a need to emphasize how different the Icelanders have become.

4.4.4 *Icelandic kinship terminology: cousin terms*

The Icelandic interest in genealogies has not declined over the centuries and the kinship terminology implicit in these charts has remained essentially unchanged from the earlier period, whilst the other Scandinavian languages have absorbed foreign terms. Whilst one witnesses continuity in kinship terminology, one finds also small fragments of evidence of Icelandic lexical innovations. Cousin terms such as *næsta bræðra* ('second cousins'), *annarra bræðra* ('third cousins') and *þriðja bræðra* ('fourth cousins') do not appear in other Norse legal codes, but are attested in *Grágás* for example (*Grágás*, Ia: 62, 136, 158, 170, 194, 202 as well as *DI*, I: 185).

These terms acted as benchmarks for laws relating to wergild payments, but also to marriage, incest, inheritance and rights and duties of prosecution. Since their relevance is a purely legal one, it is tempting to think of them not really in the sense of consanguinity, but much more in the context of lawsuits. The term *næsta bræðra* and the phrase *næsta bræðri eða nánari* 'second cousins or closer kin' occur throughout *Grágás* on occasions when it is necessary to draw a legal distinction on the basis of proximity within kin. There are fewer references to *annarra bræðra* with most legal provisions concerning second cousins or closer kin. There are also relatively few references to *þriðja bræðra* in *Grágás*.

The terms *annarra bræðra* and *þriðja bræðra* are wholly absent from *Jónsbók*, the law code written under Norwegian rule. There are references to 'third cousins' and 'fourth cousins' that appear in contexts (inheritance, manslaughter etc.) similar to *Grágás*. The terms used, however, are *þrímenningr* ('third cousin') and *fjórmenningr* ('fourth cousin') (*Jónsbók*, 1970: 40, 41, 46, 85). These appear intermittently in the Norwegian legal corpus too (*NgL* V, *Gulaþingslög*: 740 and *Íf* XII, *Brennu-Njáls saga*). The 'Icelandic' legal lexicon may have been influenced by lexical usage in Norway at this point. Alternatively, these semantically more transparent terms may have had more appeal and some degree of standardisation of terminology may have been thought useful from an Icelandic perspective too; it could also have become 'fashionable', as did some Norwegian spellings in fourteenth-century Iceland. It is even possible that some of the Icelanders had problems with their own technical terminology.

At the same time, it is difficult to explain the emergence of new cousin terms which were absent in Norwegian society. These may have been simply the creation of a legalistic mind. Even if in individual instances a person did not know who his fourth or fifth cousin was, a legalistic mind (and it appears there were many in early Iceland) may have wished to set up principles of payment and receipt of property. The question would just be why this particular numeric patterning was chosen. However, traditional societies (and certainly pre-literate societies) tend to have extensive genealogical knowledge. Iceland today is peculiar by modern western standards in that many Icelanders are able to name all their great-grandparents. So it may not be too surprising to discover that Icelanders living in the thirteenth century knew their fourth or fifth cousins.

The individualistic *landnám* led to a disruption in kin-organisation. The absence of *óðal* in Iceland is likely to have affected in particular the kinship-locality relationship; the main effect of the non-existence of ancestral land in Iceland was, however, a change in the principle of land-transfer which distinguished it from other Norse colonies. To assert that the writing of genealogies was motivated by attempts to establish rights to this land would be contentious. From the time of the Settlement, it is clear, however, that genealogies became a means for settlers to recognise their past, but also facilitated their self-identification as Icelanders.

Similar to other social structures that have been discussed in this chapter, the characteristics of Icelandic kinship structure appear to be both archaism and innovation. Unlike mainland Scandinavia, kinship terminology has remained consistent, but has accommodated the odd lexical innovation specific to the legal register.

4.5 CONCLUSION

Early Iceland's social structures were unique to a degree and were recognised as such at the time. It would seem that the Icelanders wanted to create a different society. It is impossible to know precisely what the motivation for this may have been. I would contend that the uniqueness of the social structures may be intertwined with the *landnám* itself. It was the *unsettled* land that gave the Icelanders the freedom to create their own society. In establishing social structures, the settlers may have wanted to avoid the perceived deficiencies of the models they were familiar with. Equally, they may have just exercised their freedom and chose an arrangement that they considered was most appropriate for a scattered population. The settlers were clearly not restricted to following any particular model, but they must have thought within certain parameters. They would have had some premises and mind-sets: one cannot exclude models altogether; it may be that they chose to adapt for whatever reason aspects of archaic institutions.

The terminology used for these social structures reflects a changing social and individual identity in early Iceland. Significantly, it is terminology that applied across the land, and not just in a specific region. All the Icelanders were united by one law and bound by the socio-legal terminology referring to the legal institutions and their functions: the social structures put in place reified the sense of a 'whole' that the Icelanders had because they were relevant to the whole land. This can be seen from the process of Quartering. The term *fjórðungr* ('Quarter') shows inherently that the whole land was divided up, since a Quarter could only have any meaning with reference to the whole. Thus, the establishment of Icelandic social structures during the Commonwealth Period both informs, and is informed by, the collective identity of what we may call the Icelandic nation.

5

PERCEPTION AND USE OF LANGUAGE AS AN IDENTITY MARKER

5.1 INTRODUCTION

The previous two chapters have addressed the issues of norm-establishment and identity construction in early Iceland: how a linguistic norm was established, and how language reflected new social and individual identities within the framework of social structures. Having determined in Chapter 2 that linguistic norms are used to indicate group identity, the aim of this chapter is to examine how language was used and perceived as an identity marker amongst the Icelanders, but also in subsequent encounters with non-Norse speakers. This question will be answered from a number of different perspectives, using a range of grammatical variables and data from various registers. The underlying principle will remain, as mentioned in Section 2.7.1, that the linguistic identity of a group of people living in a distant historical period can only be understood by analysing with equal measure the representations of the 'self' and the 'other'.

The starting-point for the study of the linguistic 'other' is to consider Icelanders' perceptions of *foreign* languages and their speakers. For the purpose of Section 5.2 where the focus is the literary sources, the term *foreign language* is taken to mean a language that was unequivocally *not* understood by the Norse-speaking Icelanders. As the chapter proceeds, it will become clear that mutual intelligibility is at times and in certain geographies a moot point. Section 5.2 will show moreover that there was an appreciation of other linguistic identities by Icelanders and other Norsemen and that this is reflected, albeit sparsely, in the literature. In the context of linguistic encounters in non-Norse-speaking regions, the unfamiliar language acted as an identity boundary in the obvious sense that it was simply not understood. As for non-Germanic languages that may have been spoken in Iceland in the early period, one is restricted to the controversial and poorly understood Celtic or Common Gaelic issue discussed in Chapter 3. Section 5.2.2 is concerned with references to Common Gaelic (as defined in Section 3.1) in the Icelandic literature, and presents the scant evidence of what is described as spoken Irish in the literary sources.

Linguistic and cultural perceptions may be anchored in subtle socio-linguistic differences such as dialectal variation. This issue and in particular terms such as *dönsk tunga* and *norræna* are discussed in Section 5.3. These labels imply a degree of linguistic homogeneity. It will be considered whether the relatively 'homogenous' language acted as an identity marker and whether the above terms and their implications of linguistic uniformity overshadowed differences in cultural perceptions between Scandinavians. Ideally, the usage of linguistic labels would hint at how Icelanders symbolised their own identity, even if they spent most of their time talking to other Icelanders. Language is, however, perceived as either *dönsk tunga* or not *dönsk tunga*.

An attempt is also made to understand what the notion *útlenzkr* ('foreign') signified in a Norse-Norse context and to whom it applied. This is discussed with reference to socio-legal inclusion. Socio-legal inclusion is significant because, as we have seen, this was an important factor in defining a settlers' identity. There are a select number of legal documents that outline the rights of Icelanders in Norway and *vice versa* and these are useful in this regard.

Grammatical variables are analysed in Section 5.4 in order to see how language was used as an identity marker in the earliest Icelandic texts. Section 5.4 starts by investigating the use of what will be called 'agreeing possessive adjectives' and their patterns of occurrence.[1] The fundamental issue of how Icelanders and non-Icelanders perceived *várt mál* ('our language') lies at the heart of this chapter. It is easier to determine when the settlers first distinguished themselves as 'Icelanders' than it is to know with any certainty when they first considered their language to be definitively Icelandic. Section 5.4 is also concerned with the semantics of pronominal usage, and the reader will benefit at this point from referring back to the brief theoretical discussion on pronouns in Section 2.8.4. References are made here principally to legal and historical texts. The reason for this is that a sense of the opposition between 'us' and 'them' pervades some of these documents – the impression of cultural opposition or difference is less explicit in the sagas and the poetry. The findings should be assessed in their correct historical context. It is tempting to assume that a certain pronominal usage may be a marker for social cohesion or contrast, but the medieval scribes' and authors' motivation for using these variables may have been quite different from modern conventions.

A rich system of spatial deixis existed in Norse and aspects of this grammar of space are analysed in Section 5.5. Spatial deixis and pronominal usage are discussed because, in accordance with Section 2.8.4, they both can serve as identity markers, anchoring the location of the speaker to a speech-event. Spatio-directional terminology is a promising area of research in the context of identity as the sense of how one group of people and their movements are defined relative to another is often implicit in these deictic terms. The terms discussed here are of special relevance to

---

[1] The term 'agreeing possessive adjective' refers to phrases such as *várt mál* ('our language') and *vár lög* ('our laws').

Norwegian-Icelandic relations in this early period, but may even apply on a different level within Iceland itself.

5.2 ICELANDERS' PERCEPTIONS OF FOREIGN LANGUAGES

5.2.1 *References to a foreign language*

We start by referring to the *Íslendingasögur*, which provide us with written accounts of how people viewed themselves and others. They *should* offer therefore a fertile and comprehensive source for the study of linguistic relations between Norse and non-Norse speakers, and thus the issue of linguistic identity.

There are references to foreign languages in the sagas and much of the evidence has been examined by Townend (2002: 145–61), although he focuses much more on whether the Anglo-Saxons and the Norsemen understood each other than on Icelanders' perceptions of foreign languages.[2] Given the amount of contact the Norsemen had with non-Norse speakers on their travels and taking into account the subject matter of the sagas, it is surprising that there are not more insightful references to linguistic unintelligibility. The scraps of evidence in the literary sources become disproportionately interesting mainly because they are so few. There are many contexts where one can speculate whether the Norseman spoke the foreign language. On the basis of his campaigning in the Greek Islands, one assumes that Haraldr Sigurðarson spoke Greek; churchmen will have spoken Latin – but there are very few references to it.

A number of these references tell us little more than that the language in question was not understood by Norsemen as is the case with German in *Grænlendinga saga* for example: *Hann talaði þá fyrst lengi á þýzku [...] en þeir skilðu eigi, hvat er hann sagði* 'He first spoke for a long time in German [...] and they couldn't understand what he was saying' (*Íf* IV, *Grænlendinga saga*: 252). Other passages offer more promising linguistic insights such as the account in *Örvar-Odds saga* (Boer, 1888: 28 (M-version)):

> 'Skilr þú hér nökkut mál manna?' segir Oddr. 'Eigi heldr en fugla klið,' segir Ásmundr, 'eða þykkiz þú nökkut of skilja?' segir Ásmundr. 'Eigi er þat síðr,' segir Oddr. 'Þat muntu sjá,' segir hann, 'at einn maðr skenkir hér á báða bekki, en þat gefr mér grun um, at hann muni kunna at tala á norrœna tungu'

> 'Can you understand anything of the language of the people here?' asked Oddr. 'No more than the noise of birds,' said Ásmundr. 'Can

---

[2] See also Kalinke (1983: 850–61) for a discussion of the role of foreign languages in the *riddarasögur*.

you understand anything?' asked Oddr. 'No more than you,' said Oddr. 'But you can see that man there serving drink to both the benches – well, I suspect that he may well know how to speak Norse'

The Norse identity marker in this instance may be a cultural one: Oddr might have recognised a Norse drink-serving practice, but it may be simply that the man serving the drinks looks like a Norseman. As far as the sagas are concerned, Bjarmian, German and Wendish are languages that are represented as clearly unintelligible to monolingual Norse speakers.[3] Elsewhere, there are references to what appear to be Armenian and Greek/Russian, but any linguistic detail is glossed over: *Ef byskvpar koma vt hingat til landz eþa prestar. þeir er eigi erv lærþir. a latinv tungv. huartz þeir erv hermskir eþa girskir...* 'If bishops or priests come to this country who are not versed in the Latin language, whether they are 'Armenian' or Russian...' (*Grágás*, Ia: 22); *Íf* Ii (*Íslendingabók*: 18): *Enn kvómu hér aðrir fimm, þeir es byskupar kváðusk vesa: Örnolfr ok Goðiskolkr ok þrír ermskir: Petrus ok Abraham ok Stéphánus* 'In addition, five others came here who called themselves bishops: Örnolfr and Goðiskolkr and three Armenians: Petrus, Abraham and Stéphánus' (cf. Magnús Már Lárusson, 1959: 81–94 for a discussion of Armenian bishops). Beyond the Anglo-Norse context, linguistic observations are otherwise conspicuous by their absence: no mention is made of the language of the Skrælingjar in *Eiríks saga rauða* for instance.[4] If we are not told explicitly that the language is unintelligible, then it is just assumed that this is the case and that it is not necessarily noteworthy.

5.2.2 *References to Irish*[5]

According to the genetic research referred to in Section 3.3.1, a significant number of the female settlers were of Irish stock. There is little evidence, however, in the sagas of bilingualism or Common Gaelic being spoken and almost no mention of communication problems between speakers of Norse and Common Gaelic. As mentioned in Section 3.3.1, it is assumed that the reason for this is that the female

[3] This does not represent a comprehensive list. See Ross (1981: 29–41) for descriptions of Bjarmaland which refers to the south shores of the White Sea and *Saga Óláfs Tryggvasonar af Oddr Snorrason munk* (edited by Finnur Jónsson, 1932: 209) for an incident showing the response of fellow Norwegians to Óláfr Tryggvason speaking Wendish: the language is described as *ukunnr* ('unknown'). The passage appears to be designed to show the king's superior knowledge.

[4] See *Íf* IV (*Eiríks saga rauða*: 227) where detailed physical descriptions are given: *Þeir váru svartir menn ok illiligir, ok höfðu illt hár á höfði; þeir váru mjök eygðir ok breiðir í kinnum* 'They were dark, ugly men who wore their hair in an unpleasant fashion; they had big eyes and broad cheeks'.

[5] The term 'Irish' is used when the relevant references in the Norse refer to the language as *írsk* ('Irish'). In other contexts, the 'language' is referred to as 'Common Gaelic', as discussed in Section 3.1.

Celts were Norse speakers by the time of the Settlement, having integrated and married into Norse-speaking communities in the British Isles prior to the Settlement.

There are few references in the literature to the problem of Norse-Common Gaelic intelligibility and research has tended to focus on the issues of Common Gaelic loan-words, place-names and personal names in Iceland.[6] As for the literary evidence of spoken Irish, one must turn principally to *Laxdæla saga* written in approximately 1250 A.D. (Jónas Kristjánsson, 1988: 264). It has been observed that the scene between Óláfr, the son of an Icelander, the Irish princess Melkorka and the Irish guards shows that the Norsemen required interpreters to communicate with the Irish.[7] Furthermore, we are told that Óláfr has been taught Irish by his mother, and that it is the 'best' Irish: *Auðsætt er þat á Óláfi þessum, at hann er stórættaðr maðr, hvárt sem hann er várr frændi eða eigi, ok svá þat, at hann mælir allra manna bezt írsku* (*Íf* V, *Laxdæla saga*: 57) 'It's clear that, whether or not he's our kinsman, this Óláfr is a high-born man, and also that he speaks, of all people, the best Irish'. There is also an ambiguous reference in the same saga. As Óláfr is about to depart on his travels, his mother Melkorka says good-bye and reassures him that: *Heiman hefi ek þik búit, svá sem ek kann bezt, ok kennt þér írsku at mæla, svá at þik mun þat eigi skipta, hvar þik berr at Írlandi* (*Íf* V, *Laxdæla saga*: 51) 'I have prepared you for leaving home as best as I could, and have taught you to speak Irish, so that it won't make any difference to you in which part of Ireland you land'. Townend (2002: 149) suggests that the last clause in the sentence implies that in those parts of Ireland where Norse was spoken no language difficulties would arise. This is certainly a plausible interpretation, but alternatively it may mean that Óláfr would not have trouble understanding Irish dialects as he had received such good instruction.[8] The clause remains ambiguous, but the temptation remains to perhaps over-analyse the fragmentary linguistic evidence to be found in these literary accounts.

In the context of *foreign* languages as previously defined in Section 5.1, the sagas are therefore not especially informative when it comes to the linguistic identity of the non-Norse speakers that the Norsemen encounter. The literary sources show that there was a degree of

---

[6] See Hermann Pálsson (1996: 150–207) for a discussion of over 100 Common Gaelic personal names; Jakobsen (1901: 177–78) for a discussion of Irish place-names in the Shetland Isles; Matras (1965: 22–32) on Celtic loan-words in Faroese; Helgi Guðmundsson (1997: 120–68) for Celtic loan-words in Icelandic.

[7] Townend (2002: 149); *Íf* V (*Laxdæla saga*: 55): Óláfr tells the Irish guards that the property forfeit law applies *ef engi væri túlkr með kaupmönnum* 'if no interpreter were with the traders'.

[8] O'Rahilly (1988: 248) argues that it is not correct to speak of Irish dialects at this point of time.

linguistic awareness and saga characters are on occasions celebrated as polyglots.[9] With a few noteworthy exceptions such as the atypical explicit references to Irish in *Laxdæla saga*, information on foreign languages is, however, invariably absent. It may be that the linguistic identity of the 'self' is more prominent and in order to determine that one needs an appreciation of how the Icelanders presented themselves linguistically.

5.3 A VERNACULAR IDENTITY: *DÖNSK TUNGA, NORRÆNA* AND ITS SPEAKERS

5.3.1 The *dönsk tunga* as an identity marker

In order to analyse how the Icelanders presented themselves linguistically, it is necessary to examine the use of certain linguistic labels. We start our analysis by looking at the term *dönsk tunga*. The intention is not to provide a full discussion or history of the term, but to understand how it may have been used as an identity marker in early Iceland and other Norse-speaking areas. This is a problematic undertaking as it is not clear to what degree the linguistic communality implied in the term *dönsk tunga* was a major factor in creating an identity for Norsemen, let alone Icelanders. In his comprehensive study of the term, Melberg (1951, I: 841–924) concludes that the Scandinavian languages are all offshoots of Danish. As Melberg's own examples show, *dönsk tunga* refers often unambiguously to Norse and not Danish. All the evidence shows that the language was widely considered uniform in the relevant period, at least to the extent that it was referred to in a number of different registers using the same term.

On the basis of its attestations, it is not obvious what kind of identity the term *dönsk tunga* reflects. For a term that is widely used in the secondary literature, there are relatively few references in the Icelandic primary sources written in the vernacular. Some of the references discussed by scholars are to *tunga* and not just *dönsk tunga*, cf. Karker (1977: 482). For the purpose of this analysis, the focus has been only on clear and unambiguous references to *dönsk tunga*. According to *KLNM*, the term is used infrequently in a reasonably wide range of registers. It is found in the *þingskapa-þáttr* and *arfa-þáttr* sections of *Grágás, Jónsbók*, as well as in the saga material, diplomas, grammatical treatises and poetry or texts which

---

[9] Finch (1965: 23) (*Völsunga saga*): *Hann kenndi honum íþróttir, tafl ok rúnar ok tungur margar at mæla sem þá var títt konungasonum, ok marga hluti aðra* 'He taught him various accomplishments, chequers, runes, and also how to speak many languages, as was then customary for princes, and much else besides'; Olson (1912: 12) (*Yngvars saga víðförla*): *Þar uar Ynguar iij uetur ok nam þar margar tungur at tala* 'Yngvar was there for three winters and learnt to speak many languages'.

are concerned with poetry.[10] Elsewhere, the 'danish tongue' is referred to by historians writing in Latin: *cum debito quod Danico uocabulo dicitur mithsumeres chield* 'with the debt which is called 'mithsumeres chield' in Norse' (1140 A.D.) (*DD*, 1. række II: 153).

It would help if one could know whence the term originated. Whilst it is unlikely that the term was created *ex nihilo*, its history remains rather opaque. In *Monumenta Germaniae historica, Scriptores* IV (1841: 97), Dudo uses the phrase *Dacisca lingua* in his history of the dukes of Normandy, written at the beginning of the eleventh century. It is difficult to know how to interpret this because *lingua* is the normal Latin word for 'language', not necessarily reflecting *tunga*. It is unclear if Dudo was known in Iceland: Icelandic writers do not demonstrate much knowledge of Normandy, but do seem to assume it.

In accordance with the *communis opinio*, Karker (1977: 481) suggests that the term was probably coined by foreigners, mostly southern neighbours, either the Saxons or the Anglo-Saxons.[11] It is clear from the earlier references that the *dönsk tunga* referred to the language of all Norsemen, and not to 'Danish' which was a much later development. It has been claimed that the term is a source of ambiguity in the context of twelfth- and early thirteenth-century texts, but Saxo's (the Danish historian's) references to *Danice* mean Norse (Karker, 1977: 482). It is not obvious whether Saxo had the terminology to distinguish between Danish and Norse writing at the beginning of the thirteenth century. One may even question whether he had the concept of the two as separate languages: the notion of mainland Scandinavian languages as *national* separate idioms came later.

Where the term *dönsk tunga* was used, it must surely mean that it was recognised that among a potentially wide range of dialects there were enough common characteristics to warrant the appellation. Old Icelandic was recognised as part of this linguistic family, and *dönsk tunga* represented the speech of the wider Scandinavian community and not just that of the settlers. One can be reasonably sure of this because there are in the laws references to 'foreigners' speaking *dönsk tunga*: *Ef her andaz utlendr maðr* [*af danskri tungo þa scal fe hans biða her erfingia leigo lavst*] 'If a foreigner dies here [whose language is Norse, then his property is to wait here for an

---

[10] See *KLNM* II (662–64) and Melberg (1951: 89–146) for a complete list of references. Specific references in the poetry may include Finnur Jónsson (1912, Vol. 1. B: 216): Sigvatr Þórðarson's *Víkingarvísur* v. 15, whose subject matter is the reign of St Óláfr Haraldsson and was composed before 1030 A.D.; Kock (1946: Vol. 1: 207) Markús Skeggjason's *Eiríksdrápa* v. 27; Kock (1949: Vol. 2: 212) Eysteinn Ásgrímsson's *Lilja* v. 4, composed about 1340 A.D.

[11] Cf. Maurer (1867: 48–9); Steenstrup (1878 (reprint 1972): 321–22); Karsten (1925: 151–53); (1928: 144–45); Indrebø (1951: 92); Hammerich (1953: 120–1). If it is calqued out of Latin, the phrase is unlikely to have been coined in eleventh-century Norway: one would not look for so much easy acquaintance with Latin there then. The phrase may well be of English origin: a Danelaw term, in which case it could go back to a period at which *danskr, Denisc* etc. did not specifically refer to Danes (a time earlier than the late tenth century).

heir and without interest'] (*Grágás*, Ia: 229). The term conveys a communal linguistic identity for all Norsemen and not just Icelanders (*Grágás*, Ia: 172, 173, 239, 244). It is worth reflecting on what may have been the precise meaning of the term *tunga*. There is an intriguing passage in the Icelandic Homily Book where there is a distinction drawn between what may be termed 'language' and 'idiom':[12]

...hve mjök vér erum vanbúnir við því es vér skulum guði þjóna á þá tungu ok á þá mállýsku es ér kunnuð iamt skilja og umb at mæla sem vér

how unprepared we are to serve God in that language [tunga] and in that idiom [mállýska] which you understand and speak as well as us

The term *tunga* might have referred generally to *speech*; a notion of language not constrained or defined by national boundaries,[13] whereas *mállýska* (in the above example) might refer to the speech of Icelanders, as it does seem that the term can be applied to a fully-formed free-standing language such as Latin. However, there is one difficulty with making a concrete distinction between 'language' (*mállýska*) in the sense of the group of linguistic features specific to the Icelanders, and a larger, less well-defined notion of language as a spoken form (*tunga*): the terms are not used consistently in the same context. The First Grammarian in his attempt to codify this vernacular identity for the Icelanders uses *várt mál* 'our language' and *várrar tungu* (*sic*) 'our language' interchangeably for instance: *beði latinv stofvm öllvm þeim er mer þottí gegna til vars mals vel* [...] *er æigi gegna atkvæðvm várrar tvngv* 'I have used all the Latin letters that seemed to fit our language well [...], while those were taken out that did not suit the sounds of our language' (Hreinn Benediktsson, 1972: 208). These pronominal phrases form the subject matter of Section 5.4.1, but before we turn our attention to these references we need to comment on the term that succeeded *dönsk tunga*, namely *norræna*.

5.3.2 *norræna* as an identity marker

It is not clear *why* exactly *norrænt mál* (or *norræn tunga*, *norræna*) superseded *dönsk tunga* as a language label, but it seems that from the late twelfth century onwards the term *norræna* was used initially in a very similar way to *dönsk tunga*, i.e. to refer to an area (as well as the language) where Norse was spoken. The term is widely attested across registers to refer to the Norse language in West Norse (Icelandic and Norwegian)

---

[12] Cf. Pétur Knútsson (2004: 40); Leeuw van Weenen (1993: lv); see also the same passage quoted in Sverrir Tómasson (1998: 294). It is unclear what '*mállysku*' means in this context, but one is reluctant to adopt Pétur's translation of the term as 'dialect' in its modern sense.

[13] Gunnar Harðarson (1999: 11–30) claims that the coining of the term *dönsk tunga* may have preceded literacy in Iceland.

textual sources, appearing in the sagas as well as the laws and poetry.[14] Karker (1977: 484) suggests that the evidence from *Hákonar saga Hákonarsonar* (c. 1264–65 A.D.) may show that the term was originally synonymous with *dönsk tunga*. In this text, Sturla calls the prior of the Dominican province of Dacia *próvincíalis* [...] *af öllum predikaraklaustrum á norræni túngu* 'province of all Norse-speaking monasteries', and it is clear from the quote that *á norræni túngu* cannot refer to Norwegian because Dacia tended to be used by the Roman Catholic Church to refer to the whole of Scandinavia (and sometimes Denmark alone).[15]

It should be borne in mind, however, that the term refers to a more specific and different geography from the one that is presented above. The terms *dönsk tunga* and *norræna* may have been synonymous originally but *norræna* came to refer subsequently to a West Norse (Icelandic-Norwegian) linguistic identity at some point in the late twelfth century. It appears that at this early stage there was an appreciation of linguistic differences within Norse itself (cf. Kjartan G. Ottósson, 2002: 789–90). The author of the Third Grammatical Treatise, Óláfr Þórðarson hvítaskáld, writing in the mid-thirteenth century, makes the explicit distinction between Danish and West Norse: *þýðerskir menn ok danskir hafa* [...] *þat er nú ekki haft í norrænu máli* 'Germans and Danes have it [...] but it is not present in Norse'.[16] A distinction is being made between Danish and Norse, but where Norse refers to Norwegian-Icelandic and not the language of all Norsemen. The reason that one can be sure of this is that the author explicitly contrasts *danskir* and Norse, although *danskir* had always been part of Norse. The term *norræna* therefore reflects two linguistic identities with the West Norse one acting as a subset of the wider Norse identity. It is not known to what degree the term disguised any intra-Norse dialectal variation. In order to answer this question, one needs to examine the small number of (foreign) accounts and narratives that mention variation.

5.3.3 *Norse dialectal variation and Anglo-Norse intelligibility*

There are historical accounts written in Latin that testify to the supposed homogeneity of the Norse language (Karker, 1977: 483), but there are also passages that provide a little more linguistic colour and refer to dialectal variation (in mainland Scandinavia at least). There is for example an instance where the Holy See assumed a strong discrepancy between the

---

[14] Cf. twelfth-century skaldic poetry references: Finnur Jónsson (1912, Vol. 1. A: 545): Hallar-Stein's *Rekstefja* v. 8.

[15] See *Fornmannasögur* X (76–77); cf. Jakobsen in *KLNM* XII (356–57) and the list of quotations in Melberg (1951: 116–37).

[16] See Björn M. Ólsen (1884: 87): the quote is in reference to Óláfr Þórðarson hvítaskáld's observation that the *v* had been preserved before *r* in German and Danish, but not elsewhere in Norse.

idioms of Nidaros and Oslo in 1376 A.D.: *dummodo jdem Johannes Alfuerj de prouincia Nidrosiensi* [...] *sciat loquj et intelligere ydioma quod locuntur habitatores ciuitatis Osloenssis* 'If the same Johannes Alfueri of the province of Nidaros [...] knows how to speak and understand the dialect which the inhabitants of Oslo speak'.[17] One needs to be cautious in analysing these foreign accounts: it might for instance be understood as having a Vatican perspective, and the author might have been ignorant of any languages spoken in Norway other than that which Johannes could speak. Those reservations aside, it is an insightful observation and it is obviously written from a Trondheim perspective, commenting on the spoken language of the Oslo area. The implication is that the 'official vernacular language' of the archdiocese in Trondheim in 1376 A.D.,[18] was probably still Old Norwegian. This contrasts with the spoken language of the Vík which is unlikely to have differed much from Old Danish at any period.

The statement from Saxo Grammaticus in his fifth book on the history of Denmark gives us the Scandinavian perspective on Norse linguistic variation at the beginning of the thirteenth century. The account tells how the Norwegian captain Ericus Disertus (Eiríkr *inn málspaki*) sent two scouts ashore in Denmark: *Tum Ericus duos Danicæ facundos linguæ eo* [...] *proficisci iubet*, 'Then Erik ordered two men who spoke fluent Danish [...] to set out for that place' (Ellis Davidson, 1979: 125) [Saxo Grammaticus *Gesta Danorum*]. Scholars have taken this as evidence of a marked difference between the speech of Danes and Norwegians in Saxo's time (c. 1200 A.D.) (Karker, 1977: 484; Kristján Árnason, 2003b: 268). It is unclear, however, if that is the correct interpretation; the relevant part of the passage could just as well be understood to mean 'eloquent Norse' and not necessarily 'fluent Danish'. It need not refer to the scouts being sent because they had knowledge of a different (but related) idiom; it may be simply that they were chosen for their eloquence. Saxo was probably aware of minor linguistic differences, but is unlikely to have couched any subtle distinction in terms of different national languages.[19] There is little firm evidence of intra-Norse dialectal variation. It should not be inferred from this that it was not present; merely that it is difficult to prove that it existed in the earliest period.

---

[17] *DN* (VII: 313); Karker (1977: 483) for a discussion of this and other historical foreign accounts.

[18] See Haugen (1976: 181): in 1152 A.D. a separate Norwegian archbishopric was created in Trondheim (Nidaros).

[19] See Olrik & Ræder (1931: 7) (Saxo Grammaticus *Gesta Danorum* I: 7): *regio hæc Suetiam Norvagiamque tam vocis quam situs affinitate complecitur* 'this region includes Sweden and Norway because of the affinity in both language and location'. This is a reference to the Norwegians and Swedes speaking similar idioms, in accordance with their geographic proximity. The point that Saxo is making is a specific one as *vox* is a technical term in classical and medieval grammar.

The *dönsk tunga* acted as an identity marker in a broader geographical context. Townend (2002: 183) concluded his study of Anglo-Norse intelligibility by saying that there was a degree of pragmatic intelligibility between the Icelanders and the people of Danelaw. A twelfth-century formulation of the linguistic distinction between Norse and English is given by the First Grammarian: *allz ver ervm æinnar tvngv þo at giorz hafí miök onnvr tveggía eða nakkvað bááðar* 'we are of one tongue [with the English], even though one of the two has changed greatly, or both somewhat' (Hreinn Benediktsson, 1972: 208).

Whilst Norse and English may have been mutually intelligible, they were unambiguously different languages. Norse and English speakers may have shared a linguistic identity, but a Norse speaker was considered linguistically 'different'. One witnesses in The First Grammatical Treatise an explicit objective to codify this Norse vernacular and thus establish a firm linguistic identity for all Norsemen, and more importantly Icelanders. The First Grammatical Treatise incorporates speakers of English as part of this linguistic identity. Narrative evidence such as the passage cited below in *Gunnlaugs saga ormstungu* shows that this Anglo-Norse linguistic identity was short-lasting, however (*Íf* III, *Gunnlaugs saga ormstungu*: 70):[20]

> Ein var þá tunga á Englandi sem í Nóregi ok í Danmörku. En þá skiptusk tungur í Englandi, er Vilhjálmur bastarðr vann England, gekk þaðan af í Englandi valska, er hann var þaðan ættaðr

> The language in England then was the same as in Norway and Denmark. But the languages changed in England when William the bastard conquered it; from then on French became current in England, because he was from France

The basic claim of the author of *Gunnlaugs saga ormstungu* is that the English and Norse languages were the same – *ein tunga* – albeit for a defined, and relatively short period of time. Townend (2002: 150) considers this to be an example of Anglo-Norse intelligibility and not variation between the Norse spoken elsewhere and the Norse of Scandinavian England. Boucher (1983: 76) believes that *ein tunga* refers to the Scandinavian language still spoken in large areas of Eastern England. There is little we can say about Norse dialectal variation, but the linguistic homogeneity of West Norse outlasted Anglo-Norse intelligibility.

---

[20] Cf. Magnús Fjalldal (1993: 601–09) for a discussion of this passage. Bishop Friðrekr from Saxlandi (Saxony) does not understand Norse on his visit to Iceland as stated in *Kristni saga* (*Íf* XV: 6) which is preserved in Hauksbók, dated to c. 1306–10 A.D.

5.3.4 *Representations of identity within West Norse*

As well as the issue of Anglo-Norse intelligibility, we need to understand better the notion of an intra-Norse linguistic and social identity. We can examine how Norsemen referred to their shared language, but also how Norse speakers defined themselves through the use of language. It is impossible to do this major topic justice here, but a cursory glance at Norse cultural representations in different registers will give us a reasonable understanding of the issue.

It is known from *Grágás* that Icelanders considered Norwegians, and indeed all other Norse speakers as *útlenzkr* ('foreign') (*Grágás*, Ia: 172). Equally, one witnesses in *Gulaþingslög* Norwegians calling Icelanders *útlendir menn*: *Islendingar eigu hauldzrett* [...] *aller aðrer utlenzker menn* 'Icelanders have the rights of a *hauldr* [...] all the other foreigners' (*NgL*, I: 71). The earliest legal evidence shows that a distinction was drawn between Icelanders and other Norsemen with Icelanders referring specifically to Swedes, Danes and Norwegians.[21] Despite linguistic intelligibility between Norsemen, the Icelanders saw themselves as (culturally) independent and made that explicit in the formulation of the grammatical treatises and the laws. This should not be inferred, however, from the use of the term *útlenzkr* whose connotations in medieval Scandinavia were different from 'foreign': it was less subtle. It is to be understood simply as 'coming from another land': everybody beyond their respective lands were *útlendir menn*.

One finds a number of references to Norwegians in the sagas.[22] Caution is required in using this evidence because passages can be taken out of context – one has to consider them in the light of the characterisation of a particular saga. It would not be unreasonable to suggest, however, that the Icelandic authors highlighted on occasions different cultural perspectives in Iceland and Norway. Norwegians are for instance described on one occasion as *hin versta þjóð* 'the worst people': *ek veit eigi, hví þér sýnisk at fara til innar verstu þjóðar, ok frelst hefir þú þik um tíðendasögn við mik* 'I don't know why you like visiting that worst of nations; anyway, you needn't tell me any more news' (*Íf* IX, *Víga-Glúms saga*: 7–8).

There are relatively few references in Old Icelandic poetry to Norwegians or other Norsemen, but there is an early reference to 'Icelandic' in skaldic verse:

> Os hafa avgun þessi
> isleNZC konan vísat

---

[21] *Grágás* (Ia: 170): *Ef utlendr maðr noröN eða or noregs konvngs veldi her quangaðr alanði, verðr vegiN* ... 'If a foreigner from Norway or the realms of the king of Norway who is married in Iceland is killed...'; *ibid.* (Ia: 172): *Ef utlendir menn verða vegnir her a lanðe danscir. eða sønskir eða noRønir...* 'If foreigners are killed here in the country, Danish or Swedish or Norwegian...'.

[22] See Bogi Th. Melsteð (1914: 16–33) who has dealt thoroughly with the evidence.

brattan stig at bavgi
biortum langt hin svorto
sia hefir mioðnaNan maNe
miN okuNan þinom
fótr a fornar bravtir
fulldrengila gengit

These black Icelandic eyes, woman, have directed me far along the
steep path; Oh maid of the mead, this leg/foot of mine has gone
boldly on the ancient, unknown roads[23]

The verse is well known and has been widely discussed (Bogi Th. Melsteð,
1914: 23–4). Its interest lies in the fact that 'Icelandic' is referred to in
writing at the beginning of the eleventh century, and this may represent the
first reference to *íslenzk*. It is not known whether this is an early example of
a Norwegian-Icelandic cultural distinction. The poet's concern may
actually be to distance himself from the pagans amongst whom he now
finds himself, or at least so one would judge from the accompanying prose
(*Íf* XXVII, *Heimskringla*: 140). This introduces us to another dynamic of
identity (Christian *versus* heathen) which will be discussed briefly towards
the end of this chapter.

In summary, the term *dönsk tunga* reflects an identity for all Norsemen. The
term refers unambiguously to the Norse language, and not to Danish. The
sources provide us seldom with insights into how the Icelanders viewed or
described their own language, other than generic references to *várt mál* (see
below). The term *dönsk tunga* did not reflect a sense of national identity in any
way, but instead an ill-defined and indistinct notion of Norse speech: a
collective recognition that the speech of the people of the Norse colonies was
similar, if not the same. The use of the term suggests that it referred more to
the geographic origin of the speaker than to any specific linguistic features.

With the term *norræna*, there is evidence of a West Norse identity
emerging. The coining of the term may have been motivated by linguistic
factors. Once again, this label implies a high degree of linguistic
communality.

5.4 GRAMMATICAL VARIABLES AS IDENTITY MARKERS

5.4.1 *Agreeing possessive adjectives*

We move on now from an analysis of linguistic labels to look at the usage of
grammatical variables as identity markers. By focusing on the manner in

---

[23] Finnur Jónsson (1912, Vol. 1. A: 238): Sigvatr's *Austrfararvísur* v. 15: Sigvatr was one of St
Óláfr's poets and the poem can be dated to approximately 1016–1030 A.D.

which pronouns are used, we can gain an insight into how in-group identities were formed. According to the legal texts and the First Grammatical Treatise, Icelanders would typically refer to their language not as *dönsk tunga* or *norræna*, but as *or tunga, vár tunga* or *várt mál*.[24] These phrases have been termed here 'agreeing possessive adjectives'. This is not a feature peculiar to Icelandic, but is common in medieval legal and historical accounts written in Norway as well as documents written in Latin.[25] The expression *vár tunga* could be equally self-referential in each of the law codes, but just signalling a different group of users each time. It could also have been a register-specific (medieval) stylistic measure and not an explicit expression of identity.

When the phrase *vár tunga* is used, it is not always clear which group of speakers it refers to. It would help if we knew who the intended *Grágás* readership was. The major practical purpose of *Grágás* manuscripts was for intended use within Iceland, but that cannot be seen as an absolute limitation. Some manuscripts may have even been considered prestigious and were valued as objects.

It is not surprising that the *language* spoken in twelfth-century Iceland was not generally referred to as *íslenzk* because the notion of languages as 'national' constructs had not yet been fully established. This does not mean to say that the adjective *íslenzkr* was not used, just that the language was not referred to as such at this time (Kjartan G. Ottósson, 2002: 789–90). According to Melberg (1951: 82), the first use of *íslenzk* to refer unambiguously to the language is to be found in a list of books written by the Icelandic bishop Gizurr Einarsson in 1542 A.D., and included in the manuscript AM 266 folio. (cf. *Grágás*, Ia: 49: *Ef rypiandIN sa eigi huern goþIN nefnði i dóm* [...] *oc sva foþvr hans. eþa moþvr ef þav voro islendzk* 'If the challenger did not see whom the chieftain nominated to court [...] and also his father or mother if they were Icelandic'). Referring to a language spoken by people of a specific region (if one assumes the intended *Grágás* readership was Icelandic) as 'our language' renders it difficult to infer anything about representations of Icelandic linguistic identity. In other Norse registers, languages are seldom referred to by name and there are few language-naming insights to be gleaned from the saga material or the poetry.

Agreeing possessive adjectives were used not just to describe language, but also 'land' *alandi voro* ('our land') and 'laws' *vár lög* ('our laws') (*Grágás*, Ia: 96; II: 70; *NgL*, I: 12, 13, 130, 339; *Íf* Ii, *Íslendingabók*: 23–4).

---

[24] *Grágás* (Ia: 38, 172, 239, 244; Ib: 198; II: 70, 338, 340); Hreinn Benediktsson (1972: 208, 212).

[25] *NgL* (I: 11): *aller menn a vara tunga* 'all men of our language'; Storm (1880: 24) (*Monumenta historica Norvegiæ*): reference here is actually to 'our mother tongue': *prope Slaviam quam nos materna lingua Vinnlandiam vocamus* 'nearby Slavia which we in our mother tongue call Vinland' (c. 1180 A.D.).

The phrase *vár lög* appears as the formulaic opening of a number of West Norse legal codes: *Þat er upphaf laga varra at ver scolom...* 'It is at the beginning of our laws that we should...' (*NgL* I: 1). Hastrup (1985: 121) claims that this was an important concept in early Icelandic culture where law and society were co-terminous and brought together under this expression. Hastrup notes that there was actually no word for 'society' in Old Norse: *vár lög* appears to be an all-encompassing notion, and a means of defining the community of Icelanders *vis-à-vis* the outside world. Hastrup's (1984: 235) claim that medieval Icelanders would use *vár lög* whenever they spoke of their society and that they would simply refer to their country as *land* is, however, difficult to verify. Furthermore, references to *vár lög* in Icelandic and Norwegian texts do not typically refer to 'society' at all, but very simply to 'our laws'. (*NgL* I: 1, 11). It is difficult to be certain how the Icelanders referred to their country and society in *speech*.

References such as *vár tunga*, *vár lög* and *várt land* in the legal code(s) are not explicit attempts at linguistic or community self-definition. The phrase *vár lög* may have come from Norway with the settlers as *lög* was used there in the same manner to denote a conceptual merging of geographical and socio-legal space (c.f. *Gulaþingslög*, Danelaw etc.). *Gulaþingslög* and Danelaw both referred to geographical regions of Norway and England respectively, as well as the local law(s) or society.[26] One obvious difference is that *vár lög* referred to the whole country or land mass that we now know as Iceland, whereas *Gulaþingslög*, *Trøndelag* etc. referred to provinces of a larger region. One gets the impression therefore that in the case of Iceland the whole country was akin to a 'legal zone'.

Prior to the use of terms such as *vár lög*, Iceland (unlike Norway) represented a *tabula rasa* in terms of social structures and therefore a degree of self-definition was required. The usage of phraseology such as *vár lög* does not enhance our understanding of an Icelandic linguistic identity. The only evidence of any distinct *social* identity at this early stage was legal separateness; Iceland was simply a separate legal zone in a distinct geography.

Other very early texts such as the First Grammatical Treatise or *Íslendingabók* contain references similar to these. Although Ari is writing at an early period in Iceland's history, it is clear (but surprising) that the author has an 'Icelandic' perspective. There are references to *byskupum órum* 'our bishops', *óru tali* 'our reckoning' and *oss landa* (*sic*) 'our countrymen' (*Íf* Ii, 3, 4, 6, 8). One of the objectives of the First Grammatical Treatise is to create Icelandic linguistic self-awareness. One finds passages such as, *hefir ek ok ritað oss íslendíngvm staf rof* (*sic*) 'I have written an alphabet for us Icelanders too', *várs máls* (*sic*) 'our language' and

---

[26] See *DI* (I: 606) as evidence that *Gulaþingslög* is a region: *Þar sóru eiða lendur menn ok bœndr úr öllum Gulaþingslögum, ok af Orkneyjum, Hjaltlandi ok Íslandi* 'There swore oaths either *lendur menn* or householders from the whole of Gula, and from Orkney, Shetland and Iceland'.

vár tunga 'our language'.[27] Ari's decision to write in Icelandic rather than in Latin, which was probably not obvious at the time, restricted his audience to Norse speakers – rather than opening it to a more international audience. The First Grammarian chose not only to write in Icelandic, but also to use Norse (and not Latin) terminology such as *raddarstafr* (not *vocalis*) and *samhljóðandi* (not *consonans*) (Baldur Jónsson, 2006: 18). The Latin terms were known, readily available and perhaps readily established, and yet in a process reminiscent of the much later linguistic purism of the nineteenth century, the Norse terms were used. In the opening paragraphs of the text, the author was taking, however, 'our language' to mean Icelandic and not Norse, when Norse was still a (fairly) homogenous language at the time of writing (early twelfth century).

The First Grammatical Treatise represents the first evidence of Icelandic cultural nationalism, or at least it exhibits a confident cultural self-awareness on the part of the author. This is also one of the few instances where an agreeing possessive adjective acts as an identity marker. The First Grammarian may be invoking ideology when he clearly defines the Icelanders, and implies that the 'them' are those who do not speak (or at least write) the Icelandic language. There is in the text an expectation that legal codes are written in the 'national' language, but interestingly the author refers to it as generally *várrar tvngv* (*sic*) and not explicitly *íslenzkr* (Hreinn Benediktsson, 1972: 208).

The use of the agreeing possessive adjectives discussed here tends to be a register-specific phenomenon, found only in legal codes, historical texts and grammatical treatises. In other genres, as in the sagas for example, Iceland tends to be referred to simply as *Ísland*. Such references can be found throughout the sagas: *Íf* II (*Egils saga Skalla-Grímssonar*: 77–78: *kom hann til Íslands* 'he came to Iceland'); *Íf* IV (*Eyrbyggja saga*: 7: *hafði farit at byggja Ísland* 'had come to settle Iceland'); *Íf* XII (*Brennu-Njáls saga*: 20: *Villt þú til Íslands?* 'Do you want to go to Iceland?'). One explanation for this pattern of occurrence may be simply chronology. The laws, *Íslendingabók* and the First Grammatical Treatise were amongst the earliest texts in Norse to be committed to writing. Alternatively, these agreeing possessive adjectives may have been used because in the early period 'law' was one of the few means in which the Icelanders could define themselves relative to any other Scandinavians: they were *í lögum við* 'in law with' each other, and not (except perhaps through treaties, *sáttmálar*) with other Norsemen.[28] If the 'law' was a

---

[27] Hreinn Benediktsson (1972: 208): *raddar stafir e[rv] öngvir or teknir, enn i gjorfir miog margir þviat váár tvnga hefir flesta alla hlióðs eða raddar* 'No vowels were rejected, but a good many were added, since our language has the greatest number of vowel sounds'.

[28] *Grágás* (Ia: 44, 64): *oc varþar þing maNinvm eigi við log* 'his assembly man is under no legal penalty'; *EN ef sa verðr at liug quið. þa varðar þeim þat ecki við lög er aNat villdo bera. er þeir hafa þeim orðom mælt at domi* 'But if that proves to be a false verdict, those who wished to give a different verdict are under no legal penalty if they spoke those words in court'.

basis for self-definition at this early stage of Icelandic history, then it is perhaps not surprising to find such self-references within this register.

Whilst one could argue that the First Grammatical Treatise and *Íslendingabók* were written from an Icelandic perspective and marked an Icelandic and not a Norse identity, it is difficult to claim that the use of agreeing possessive adjectives in early Icelandic legal texts acted as an identity marker. It is also the case that the First Grammatical Treatise and *Íslendingabók* were both exceptional texts without obvious Norse parallels and that their patterns of grammatical usage may therefore not be directly comparable to those in other works.

5.4.2 *Pronominal usage in the early Icelandic law codes*

Coupled with the difficulty of analysing so-called agreeing possessive adjectives is the general issue of how one interprets pronominal usage in the context of identity. These agreeing possessive adjectives are formulated using the possessive pronoun. It is tempting to consider such pronominal usage as an identity marker, encoding social relations and implicitly or explicitly contrasting with another identity. As the above analysis has shown, there is in fact little evidence of these agreeing possessive adjectives being used for this purpose.

If one examines *Grágás*, one finds that the first person plural pronoun, *vér* ('we') is used intermittently. Contextually, the *vér* is employed in phrases marking a sense of communal responsibility, often followed by the modal verb (*at*) *scolo* ('to be obliged to'), to show what the collective community should do or will do in the future.[29] It is found frequently in the Christian section of the laws, where the requirements of the Icelander's Christian beliefs are listed (*Jónsbók*, 1970: 17–18). Otherwise, the non-referential third person *maðr* ('one') is used in the omnipresent *Ef maþr* [...] *oc...*'if one [does such and such], then....' type construction. With the use of the first person plural pronoun, we have once again a feature which may be a purely stylistic one, and one that is specific to a certain register.

Attempting to understand the manner in which pronouns are employed in the law codes raises a number of fundamental issues: it is not immediately obvious if the first person plural pronoun is inclusive or exclusive. More fundamentally, it is not certain if the *vér* ('we') is contrastive, let alone which persons or social groups actually make up the *vér*. One way to understand the 'we' may be to define the 'they'. In doing so, one should remember that the process of defining the other may take place at many different levels and that social categories and conceptual distinctions between 'we' and 'they' may not be fixed.

---

[29] *Grágás* (Ia: 19, 23) and *Jónsbók* (1970: 17): *Vér skulum trúa á várn drottin Jesum Christum* 'We should believe in our Lord Jesus Christ'.

5.4.3 *The 'they'*

Non-Icelanders and their rights are acknowledged in a number of different passages in *Grágás*. The majority of these non-Icelanders were Norse speakers or at least people who had an understanding of Norse.[30] These groups are referred to as *útlendir menn* – a term which has been previously discussed, and the obvious candidate for the 'they'.

Where legal rights are concerned, the linguistic identity of the settler or visitor was certainly important. One could be considered *útlenzkr*, but if one spoke the *dönsk tunga* and had lived in Iceland for a period of three years, one was entitled to participate in the legal system: *Þan man scal eigi i dom nefna. er eigi hefir mal nvmt. i barn æskv. a danska tvngv. aþr hann hefir verit .iij vetr a íslandi. eþa lengr* 'A man who has not learnt to speak the Norse language in his childhood is not to be nominated to join a court until he has been in Iceland three winters or more'.[31] The laws made a provision for people who learnt Norse as a second language: this group of people might have been traders or English-speaking merchants from what had been the 'Danelaw'. It is unlikely, however, that traders stayed in Iceland for three winters. Alternatively, the target group may have conceivably been foreign churchmen, including bishops and other missionaries. The fact that such a passage was formulated in the laws suggests that the scribe had some sort of group of speakers in mind. It is significant because it made linguistic identity a legal issue.

The language that one spoke was not only a criterion for participation in the legal system at a certain level (in the sense of joining a court), but it determined one's legal rights and in some cases privileges. This was the case for various aspects of the law, but it is particularly notable in clauses dealing with homicide and rights to claim inheritance on Icelandic soil.[32] This remained the case, albeit to a lesser extent, in the later Icelandic legal code *Jónsbók* where *dönsk tunga* speakers are given more favourable inheritance rights in Iceland than non-*dönsk tunga* speakers: *En af ollum tungum öðrum en danskri tungu skal engi maðr at frændsemi taka arf hér, nema faðir, son eða bróðir, nema þeir hafi lögligt umboð til* 'And as for speakers of all other languages other than Norse, neither the father nor the brother of the kinsman has inheritance rights here unless they have legal charge' (*Jónsbók*, 1970: 94). As we have seen, the laws formed the backbone of Icelandic society and they were a means of defining different levels of social inclusion. There were probably a number of factors that determined

---

[30] *Grágás* (Ia: 229): provision for the death of Englishmen in Iceland.

[31] *Grágás* (Ia: 38): *barnæska* is young childhood and younger than our word sometimes suggests; it may be closer to babyhood.

[32] *Grágás* (Ia: 173): *Sva scal fara vm vig sacir utlendra manna sem her er tínt. nema her se alande or varre tungo frændr eNa vegno manna* 'The procedure in cases of killing foreigners is to be as here rehearsed unless kinsmen of the men killed who share our language are here in the country'.

an individual's degree of social inclusion in Icelandic society, but language was one of the more prominent amongst them.

There are two observations to be made here with regard to identity: the evidence from legal texts appeals to a Norse identity, unlike texts such as *Íslendingabók* and the First Grammatical Treatise whose perspectives are unambiguously Icelandic. The second point is that an identity distinction is framed in terms of language. The linguistic criterion is normally whether the claimant or legal subject speaks the *dönsk tunga* or not.

The community of *dönsk tunga* speakers appears as a homogenous linguistic block in the laws. But, there is reason to believe that the 'they' do not always form a uniform group in *Grágás*. In accordance with Icelandic law, the Norse kinsmen of the three kingdoms of Norway, Sweden and Denmark were not equally close to the Icelanders. Within the category of Norse speakers outside Iceland, Norwegians had a special position. *noregsmenn* ('Norwegians') for example were exempted from paying the *hafnar toll* ('harbour toll'): *Allir menn scolo gialda hafnar toll nema noregs menn öln vaðmals eða ullar reyfi þat er vi. gøri hespo eða lambs gæro...* 'Everyone is to pay a landing-place toll except men from Norway, an ell of homespun or raw wool amounting to one sixth of a hank or a lamb's fleece' (*Grágás*, Ib: 71). The relationship between Icelanders and Norwegians was a special one. There were even treaties outlining the rights and benefits in the 'other' country. From examining these, information can be gleaned on aspects of a West Norse identity.[33] The special relationship between Icelanders and Norwegians is outlined in a treaty sometimes known as the *Óláfslög* which can be dated to approximately 1030 A.D.[34]

The treaty was written in Norway and concerns the rights of the Norwegian king in Iceland and of Icelanders in Norway. It is significant because it grants Icelanders *hauldsréttr* in Norway, legal privileges of a free farmer on inalienable ancestral land (*Grágás*, Ib: 195–97). This is evidence of Icelanders being considered as worthy of the rights of members of the upper echelons of Norwegian society. The same passage appears in the Norwegian *Gulaþingslög* (*NgL*, I: 71). These and other passages show that there are a number of parallels in how Icelanders and Norwegians perceived each other.

In addition, one finds in *Gizurarsáttmáli*, the name of the agreement which effected the union of Iceland and Norway in 1262–64 A.D., a clear perspective on Icelandic-Norwegian relations written from a Norwegian perspective.[35] There was a high degree of contact between Icelanders and

---

[33] A West Norse legal identity is taken here to refer to just Norway and Iceland, and does not include the Faroe Islands where the sources are lacking.

[34] See Boulhosa (2005: 44–45) where she refers to the treaty as *Óláfslög*.

[35] See *DI* (I: 602–716); Bouhlhosa (2005: 87–90): this is the name given to an agreement which is believed to correspond to the decision – as it is described in certain sagas – reached at the *alþingi* in 1262 A.D., when Icelanders from the Northern and Southern Quarters of the country formally submitted to the Norwegian king, King Hákon Hákonarson.

Norwegians and a willingness to recognise each other's legal rights. Iceland was settled principally by Norwegians and one would expect close historical links to have been preserved.

5.4.4 The 'we'

It is not easy to define the 'they' in early Iceland. One reason for this is the fact that there were different levels of social inclusion which were in part determined by the language one spoke. Providing the linguistic conditions had been met and the individual resided in Iceland, one was considered part of Icelandic society. The other difficulty is that the presence of a West Norse legal identity renders it difficult to tease one identity apart from another. In defining the 'we' one is faced with similar problems.

The *vér* ('we') of the law codes is not specifically defined, but one assumes that it is the group of people that lived in Iceland for at least three years, spoke *dönsk tunga* and whose position in society could be defined as *í lögum við* ('in law with') or *í þingi með* ('attached to an assembly-attending householder'). It is not the case that all the people residing in Iceland at the time met these criteria. Those who did not speak Norse or did not live in Iceland were unequivocally not part of the 'we' as has been previously established. However, it is not the case that all the remaining people were accepted in to Icelandic society. There were in fact groups that were socially excluded, and this social exclusion acted as a significant identity marker. These people were for example the homeless such as *göngu-menn* ('vagrants'): they were not *lögfestir* 'attached to the law', and were thus excluded from all aspects of society.[36] *skógarmenn* and *fjörbaugsmenn*, full and lesser outlaws respectively, would also not have been considered part of society.[37]

Legal compliance or lawfulness acted alongside language as an identity marker. It became a means of differentiating between insiders and outsiders: an important notion in all societies, but particularly so in early Iceland where in-group and out-group identities were clearly defined. The language used in *Grágás* to refer to outsiders is sufficiently explicit to warrant a clear demarcation between insiders and outsiders in Iceland itself. The Icelandic legal code reflects this distinction between 'insiders' and 'outsiders' at several different levels in society with terms such as *innanþingsmaðr* ('a man of the local assembly'), *innanhreppsmaðr* ('a man of the local commune') and *innanfjórðungsmaðr* ('a man of the Quarter'). In

---

[36] See *Grágás* (Ia: 140) for a legal definition; (Ia: 229); (Ib: 14) for punishments relating to feeding or housing *göngu-menn* 'vagrants': *En ef menn gefa þeim mat þa varðar þeim fiorbavgs Garð* 'And if men give them food, then they will be sentenced to outlawry'.

[37] See *Grágás* (Ia: 174–75) for outlaws that do not have *þingreitt* 'right to attend an assembly', *EN ef þeir menn fara a alþingi oc scal þeirre söc stefna at lögbergi* 'But if such men go to the General Assembly, the summons for that offence is to be made at the Lögberg'.

the case of outlaws, people were sometimes marked as outsiders in the most visible way possible by putting an outlaw's price on their head. There is little evidence to show that full outlaws were actually sent to Norway during the Commonwealth Period. Outlaws fled allegedly to the Interior; they were not sent. Those subject to lesser outlawry tended to make their own way abroad. Outlawry (of either kind) was not a judicial sentence in our sense. It imposed no penalty. It simply allowed those who wished to take vengeance in a feud to do so without (legal) comeback. So an outlaw would not be fleeing the law, or any enforcement of the law: he would be fleeing those who wished to kill him in pursuit of a feud. Those pursuing a feud could set a bounty on somebody's head, so that someone else might kill their outlaw: *Hann lagði þá fé til höfuðs honum sem öðrum skógarmönnum ok reið við þat heim* 'He put an outlaw's price on Grettir's head, then rode home' (*Íf* VII, *Grettis saga Ásmundarsonar*: 147).

The criterion for distinguishing the 'they' on the basis of the legal code was therefore partially linguistic, whereas the means of defining the 'we' was lawfulness itself as understood in the early Icelandic legal code. The 'they' was not a gradable phenomenon, unlike the 'we' where there were different degrees of social inclusion. These observations are based on the evidence of just one register, albeit an important one.

In summary of this Section, one can say that grammatical variables played an ambiguous role as identity markers in early Icelandic legal texts – it is seldom clear if they are being used as stylistic tools or if a variable such as pronominal usage marks solidarity and actually represents the values of a group of people. Fortunately, the evidence from historical texts and the First Grammatical Treatise is more definitive as there is not only a sense of Icelandic identity but also a suggestion of contrast.

One is able to get a reasonably good idea of the 'we' and the 'they' from the legal codes. It is evident, however, that there may be several layers of identity and that it is not pronominal usage or any other grammatical variable that marks identity *per se*. One can define the *vér* ('we'), but only with the help of a sound understanding of early Icelandic society, and not just through the use of grammatical features.

5.5 SPATIAL REFERENCES: THE ISSUE OF IDENTITY

5.5.1 *Spatio-directional particles*

In addition to examining pronouns, we can analyse spatial deictic terms to see what their usage can tell us about the role that language played in the establishment of the identity of the settlers. This may show us how groups of people perceive movement, and how language reflects changing identities. Spatial references are of particular interest in Norse because there existed a rich and widely used system of spatio-directional particles; the idiomatic use of some of these particles such as locational adverbs provide insights into how one group of speakers identified themselves relative to others.

The term spatio-directional particle is used to refer to the family of adverbs in Norse that mark the threefold distinction between direction, location and the source, i.e. 'to a place', 'in a place' and 'from a place'. The most commonly occurring threefold set of spatio-directional *adverbs* in Norse is *hingað-hér-heðan* 'hither-here-hence', *þangað-þar-þaðan* 'thither-there-thence', *hvert-hvar-hvaðan* 'whither-where-whence'.[38] The particles that denote rest in a place have typically an *-i* suffix whilst an *-an* suffix indicates movement from a place. So, for example, one has in Icelandic: *inn* 'into', *inni* 'inside', *innan* 'from within'; *út*, 'out', *úti* 'outside', *útan* 'from without'; *upp* 'up', *uppi* 'above', *ofan* 'from above'; *niður* 'down', *niðri* 'below', *neðan* 'from below' and *heim* 'home', *heima* 'at home', *heiman* 'from home'.[39]

For the purpose of this study, all of these terms are referred to collectively as spatio-directional particles in order to emphasize both the spatial and the directional function. The term 'particle' has been used because some of these expressions are neither quite prepositions nor adverbs and they do not always fall easily under any of the traditional parts of speech. Ideally, one would have specific, economical and transparent terms for 'movement towards', 'rest at' and 'movement away'. In the absence of more precise terms, reference will be made to them using this terminology. The term 'spatio-directional particle' is not my own, but is used in Svenonius (2006: 6).

The most frequently used spatial deictic term in the earliest Icelandic law code is the particle *hér* 'here'. Throughout *Grágás*, Iceland is invariably referred to simply as *hér* or *á landi hér* ('in the country here'), whereas in *Landnámabók* and in the sagas, the tendency is to refer to Iceland as *Ísland* (*Grágás*, Ia: 3, 19, 21, 22). The use of the semantically imprecise *hér* is continued in the later Icelandic legal text *Jónsbók* (1970: 32). *Jónsbók* was written in Norway after the submission to the Norwegian Crown (albeit by an Icelander) and yet the Icelandic perspective is maintained. As pointed out by Ólafur Lárusson (1960: 77), the King of Norway did not simply inflict Norwegian law upon the Icelanders. Instead he created specific

---

[38] These are their modern Icelandic forms. It should be noted that all of these words are used in modern Icelandic and do not have the archaic ring of some of the English equivalents.

[39] See Stefán Einarsson (1945: 60–63). Some of the adverbs have only two of the forms such as *norðr* 'northwards' and *norðan* 'from the north', but the majority of them adhere to the tripartite system. Adverbs with the *-an* suffix combine with the preceding preposition *fyrir* to form a prepositional phrase indicating position relative to another (fixed) position, for example *fyrir norðan heiðina* 'north of the heath', *fyrir ofan húsin* 'above the buildings' and the idiomatic *fyrir norðan* 'in the north'.

Icelandic laws parallel to the Norwegian ones. This is reflected in the language where the 'colonial' Norwegian voice is mainly absent.

It is not clear if it is significant but there is a parallel between the non-specificity of pronominal phrases such as *vár lög* and deictic references such as *hér*, both of which are found predominantly in legal registers. As with the phrase *vár lög*, it is difficult to argue that this specific use of spatial deixis (*hér*) acted as an identity marker as there is no evidence of naming or explicit referencing. On the contrary, the referent appears to be almost obfuscated with deliberate vagueness. It may be anachronistic to hold such an opinion, however: these laws were not written in the context of modern political boundaries dividing nation-states. We must constantly bear in mind that, although the total geographical span of Scandinavia in Europe has not changed much, both external and internal boundaries were then irregular and in some cases very different from now (Foote & Wilson, 1970: 1). The scribes may not have felt the need to refer to Iceland explicitly by its name, thinking that their readers were entirely within the land's boundaries.

Clunies Ross (1997: 12) comments on the use of spatial deixis in *Íslendingabók* and claims that there is a degree of semantic differentiation between Christian space and heathen space.[40] According to her, the Irish Christian monks (*papar*) occupy an undefined social space. In *Íslendingabók* (*Íf* Ii, 5), they are simply described as *váru hér* ('were here'), whereas the Norsemen are referred to as *landnámsmenn* ('settlers'), terminology that perhaps implies that the *papar* had no legitimate right to the land. The term *landnámsmenn* brought together people of different ethnic groups, and yet they appear to be conceived as 'common stock' through their settling the land. The view that Christians occupy undefined space is contradicted, however, by references in *Grágás* to Christians coming to Iceland: *I þan tið er cristni com ut hingat til islandz gecc her* 'at the time when Christians came here to Iceland (from Norway)', where Iceland is named explicitly (*Ísland*) and is not just *her* (*Grágás*, Ib: 192). The argument that certain spatial deictic terms are reserved for specific ethnic or religious groups is probably unfounded or at least requires further analysis. These references are not revealing for what they tell us about social identity, and for the moment at least can only be assigned to the peculiarities of register-specific language.

Two other aspects of spatial references are, however, more relevant to an early Iceland identity: the idiomatic use in Norway *and* Iceland of some of the previously mentioned spatio-directional particles and the system of cardinal and intermediate orientation terms used at the time.

---

[40] Sverrir Jakobsson (2005: 364) believes that the Christian-pagan dichotomy was the most important way of separating and classifying people in Iceland in the period 1100–1400 A.D.

5.5.2 *Idiomatic use of spatial grammar*

The sagas show us that the settlers brought with them a rich spatio-directional grammar. It was idiomatic to speak of travel from Norway to Iceland as *að fara út*, an abbreviated form of *að fara frá Noregi út til Íslands*, 'to go (or sail) from Norway out to Iceland' (*Íf* IV, *Eiríks saga rauða*: 208). The Norse system of spatio-directional particles was based largely on the sea (unsurprisingly) and *út* is often (but not always) to be understood as travelling 'out to sea'. One may compare it to the American usage of 'out west'. If the speaker were in Iceland, travel from Norway to Iceland would be typically described as *að koma út* (*hingað*), literally 'to come out (here)', *hingað* being the directional adverb.[41] The particle *út* may imply a sense of geographical remoteness and not just refer to the logistics of traversing the sea to get to Iceland. It is also noteworthy that the Icelanders described their geographical remoteness in the same terms as the Norwegians. The Icelanders reapplied the particle *út* in different geographical contexts too, describing for instance travel from Russia (*Garðaríki*) to Constantinople (*Miklagarð*) in terms of *að fara út*. Travel to Byzantium was described in these terms, whilst travel to Rome was described as *að fara suðr* ('to travel south'). Crossing was not a specific requirement of itself. For instance, travel to the British Isles is described as *vestr um haf* 'west over the sea', not *út* (*Íf* XII, *Brennu-Njáls saga*: 197).

The inverse to this, i.e. travelling from Iceland to Norway was formulated as *að fara útan* which one may translate literally as 'to travel from without' and the phrase was used in the sagas: '*þat ætla ek*', *segir Þórólfr*, '*at Björn vildi helzt fara til Noregs*' [...] *ok fekk menn til útanferðar um sumarit* 'I intend', said Þórólfr, 'Björn to travel (preferably) to Norway' [...] and that he gets men for the journey to Norway in the summer' (*Íf* II, *Egils saga Skalla-Grímssonar*: 88–89). Passages in the Icelandic laws discuss the treatment of outlaws travelling from Iceland to Norway and their movement is expressed as *að fara útan heðan* (*sic*), i.e. literally to 'travel from without (from here or hence)' (*Grágás*, Ia: 226). The same movement is sometimes referred to using the phrase *að koma útan heðan* as in *Íslendingabók*, the history of Iceland written by Ari Þorgilsson: *En þat sumar it sama kómu útan heðan þeir Gizurr ok Hjalti ok þágu þá undan við konunginn* 'But that same summer Gizurr and Hjalti came from Iceland ('from outside') and got the King to release them' (*Íf* Ii, 15). Ari is emphasizing that although the action is set in Norway, it is being recounted from an Icelandic authorial perspective. This mirrors the phraseology *að koma út hingað* used for travel to Iceland, but from an Icelandic perspective employing the source adverb and not the directional, i.e. *heðan* and not *hingað*.

---

[41] This is also described as *at fara ut hingat*, see *Grágás* (Ib: 20) and *Íf* IX (*Svarfdæla saga*: 160).

As previously stated, Iceland was settled by Norwegians and people from the British Isles, and it is not surprising therefore to discover that the settlers used the same spatial grammar as their Norwegian ancestors. The consistency of usage was such, however, that the emigrants many centuries after having settled in Iceland were still describing travel to Norway from a Norwegian perspective, i.e. Icelanders described travel to Norway as 'travelling from without' (*að fara útan*).[42]

This is significant for two reasons: it seems to contradict the evidence found elsewhere in legal and historical documents which shows Icelanders presenting an Icelandic identity, employing new terms to refer to Icelandic social structures, writing grammatical treatises to develop alphabets for *oss islendíngvm* (*sic*) 'us Icelanders' and insisting on the retention of Icelandic laws (*íslenzkum lögum*). Secondly, the phrase *að fara útan* used when travelling from Iceland to Norway implies that Iceland, the locative, was *úti* or 'outside'.

The use of these spatio-directional particles was partially reapplied by the Icelanders to describe travel to Greenland. Evidence for the use of these terms comes principally from *Eiríks saga rauða* and *Grænlendinga saga*, thirteenth-century texts concerned with the settlement of Greenland in the latter half of the tenth century. Travel or movement to Greenland from both Iceland and Norway is phrased as *að fara út*, (*Íf* IV, *Grænlendinga saga*: 248) or as *að koma* (*út*) *þangat: sá hafði háttr verit á Grænlandi síðan kristni kom þangat* 'that had been the custom in Greenland since the arrival of Christianity (out) there' (*Íf* IV, *Eiríks saga rauða*: 217). There are not, however, references to travel from Greenland to Iceland being described as *að fara útan*. Travel from Greenland to Norway is described in one instance as *kom útan af Grænlandi* (*Íf* IV, *Grænlendinga saga*: 248). It may imply that whilst Greenland was conceived by Norsemen as a geographically outlying (remote) land and thus *úti*, its remoteness had not been fully internalised. This may reflect the fact that Greenland was settled principally by Icelanders and not Norwegians, and thus their perspective was different. It must also be borne in mind that the textual evidence postdates the settlement of Greenland by three hundred years, and that is long enough for perspectives to change. Equally, both Iceland and Greenland might have been considered *úti*, even by their inhabitants. It may not be so much a question of remoteness as the question of crossing a boundary.

---

[42] See *Íf* X (*Ljósvetninga saga*: 23, 44): *En um haustit fór hann útan ok var þá í Nóregi þann vetr* 'And in the autumn he travelled to Norway and stayed there that winter'; *Íf* X (*Vöðu-Brands þáttr*: 126–7). On occasions, it seems that any travel by sea eastwards from Iceland is described as *að fara útan*, without actually specifying or implying Norway (*Íf* X, *Ljósvetninga saga*: 6). The same phrase was used for travel from Iceland to Shetland and Orkney (*Íf* X, *Ljósvetninga saga*: 43).

5.5.3 *Semantics of orientation: the Norwegian system*

As well as spatio-directional particles, the emigrants to Iceland brought with them in the latter half of the ninth century the cardinal directions *norðr*, *suðr*, *austr* and *vestr* ('north', 'south', 'east' and 'west'). Evidence from historical texts, the saga narratives and skaldic poetry show us that the Icelanders used additionally intermediate terms (*Íf* IX, *Svarfdæla saga*: 160: *útnorðr*; *Íf* XII, *Brennu-Njáls saga*: 433: *landsuðr*; Unger, 1862: 88: *útsuðr*; Finnur Jónsson, 1912, Vol. 1. A: 110: Styrbjörn's *Lausavísur*: *vt nordr* (*sic*)). These terms discussed by Stefán Einarsson (1944: 265–85) and Haugen (1957: 447–59) were based on the contour of the Norwegian west coast and in the absence of compasses could only have been determined by celestial observation. For example, north-east was referred to as *landnorðr* ('north-wards by the land'), south-east as *landsuðr* ('southwards by the land') whereas north-west was referred to as *útnorðr* (i.e. northwards and out to the sea which meant 'west') and south-west as *útsuðr*.[43] These terms seem obscure, but if one considers the shape of the Norwegian coast line (with the exception of the Vík area) then their derivation becomes apparent.

The relevant point is that these terms were adopted in Iceland even though they were peculiar to the geography of Norway.[44] Interestingly, the *Icelandic* settlers to the Norse colony of Greenland adopted the Norwegian system of orientation too. The terminology of Eystribyggð ('Eastern Settlement') and Vestribyggð ('Western Settlement') had the same skewing of the terms of direction to the north-east, reflecting once again the shape of the Norwegian coast line. Vestribyggð is more northerly than westerly. In both Iceland and Greenland, the Norse settlers did not modify terminology as fundamental as spatial orientation to reflect their new geographies.

5.5.4 *Semantics of orientation: the Quarter-based system*

However, it would be wrong to believe that the orientation system used in early Iceland was based entirely on the Norwegian model. The Icelanders developed their own system based on the different Quarters of Iceland; the land was administratively divided into Quarters (*fjórðungar*) named after the cardinal directions in 965 A.D. This led to 'incorrect' or 'proximate' usages of cardinal terms whereby Icelanders would for instance indicate they were travelling 'south' to the Southern Quarter, irrespective of the fact that the actual direction of travel might be west (see Map 2 below).[45] Similarly, Icelanders living on the tip of the Reykjanes peninsula would

---

[43] The map and its directions are only an approximation. No modern map can correspond exactly to the 'mental maps' of the Norsemen.

[44] According to Gaffin (1996: 73), these terms were taken to the Faroe Islands too and are still used today for wind directions.

[45] See Haugen (1957: 450–51). The Quarter-boundaries divided only the inhabited areas – the Interior was and is effectively undivided.

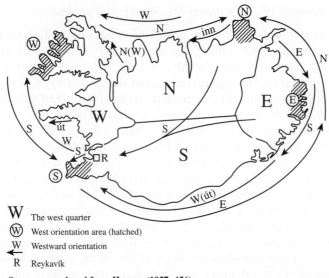

W The west quarter
Ⓦ West orientation area (hatched)
W Westward orientation
←
R Reykavík

Source: reproduced from Haugen (1957: 456).

Map 2: The spatio-directional terminology of Iceland

indicate, as Map 2 shows, that they were travelling 'west' to Snæfellsnes even if they were strictly speaking travelling almost due north just as inhabitants of Eyjafjörður speak of going north to Langanes even if the map shows that it is due east (Haugen, 1957: 450–51). Usage varies from region to region with Icelanders living in the western Quarter describing travel westwards as *út*, because it is in the direction of the sea, but those in the East use the 'correct' cardinal term, *vestur*. There is no category of words that shows more difference of usage in Icelandic than the words of orientation.[46]

The use of spatial deictic terms in the earliest Icelandic texts suggests there was a high degree of conceptual and semantic continuity between the Norwegians in Norway and the settlers in Iceland. Based on the evidence of certain spatial references, the settlers retained a Norwegian perspective. The use of these terms reflects an identity that contrasts to that evoked elsewhere in other texts. The Icelanders' use of spatial deixis in their description of Greenland suggests an absence of proximity.

The evidence from orientation (as opposed to spatial deictic) terms shows that the Icelanders developed their own systems of classification and this may reflect an Icelandic identity. This system has survived into the modern language whilst the Norwegian intermediate orientation terms and the use

---

[46] See Stefán Einarsson (1944: 265–85); Haugen (1957: 447–59). Wylie & Margolin (1981: 15) discuss complex dialectal idioms of orientation used in the Faroe Islands.

of the particle *útan* to describe movement have all but disappeared. A thousand years after the Settlement, Icelanders now describe spatial movement in their own terms.

5.6 CONCLUSION

The sources send us different messages on the role of language as an identity marker in early Iceland. For instance, the sagas tell us little about the linguistic identity of the settlers or the people the Norsemen encounter on their travels whereas language is more of a concern in the Icelandic legal code and obviously the subject matter of grammatical treatises. One approach in this chapter has been to examine the use of linguistic labels such as *dönsk tunga* and *norræna*. It is problematic to determine how or whether these terms were used as linguistic identity markers as they were not used particularly widely in the primary sources. The usage of these terms indicates that there was a degree of regional linguistic awareness and that a vernacular identity was being portrayed for all Norsemen in the case of *dönsk tunga*, and for West Norsemen subsequently in the use of the term *norræna*. The fact that there was a need for the term *norræna* referring to the linguistic or social identity of the Icelanders and Norwegians appears to be significant. As for local intra-Norse linguistic variation, there is little unequivocal evidence that it existed and there are references to Norse being apparently understood in medieval England.

For the purpose of legal rights in Iceland, *dönsk tunga* acted as an identity marker because speaking it brought with it certain legal advantages or at least a different set of rights. As far as Iceland is concerned, language was undoubtedly one of a number of factors that determined an individual's social inclusion – an important parameter in early Icelandic society.

The language used to describe spatial referencing does not mark an Icelandic identity with the settlers continuing to use terminology that was not only more relevant to their native Norway, but also that reflected a Norwegian identity. There remain, however, indications that the Icelanders intended to mark their own Icelandic identity. In the legal texts, a distinction was drawn between Icelanders and other Norsemen whilst the sagas highlight the different cultural perspectives in Norway and Iceland. This was achieved through the semantics of a Quarter-based orientation system, via the introduction of an Icelandic alphabet and it is arguably also present in the minutiae of the skalds' descriptions of 'Icelandic eyes'. The intention to portray an Icelandic identity is at its most acute in texts such as *Íslendingabók* and the First Grammatical Treatise. These works were written for an Icelandic audience and engineer respectively a clear Icelandic perspective through an account of Icelandic history and an attempt to establish an orthography for Icelanders.

6

CONCLUSION

In Section 1.1 it was suggested that language has an important role to play when people construct an identity for themselves. By looking at the first few hundred years of settlement in Iceland, I have considered what role language, language development and social structures played in the construction of the settlers' identity in this frontier society. Alongside sociolinguistic models and theories, new-dialect formation case studies aid us in understanding how settlers to a new land develop linguistic norms and how language can be used to project an identity. Models are of less help when looking at reflections of linguistic identity, and because spoken data for such a distant historical period are unavailable, we are wholly dependent on textual sources when it comes to the presentation of an identity. The information that we have on language and identity in early Iceland is therefore inevitably incomplete: we cannot know how the settlers used identity factors in speech.

Working within these limitations, one can note, however, that the language of a speech community is most likely to act as an identity marker for *all* of its speakers if linguistic norms are widely shared. It is assumed that this was the case in early Iceland as there are no references to norm variation in the relevant literature. The language community that we can reconstruct for early Iceland is a 'closed' (Andersen, 1988: 60), 'focused' (Le Page & Tabouret-Keller, 1985) one with dense and multiplex social networks. Sociolinguistic theory tells us that this should lead to the establishment and maintenance of *local* norms, but this was not the outcome in early Iceland. Instead, Iceland was arguably mono-dialectal, was certainly characterised by long-term linguistic homogeneity and remained a society where nucleated settlements barely formed over a thousand-year period. This norm maintenance gained social meaning over time (once Icelanders became aware of other linguistic norms), and emerged ultimately as an Icelandic linguistic identity marker in itself. There is no evidence that any clan-type linguistic identities formed in medieval feudal Iceland, as one might perhaps expect. There prevails instead what one could call a Settlement linguistic identity which in contemporary Iceland has taken on mythical proportions: many Icelanders today like to think that they speak the language of the original settlers.

The problem has been therefore to understand how a new dialect acquired societally shared norms and long-term stability, if sociolinguistic models indicate that the opposite should have occurred. Making sense of dialect formation and identity construction in a low-contact, scattered, rural speech community is problematic, and there have been few attempts to explain language development in this context *per se*. By looking at settlement patterns and using community-type models, I have shown, however, that it is possible to reconstruct the sociolinguistic structures of early Iceland.

In order for new linguistic norms to emerge (local or otherwise) and thus language change to take place, one needs a reconfiguration of social networks. The scope for contact (and thus 'accommodation') within the networks of the thinly-populated new society can only be gauged by assessing the dynamics of the settlements the newcomers formed, the type of communities and social structures they established and their patterns of population movement. In early Iceland the isolated, peripheral settlement pattern provided few opportunities for regular *convergence* of all Icelanders on one place (instead 'cooperative clusters' formed initially at local *þings* and *hreppar*) (Birgir T. R. Solvason, 1993: 97–125). This was combined with a lack of *sustained* non-local contact, decentralised social structures and quite high degrees of internal mobility. In theory, this sort of environment should lead (over a thousand-year period at least) to dialect splitting, and not dialect levelling. The mobility factor explains better the long-term linguistic (dialectal) homogeneity and lack of dialect fragmentation than the koineisation process itself, which is thought to have occurred at some point in the history of West Norse.

A search was therefore undertaken to find more plausible contexts for dialect levelling. It was proposed that the levelling began in mainland Scandinavia where the archaeological sources show significant population movement, social upheaval and the convergence of people on nucleated settlements: all the ingredients for dialect mixing, and if contact is sustained in one place, levelling. Dialect mixing probably also occurred in the Northern Isles prior to the Settlement because these islands were at the centre of the Viking trading routes.

It is therefore argued here that the dialect taken to Iceland may have been relatively uniform already and that Norse was the only language spoken in Iceland from the Settlement onwards. The genetic evidence indicates that a majority of the female settlers were Celtic, and yet there are almost no references in the literature to any Celtic language(s) ever having been spoken in Iceland. The most plausible explanation for this apparent anomaly is that the Celtic women who came to Iceland had already integrated into Norse-speaking households and communities in the British Isles before coming to Iceland, and were thus Norse speakers upon arrival. The question of social factors, sociolinguistic variation and prestige inevitably arises when discussing such potential dialect melting pots. Prestige in a *tabula rasa* society is only likely to be a factor if speakers are aware of other (perhaps competing) norms, but a 'founder effect' in early Iceland cannot be disregarded entirely, albeit it is difficult to quantify.

As for reflections of this linguistic identity, the identity projected in many of the texts of early Iceland is actually a Norse one. As social structures became established in Iceland, speaking *dönsk tunga* entailed certain legal advantages. The default linguistic identity at the time was clearly a regional, Scandinavian one, and at this point it was perhaps the only one that was both known and established. It seems that there was little need or interest in making explicit references to language in early Iceland: competing linguistic norms were either not known, did not exist or were apparently not worthy of comment. The Icelanders presented their new identity more conspicuously through the establishment of new (and to an extent original) social structures and through their incipient literary culture which gives us an idea of the Icelanders' undeniable and strong appreciation of their native language. These factors set them apart from Norway whence many of the settlers came.

A clear exception to the portrayal of a Norse linguistic identity is to be found in the First Grammatical Treatise whose appeal is to an Icelandic identity. The relationship between linguistic distinctiveness and an Icelandic identity has been increasingly highlighted from the nineteenth century onwards, but the beginnings of this linguistic distinctiveness date from this early period. It is difficult to know what motivated this indigenous concern for the Icelandic language from the outset, but some of the first settlers might have been attracted to an idea of a separate linguistic identity for ideological reasons.

There are many opportunities for further research in the field of language and identity in Iceland, and in modern Iceland in particular. There is for the first time unequivocal evidence of sociolinguistic variation in Icelandic, and this will have implications for the linguistic identity of the Icelanders. This might undermine the Settlement linguistic identity referred to above.

Dialect formation and identity construction in new societies are also still poorly understood, and more research is needed in particular in non-English-speaking new societies. This study has contributed to the discussion on both linguistic identity and dialect formation and has shown that Iceland does not fit neatly the models discussed in Chapter 2. The linguistic history and development of sociolinguistic structures in Iceland is in fact unique, and can only be properly understood if we take into account the peculiar settlement pattern and relevant community-type models.

To an extent, the relationship between language and identity in early Iceland remains of course nebulous and ill-defined. Nonetheless, it is beyond doubt that the Icelandic language and its rich literature became subsequently the single most important factor for the identity of the Icelanders. The foundations for this identity and linguistic culture were laid early on and were therefore rooted in the development of the language itself.

REFERENCES

ABRAMS, DOMINIC & HOGG, MICHAEL A., 1990. *Social Identity Theory: Constructive and Critical Advances*, New York: Harvester Wheatsheaf.

AKSELBERG, GUNNSTEIN, 1995. *Fenomenologisk dekonstruksjon av det labov-milroyske paradigmet i sosiolingvistikken. Ein analyse av sosiolingvistiske tilhøve i Voss kommune*. Dr. art. Avhandling, Nordisk Institutt, UiB.

ANDERSEN, HENNING, 1988. 'Centre and periphery: Adoption, diffusion and spread', in Jacek Fisiak (ed.), 39–85.

ANDERSEN, HENNING, 1989. 'Understanding linguistic innovations', in Leiv Egil Breivik & Ernst Håkon Jahr (eds.), 5–29.

ANDERSEN, HENNING, 2002. 'Preglottalization in English and a North Germanic bifurcation', in David Restle & Dietmar Zaefferer (eds.), *Sounds and Systems. Studies in Structure and Change. A Festschrift for Theo Vennemann*, Berlin; New York: Mouton de Gruyter, 15–34.

ANDERSSON, HANS, 2003. 'Urbanisation', in Knut Helle (ed.), 312–42.

ANDERSSON, THEODORE M., 1964. *The Problem of Icelandic Saga Origins*, New Haven: Yale University Press.

ANTONSEN, ELMER H., 1975. *A Concise Grammar of the Older Runic Inscriptions*, Tübingen: M. Niemeyer.

ANTONSEN, ELMER H., 2002. *Runes and Germanic Linguistics*, Berlin and New York: Mouton de Gruyter.

ARGE, SÍMUN V., 2005. 'Cultural landscapes and cultural environmental issues in the Faroes', in Andras Mortensen & Arge Símun (eds.), *Viking and Norse in the North Atlantic: Select Papers from the Proceedings of the Fourteenth Viking Congress*, Tórshavn 19–30 July, 2001, Tórshavn: Føroya Fróðskaparfelag, 22–39.

ARNÓRSSON, EINAR, 1942. *Ari fróði*, Reykjavík: Hið íslenska bókmenntafélag.

ÁRNASON, KRISTJÁN, 1980a. *Quantity in Historical Phonology: Icelandic and Related Cases*, Cambridge Studies in Linguistics, 30, Cambridge: Cambridge University Press.

ÁRNASON, KRISTJÁN, 1980b. *Íslensk málfræði: kennslubók handa framhaldss-kólum*, Reykjavík: Iðunn.

ÁRNASON, KRISTJÁN, 1990. 'Conflicting teleologies: Drift and normalisation in the history of Icelandic phonology', in H. Andersen & K. Koerner, (eds.), *Historical Linguistics 1987: Papers from the 8th International Conference on Historical Linguistics*, Amsterdam: John Benjamin Publishing Company, 21–36.

ÁRNASON, KRISTJÁN, 1999. 'Landið, þjóðin, tungan og fræðin', *Skírnir* 173, 449–66.

ÁRNASON, KRISTJÁN, 2003a. 'Language planning and the structure of Icelandic', in Kristján Árnason (ed.), *Útnorður: West Nordic Standardisation and Variation*, Reykjavík: University of Iceland Press, 193–218.

ÁRNASON, KRISTJÁN, 2003b. 'Icelandic', in Ana Deumert & Wim Vandenbussche (eds.), *Germanic Standardisation – Past and Present*, Amsterdam; New York: John Benjamins, 245–79.

ÁRNASON, KRISTJÁN, 2004. 'Á vora tungu', *Skírnir* 178, 375–404.

ÁRNASON, KRISTJÁN & ÞRÁINSSON, HÖSKULDUR, 1983. 'Um málfar Vestur-Skaftfellinga', *Íslenskt mál* 5, 81–103.

ASKEDAL, JOHN OLE, 2005. 'The standard languages and their systems in the 20th century III: Norwegian', in *The Nordic Languages: An International Handbook of the History of the North Germanic Languages*, Volume 2, Berlin: de Gruyter, 1584–1602.

AUER, PETER & HINSKENS, FRANS, 1996. 'The convergence and divergence of dialects in Europe. New and not so new developments in an old area', *Sociolinguistica* 10, 1–30.

AUER, PETER, HINSKENS, FRANS & KERSWILL, PAUL, 2005. *Dialect Change: Convergence and Divergence in European Languages*, Cambridge: Cambridge University Press.

AUER, PETER et al., 1998. 'Saliency in long-term dialect accommodation', *Journal of Sociolinguistics* 2, 163–87.

BAKHTIN, MIKHAIL, 1981. *The Dialogic Imagination: Four Essays by M. M. Bakhtin*, edited by Michael Holquist and translated by Caryl Emerson & Michael Holquist, Austin: University of Texas Press.

BALL, MARTIN J., & FIFE, JAMES, (eds.) 2002. *The Celtic Languages*, London; New York: Routledge.

Bandamanna saga, edited by Guðni Jónsson. Íslenzk fornrit, vol VII, 1936, Reykjavík: Hið íslenzka fornritafélag.

BANDLE, OSCAR, 1956. *Die Sprache der Guðbrandsbiblía: Ortographie und Laute Formen*, Kopenhagen: Ejnar Munksgaard.

BANDLE, OSCAR, 1967. *Studien zur westnordischen Sprachgeographie A*. Textband; Bibliotheca Arnamagnæna 28, Kopenhagen: Munksgaard.

BANDLE, OSCAR, 1973. *Die Gliederung des Nordgermanischen*. Beiträge zur nordischen Philologie I, Basel; Stuttgart: Helbing und Lichtenhahn.

BANDLE, OSCAR, ELMEVIK, LENNART & WIDMARK, GUN, (eds.), 2002–2005. *The Nordic Languages: An International Handbook of the History of the North Germanic Languages*. 2 Vols, Berlin: de Gruyter.

BARLAU, STEPHEN, 1981. 'Old Icelandic kinship terminology: An anomaly', *Ethnology* 20, 191–202.

BARNES, JOHN A., 1954. 'Class and committees in a Norwegian island parish', *Human Relations* 7, New York: Plenum, 39–58.

BARNES, MICHAEL, 2001. 'The Hedeby inscriptions, the short-twig runes, and the question of early Scandinavian dialect markers', in K. Düwel, E. Marold & C. Zimmermann (eds.), *Von Thorsberg nach Schleswig:*

Sprache und Schriftlichkeit eines Grenzgebietes im Wandel eines Jahrtausends, Berlin; New York: de Gruyter, 101–109.

BARNES, MICHAEL, 2003. 'Standardisation and variation in migration – and Viking-Age Scandinavian', in Kristján Árnason (ed.), *Útnorður: West Nordic Standardisation and Variation*, Reykjavík: University of Iceland Press, 47–66.

BARNES, MICHAEL, 2004. *An Introduction to Old Norse: Part I Grammar*, London: Viking Society for Northern Research.

BARNES, MICHAEL, 2005. 'Language', in R. McTurk (ed.), *A Companion to Old Norse-Icelandic Literature and Culture*, Oxford: Blackwell Publishing, 173–89.

BARNES, MICHAEL, 2006. 'Standardised fuþarks: A useful tool or a delusion?', in G. Fellows-Jensen, M. Stoklund, M.L. Nielsen & B. Holmberg (eds.), *Runes and their Secrets: Studies in Runology*, Copenhagen: Museum of Tusculanum Press, 11–31.

BARTSCH, RENATE, 1987. *Norms of Language: Theoretical and Practical Aspects*, London: Longman.

BATELY, JANET, (ed.) 1980. *The Old English Orosius*, London; New York; Toronto: Published for the Early English Text Society by the Oxford University Press.

BATELY, JANET, (ed.) 1986. *The Anglo-Saxon Chronicle*, Cambridge: Cambridge University Press.

BAUGH, ALBERT C., 1959. *A History of the English Language*, London: Routledge & Kegan Paul.

BAX, R., 2000. 'A network strength scale for the study of eighteenth-century English', *European Journal of English Studies* 413, 277–89.

BECK, HEINRICH, 1993. *Wortschatz der altisländischen Grágás*, Göttingen: Vandenhoeck & Ruprecht.

BELICH, JAMES, 1996. *Making Peoples: A History of the New Zealanders. From Polynesian Settlement to the End of the Nineteenth Century*, Honolulu: University of Hawaii Press.

BELL, A., 1997. 'Language style as audience design', in Nikolas Coupland & Adam Jaworski (eds.), *Sociolinguistics: A Reader*, Basingstoke: Macmillan, 240–50.

BENEDICTOW, OLE JØRGEN, 2003. 'Demographic conditions', in Knut Helle (ed.), *The Cambridge History of Scandinavia. Volume 1, Prehistory to 1520*, Cambridge: Cambridge University Press.

BENEDIKTSSON, EINAR, 1952. *Laust mál: Úrval*, Reykjavík: Ísafoldarprentsmiðja.

BENEDIKTSSON, HREINN, 1961–62. 'Icelandic dialectology: Methods and results'. *Íslensk tunga* 3, 72–113.

BENEDIKTSSON, HREINN, 1963. Review of Chapman 1962. *Íslenzk tunga – Lingua Islandica* 4, 152–62.

BENEDIKTSSON, HREINN, 1964. 'Upptök íslenzks máls', in Halldór Halldórsson (ed.), *Þættir um íslenzkt mál eftir nokkra íslenzka málfræðinga*, Reykjavík: Almenna bókafélagið, 9–46.

BENEDIKTSSON, HREINN, 1965. *Early Icelandic Script as Illustrated in Vernacular Texts from the Twelfth and Thirteenth Centuries*, Reykjavík: Manuscript Institute of Iceland.

BENEDIKTSSON, HREINN, 1972. *The First Grammatical Treatise*, Reykjavík: Institute of Nordic Linguistics.

BENEDIKTSSON, JAKOB, 1993. 'Landnámabók', in P. Pulsiano *et al.*, *Medieval Scandinavia: An Encyclopedia*, New York; London: Garland Publishing, 373–4.

BENVENISTE, ÉMILE, 1966. *Problèmes de linguistique générale*, Paris: Gallimard.

BENWELL, BETHAN & STOKOE, ELIZABETH, 2006. *Discourse and Identity*, Edinburgh: Edinburgh University Press.

BERGSVEINSSON, SVEINN, 1955. *Þróun ö-hjlóða í íslenzku*, [Peter Foote: Notes on the Prepositions Of and Um(B) in Old Icelandic and Old Norwegian Prose]. Studia Islandica 14, Reykjavík: H. F. Leiftur; Ejnar Munksgaard: Kaupmannahöfn.

BERGS, ALEXANDER, 2005. *Social Networks and Historical Sociolinguistics: Studies in Morphosyntactic Variation in the Paston Letters (1421–1503)*, Topics in English Linguistics 51, Berlin: Mouton de Gruyter.

BERRUTO, GAETANO, 1995. *Fondamenti di sociolinguistica*, Roma: Laterza.

BIBIRE, PAUL, 1993. 'Hungrvaka', in P. Pulsiano et al. (eds.), *Medieval Scandinavia: An Encyclopedia*, New York; London: Garland Publishing, 307.

BIDDLE, MARTIN & KJØLBYE-BIDDLE, BIRTHE, 1992. 'Repton and the Vikings', *Antiquity* 66, 36–51.

Biskupa Sögur I, edited by Sigurgeir Steingrímsson, Ólafur Halldórsson & Peter Foote. Íslenzk fornrit, vol. XV, 2003, Reykjavík: Hið íslenzka fornritafélag.

Biskupa Sögur II, edited by Ásdís Egilsdóttir. Íslenzk fornrit, vol. XVI, 2002, Reykjavík: Hið íslenzka fornritafélag.

BLANC, H. 1968, 'The Israeli koine as an emergent national standard', in Joshua Fishman, Charles Ferguson & Jyotirindra Das Gupta (eds.), *Language Problems of Developing Nations*, New York: John Wiley, 23–51.

BLOM, JAN-PETER & GUMPERZ, JOHN J., 1972. 'Social meaning in linguistic structures: Code-switching in Norway', in John J. Gumperz J. & Dell Hymes (eds.), *Directions in Sociolinguistics: the Ethnography of Communication*, New York: Holt, Rinehart & Winston, 407–34.

BLOMLEY, NICHOLAS K., 1994. *Law, Space and the Geographies of Law*, New York; London: The Guildford Press.

BLÖNDAL MAGNÚSSON, ÁSGEIR, 1989. *Íslenzk orðsifjabók*, Reykjavík: Orðabók Háskolans.

BLÖNDAL, SIGFÚS, 1920–1924. *Islandsk-Dansk Ordbog*, Reykjavík; København og Kristiania: Prentsmiðjan Gutenberg.

BLOOMFIELD, LEONARD, 1933. *Language*, New York: Holt.

BORTONI-RICARDO, S. M., 1985. *The Urbanization of Rural Dialect Speakers: A Sociolinguistic Study in Brazil*, Cambridge: Cambridge University Press.

BOSWORTH, J. & TOLLER, T. N., (eds.) 1964. 3rd edition. *An Anglo-Saxon Dictionary*, Oxford: Oxford University Press.

BOUCHER, ALAN, (trans.) 1983. *The saga of Gunnlaug Snake-tongue together with the Tale of Scald-Helgi*, Reykjavík: Iceland Review.

BOUHLHOSA, PATRICIA PIRES, 2005. *Icelanders and the Kings of Norway*, Leiden; Boston: Brill.

BOURDIEU, PIERRE, 1991. *Language & Symbolic Power*, Cambridge: Polity Press.

BRAUNMÜLLER, KURT, 1983. 'De sog. Zweite Grammatische Traktat: Ein verkanntes Zeugnis altisländischer Sprachanalyse', in H. Uecker (ed.), *Akten der fünften Arbeitstagung der Skandinavisten des deutschen Sprachgebiets, 16.-22. August 1981 in Kungälv*, St Augustin: Kretschmer, 45–56.

BRAUNMÜLLER, KURT, 2001. 'Morfologisk typology og færøsk' in Kurt Braunmüller & Jógvan í Lon Jacobsen (eds.), *Moderne lingvistiske teorier og færøysk*, Oslo: Novus Forlag, 67–89.

Brennu-Njáls saga, edited by Einar Ól. Sveinsson. Íslenzk fornrit, vol. XII, 1954, Reykjavík: Hið íslenzka fornritafélag.

BREIVIK, LEIV EGIL & JAHR, ERNST HÅKON, (eds.) 1998. *Language Change: Contributions to the Study of its Causes*, Berlin; New York: Mouton de Gruyter.

BRIEM, HALLDÓR, 1918. *Ágrip af íslenskri málfræði*, Reykjavík: Bókaverslun Guðm. Gamalíessonar.

BRIEM, ÓLAFUR, (ed.) 1968. *Eddukvæði*, Reykjavík: Skálholt.

BRITAIN, DAVID, 1991. Dialect and space: A geolinguistic study of speech variables in the Fens. PhD dissertation. University of Essex.

BRITAIN, DAVID, 1997a. 'Dialect contact and phonological reallocation: "Canadian Raising" in the English Fens', *Language in Society* 26, 15–46.

BRITAIN, DAVID, 1997b. 'Dialect contact, focusing and phonological rule of complexity: The koineisation of Fenland English', in *University of Pennsylvania Working Papers in Linguistics* 4. A Selection of Papers from NWAVE 25, Philadelphia: University of Pennsylvania, 141–70.

BRITAIN, DAVID, 2001. 'Where did it all start?: Dialect contact, the "Founder Principle" and the so-called < -own > split in New Zealand English', *Transactions of the Philological Society* 99, 1–27.

BROWN, ROGER & GILMAN, ALBERT, 1960. 'The pronouns of power and solidarity', in Thomas A. Sebeok (ed.), *Style in Language*, New York: MIT, 253–76.

BROWN, ROGER & LEVINSON, STEPHEN C., 1987. *Politeness: Some Universals in Language Use*, Cambridge: Cambridge University Press.

BRUHN, OLE, 1999. *Tekstualisering: bidrag til en litterær antropologi, med forord af Preben Meulengracht Sørensen*, Aarhus: Aarhus universitetsforlag.

BRUNSTAD, ENDRE, 2003. 'Standard language and linguistic purism', *Sociolinguistica* 17, 52–70.

BRYCE, JAMES, 1901. 'Primitive Iceland', in *Studies in History and Jurisprudence*, New York: Oxford University Press, 263–300.

BUBENIK, VIT, 1993. 'Dialect contact and koineisation: The case of Hellenistic Greek', *International Journal of the Sociology of Language* 99, 9–23.

BYOCK, JESSE, 2001. *Viking Age Iceland*, London: Penguin.

BÆKSTAD, A., 1942. *Islands runeindskrifter*, Bibliotheca Arnamagnæna 2 Gamalíelssonar, København: Munksgaard.

CAMERON, DEBORAH, 1990. 'Demythologising sociolinguistics: Why language does not reflect society', in John Joseph & Talbot Taylor (eds.), *Ideologies of Language*, London: Routledge, 79–96.

CELANDER, HILDING, 1906. *Om övergången av ð > d i fornisländskan och fornnorskan*, Lund: Berlingska boktryckeriet.

CHAMBERS, JACK K., 2002a. 'Patterns of variation including change', in Jack K. Chambers *et al.*, *The Handbook of Language Variation and Change*, Malden, MA: Blackwell, 349–72.

CHAMBERS, JACK K., 2002b. 'Dynamics of dialect convergence', *Journal of Sociolinguistics* 6, 117–30.

CHAMBERS, JACK K., 2003. *Sociolinguistic Theory*. 2nd edition, Oxford: Blackwell.

CHAMBERS, JACK K., & TRUDGILL, PETER, 1998. *Dialectology*, 2nd edition, Cambridge: Cambridge University Press.

CHAMBERS, JACK K., *et al.*, 2002. *The Handbook of Language Variation and Change*, Malden, MA: Blackwell.

CHAPMAN, KENNETH G., 1962. *Icelandic-Norwegian Linguistic Relationships*, Oslo: Universitetsforlaget.

CHEN, MATTHEW, 1972. 'The time dimension: Contribution towards a theory of sound change', *Foundations of Language* 8, 457–98.

CHRISTIANSEN, MORTEN & KIRKBY, SIMON, 2003. *Language Evolution*, Oxford: Oxford University Press.

CHRISTY, T. CRAIG, 1983. *Uniformitarianism in Linguistics*, Amsterdam/ Philadelphia: John Benjamins.

CLEASBY, RICHARD, GUÐBRANDUR, VIGFÚSSON, & CRAIGIE, WILLIAM A., 1874. *An Icelandic – English Dictionary*, Oxford: Clarendon Press.

CLIFFORD, JAMES, 1988. *The Predicament of Culture: Twentieth-century Ethnography, Literature and Art*, Cambridge, Mass.: Harvard University Press.

CLOVER, CAROL J., 1985. *Old Norse-Icelandic Literature: A Critical Guide*, Ithaca: Cornell University Press.

CLOVER, CAROL J., 1988. 'The politics of scarcity: Notes on the sex ratio in early Scandinavia', *Scandinavian Studies* 60, 147–188.

CLUNIES ROSS, MARGARET, 1987. *Skáldskaparmál. Snorri Sturluson's 'ars poetica' and Medieval Theories of Language*, The Viking Collection, Studies in Northern Civilisation 4, Odense: Odense University Press.

CLUNIES ROSS, MARGARET, 1993. 'The development of Old Norse textual worlds: Genealogical structure as a principle of literary organisation in early Iceland', *Journal of English and Germanic Philology* 92, 372–85.

CLUNIES ROSS, MARGARET, 1997. 'Textual territory: The regional and genealogical dynamic of medieval Icelandic literary production', in R. Copeland, D. Lawton & W. Scase (eds.), *New Medieval Literatures*, Oxford: Clarendon Press.

CLUNIES ROSS, MARGARET, 2005. *A History of Old Norse Poetry and Poetics*, Cambridge: D. S. Brewer.

COSERIU, EUGENE, 1974. *Synchronie, Diachronie und Geschichte: das Problem des Sprachwandels*, translated by H. Sohre, München: W. Fink.

COULMAS, FLORIAN, (ed.) 1997. *The Handbook of Sociolinguistics*, Oxford: Blackwell.

COUPLAND, NIKOLAS, 1984. 'Accommodation at work', *International Journal of the Sociology of Language* 46, 49–70.

COUPLAND, NIKOLAS, 1988. *Dialects in Use: Sociolinguistic Variation in Cardiff English*, Cardiff: University of Wales Press.

COUPLAND, NIKOLAS, 1997. 'What is sociolinguistic theory?', *Journal of Sociolinguistics* 2, 110–17.

CROFT, WILLIAM, 2000. *Explaining Language Change: An Evolutionary Approach*, Longman Linguistic Library, Edinburgh: Pearson Education Limited.

DAHLSTEDT, KARL-HAMPUS, 1958. 'Isländsk dialektgeografi. Några synpunkter', *Scripta Islandica* 1, 5–33.

Danske gamle Landskabslove med Kirkelovene, 1933–1961. Johs. Brøndum-Nielsen & Poul Johs. Jørgensen (eds.). 8 Vols, København: Gyldendal.

DAVIDSON, ELLIS & RODERICK, HILDA, 1979. *Saxo Grammaticus: The History of the Danes*. Vol. 1: Text. Translated by P. Fisher. Edited by Ellis Davidson & Hilda Roderick, Cambridge: D. S. Brewer.

DAVIES, NORMAN, 1999. *The Isles: A History*, London: Macmillan Publishers.

DEBES, H. J., 1995. *Føroya søga 2. Skattland og len*, Tórshavn: Føroya Skúlabókagrunnur.

DENCIK, L., 1998. 'Hur formas individers identiter i ett föränderligt samhälle?', in A. Emilsson & S. Lilja (eds.), *Lokala identiteter – historia, nutid, framtid*, HS-institutionens skriftserie 2 Högskolan i Gävle-Sandviken, 37–67.

DENISON, NORMAN, 1997. 'Language change and progress: Variation as it happens', in Florian Coulmas (ed.), *The Handbook of Sociolinguistics*, 65–80.

DENNIS, ANDREW, FOOTE, PETER & PERKINS, RICHARD, 1980. *Laws of Early Iceland*, Winnipeg: University of Manitoba Press.

DENNIS, ANDREW, FOOTE, PETER & PERKINS, RICHARD, 2000. *Laws of Early Iceland II*, Winnipeg: University of Manitoba Press.

DE VRIES, JAN, 1961. *Altnordisches Etymologisches Wörterbuch*, Leiden: E. J. Brill.

DILLARD, JOHN, L., 1972. *Black English: its History and Usage in the United States*, New York: Random.

Diplomatarium Danicum. 1 række. 1957–1990. Edited by L. Weibull *et al.* Vols. 1–7. København: Munksgaard.

Diplomatarium Danicum. 2 række. 1938–1960. Edited by A. Afzelius *et al.* Vols. 1–12. København: Munksgaard.

Diplomatarium Islandicum. 1857–1972. Íslenzkt fornbréfasafn, sem hefir inni að halda bréf, gjörninga, dóma og máldaga og aðrar skrár, er snerta Ísland og íslenzka menn, Vols. 1–16. Kaupmannahöfn & Reykjavík: Hið íslenzka bókmenntafélag.

Diplomatarium Norvegicum. 1847–1995. Oldbreve til Kundskab om Norges indre og ydre Forhold, Sprog, Slægter, Lovgiving og Rettergang i Middelalderen. Edited by C. A. Lange & C. R. Unger Vols. 1–32. Christiania: P. T. Mallings Forlagshandel.

DOBSON, ERIC J., 1968. *English Pronunciation, 1500–1700*. 2nd edition, Oxford: Clarendon Press.

DORIAN, NANCY C., 1994. 'Varieties of variation in a very small place: Social homogeneity, prestige, norms, and linguistic variation', *Language* 70, 631–96.

DORIAN, NANCY C., 2001. 'Review of "Language change: Advances in historical sociolinguistics" (Ernst Håkon Jahr (ed.))', *Anthropological Linguistics* 43.3, 387–9.

DUGMORE, ANDREW J., CHURCH, MICHAEL J., *et al.*, 2005. 'The Norse *landnám* on the north Atlantic islands: An environmental impact assessment', *Polar Record* 41 (216), 21–37.

DUSZAK, ANNA, 2002. 'Us and others: An introduction', in Anna Duszak (ed.), *Us and Others: Social Identities across Languages, Discourses and Cultures*, Amsterdam; Philadelphia: John Benjamins Publishing Company.

ECKERT, PENELOPE, 1989. *Jocks & Burnouts: Social Categories and Identity in the High School*, New York & London: Teachers College Press.

ECKERT, PENELOPE, 1998. 'Adolescent social structure and the spread of linguistic change', *Language in Society* 17, 83–207.

ECKERT, PENELOPE, 2000. *Linguistic Variation as Social Practice: The Linguistic Construction of Identity in Belten High*, Language in Society 27, Oxford: Blackwell.

ECKERT, PENELOPE, 2003. 'Language and gender in adolescence', in J. Holmes & M. Meyerhoff (eds.), *Handbook of Language and Gender*, Oxford: Blackwell, 381–400.

EGILSSON, SVEINBJÖRN, 1966. *Lexicon poeticum antiquæ linguæ septentrionalis.* 2nd edition by Finnur Jónsson, København: Atlas Bogtryk.

Egils saga Skalla-Grímssonar, edited by Sigurður Nordal. Íslenzk fornrit, vol. II. 1933, Reykjavík: Hið íslenzka fornritafélag.

EINARSSON, STEFÁN, 1932. 'Icelandic dialect studies I. Austfirðir', *Journal of English and Germanic Philology*, Vol. XXXI, 537–72.

EINARSSON, STEFÁN, 1942. 'Terms of direction in modern Icelandic'. Presented to George T. Flom, *Scandinavian Studies*, 37–48.

EINARSSON, STEFÁN, 1944. 'Terms of direction in old Icelandic', *Journal of English and Germanic Philology* 43, 265–85.

EINARSSON, STEFÁN, 1945. *Icelandic: Grammar, Texts, Glossary*, Baltimore; London: The Johns Hopkins University Press.

Eiríks saga rauða, edited by Einar Ól. Sveinsson & Matthías Þórðarson. Íslenzk fornrit, vol. IV. 1935, Reykjavík: Hið íslenzka fornritafélag.

ELDJÁRN, KRISTJÁN, 2000. *Kuml og haugfé. Úr heiðnum sið á Íslandi*- 2. Útgafa. Ritstjóra (editor) Adolf Friðriksson, Reykjavík: Mál og menning.

ENTRIKIN, NICHOLAS J., 1991. *The Betweenness of Places: Towards a Geography of Modernity*, Baltimore: The Johns Hopkins University Press.

ERHARDT, HARALD, 1977. *Der Stabreim in altnordischen Rechtstexten*, Heidelberg: Carl Winter Universitätsverlag.

Eyrbyggja saga, edited by Einar Ól. Sveinsson & Matthías Þórðarson. Íslenzk fornrit, vol. IV. 1935, Reykjavík: Hið íslenzka fornritafélag.

EYÞÓRSSON, ÞÓRHALLUR 1999. 'The runic inscription on the Reistad stone: The earliest *Landnámabók*', in A. Bammesberger (ed.), *Pforzen und Bergakker: Neue Untersuchungen zu Runeninschriften*, Göttingen: Vandenhoeck & Ruprecht, 189–202.

FAARLUND, JAN TERJE, 2003. 'The Nynorsk standard language and Norwegian dialect varieties', in David Britain & Jenny Cheshire (eds.), *Social Dialectology: In honour of Peter Trudgill*, Amsterdam; Philadelphia: John Benjamins Publishing Company, 311–325.

FAARLUND, JAN TERJE, 2004. *The Syntax of Old Norse*, Oxford: Oxford University Press.

FARRAR, K. & JONES, MARI C., 2002. 'Introduction', in Mari C. Jones & Edith Esch, *Language Change: the Interplay of Internal, External and Extra-linguistic Factors*, Berlin; New York: Mouton de Gruyter, 1–16.

FAULKES, ANTHONY, 1978–9. 'Descent from the Gods', *Medieval Scandinavia* 11, 92–125.

FAULKES, ANTHONY, (ed.) 1991. *Edda: Háttatal*, Oxford: Clarendon Press.

FEIST, SIGMUND, 1939. *Vergleichendes Wörterbuch der gotischen Sprache mit Einschluß des Krimgotischen und sonstiger zerstreuter Überreste des Gotischen*, Leiden: E. J. Brill.

FERGUSON, CHARLES A., 1959. 'The Arabic koine', *Language* 35, 616–30.

FERGUSON, CHARLES A., 1962. 'The language factor in national development', *Anthropological Linguistics* 4.1, 23–7.

FINCH, R. G., (translator) 1965. *The Saga of the Volsungs*, London: Nelson.

FINK, HANS, 1991. 'Om identiteters identitet', in Hans Fink & H. Hauge (eds.), *Identiteter i forandring*, Aarhus: Aarhus Universitetsforlag, 204–27.

FINNBOGASON, GUÐMUNDUR, 1971. *Íslendingar*, Reykjavík: Almenna bókafélagið.

FINSEN, VILHJÁLMUR, 1849. Fremstilling af den islandske familieret efter Grágás, 1. *Annaler for nordisk oldkyndighed og historie*, København: I Commission i den Gyldendalske Boghandel.

FISHMAN, JOSHUA A., 1972. *The Sociology of Language: an Interdisciplinary Social Science Approach to Language and Society*, Rowley, Mass.: Newbury House.

FISIAK, JACEK (ed.), 1988. *Historical Dialectology: Regional and Social*. Trends in Linguistics, Studies and Monographs 37, Berlin; New York; Amsterdam: Mouton de Gruyter.

FIX, HANS, 1984. *Wortschatz der Jónsbók*, Frankfurt am Main: Peter Lang Verlag.

FIX, HANS, 1993. 'Grágás', in P. Pulsiano *et al.*, *Medieval Scandinavia: An Encyclopedia*, New York; London: Garland Publishing, 234–5.

FJALLDAL, MAGNÚS, 1993. 'How valid is the Anglo-Saxon Scandinavian language passage in *Gunnlaug's saga* as historical evidence?', *Neophilologus* 77, 601–09.

FOOTE, PETER, 1974. 'Secular attitudes in early Iceland', *Medieval Scandinavia* 7, 31–44.

FOOTE, PETER & WILSON, DAVID M., 1970. *The Viking Achievement: The Society and Culture of Early Medieval Scandinavia*, London: Sidgwick & Jackson.

Fornmannasögur eptir gömlum handritum. Útgefnar að tilhlutun hins konúnglega norræna fornfræða félags. Vol X. 1835. Kaupmannahöfn: S. L. Möllers.

FORTESCUE, MICHAEL, 1997. 'Dialect distribution and small group interaction in Greenlandic Eskimo', in P. McConvell & N. Evans (eds.), *Archaeology and Linguistics: Aboriginal Australia in Global Perspective*, Oxford: Oxford University Press, 111–22.

FOX, ROBIN, 1978. *The Tory Islanders: A People of the Celtic Fringe*, Cambridge: Cambridge University Press.

Færeyinga saga, Óláfs saga Tryggvasonar eptir Odd munk Snorrason, edited by Ólafur Halldórsson. Íslenzk fornrit, vol. XXV. 2006, Reykjavík: Hið íslenzka fornritafélag.

GADE, KARI ELLEN, 2000. 'Poetry and its changing importance', in Margaret Clunies Ross (ed.), *Old Icelandic Literature and Society*, Cambridge: Cambridge University Press, 61–95.

GAFFIN, DENNIS, 1996. *In Place: Spatial and Social Order in a Faeroe Islands Community*, Prospect Heights, Illinois: Waveland Press.

GAL, SUSAN, 1979. *Language Shift: Social Determinants of Linguistic Change in Bilingual Austria*, New York: Academic Press.

GERGEN, K. J., 2001. *Social Construction in Context*, London; Thousand Oaks; New Delhi: Sage Publications.

GIDDENS, ANTHONY, 1984. *The Constitution of Society: Outline of the Theory of Structuration*, Cambridge: Polity Press.

GIDDENS, ANTHONY, 1991. *Modernity and Self-Identity: Self and Society in the Late Modern Age*, Cambridge: Polity Press.

GILES, HOWARD, 1973. 'Accent mobility: A model and some data', *Anthropological Linguistics* 15, 87–105.

GILES, HOWARD, BOURHIS, R. Y. & TAYLOR, D. M., 1977. 'Towards a theory of language in ethnic group relations', in Howard Giles (ed.), *Language, Ethnicity and Intergroup Relations*, London: Academic Press.

GILES, HOWARD & COUPLAND, NIKOLAS, 1991. *Language: Contexts and Consequences*, Milton Keynes: Open University Press.

GILES, HOWARD & POWESLAND, PETER F., 1975. *Speech Style and Social Education*, New York and London: Academic Press.

GILES, HOWARD & POWESLAND, PETER F., 1997/75. 'Accommodation theory', in Nikolas Coupland & Adam Jaworski (eds.), *Sociolinguistics: A Reader*, Basingstoke: Macmillan, 232–39.

GILES, HOWARD & SMITH, PHILIP M., 1979. 'Accommodation theory: Optimal levels of convergence', in Howard Giles & Robert N. St. Clair (eds.), *Language and Social Psychology*, Language and Society 1, Oxford: Blackwell, 45–65.

GILLES, PETER & MOULIN, CLAUDINE, 2003. 'Luxembourgish', in Ana Deumert & Wim Vandenbussche (eds.), *Germanic Standardisation – Past and Present*, Amsterdam; New York: John Benjamins, 303–27.

Gísla saga Súrssonar, edited by Björn K. Þórólfsson & Guðni Jónsson. Íslenzk fornrit, vol. VI. 1943, Reykjavík: Hið íslenzka fornritafélag.

GJERSET, KNUT, 1925. *History of Iceland*, New York: The Macmillan Company.

GORDON, ELIZABETH et al., 2004. *New Zealand English: its Origins and Evolution*, Cambridge: Cambridge University Press.

GRANOVETTER, MARK S., 1973. 'The strength of weak ties', *American Journal of Sociology* 78, Issue 6, May, 1360–80.

Grágás. Islændernes Lovbog i Fristatens Tid, ed. Vilhjálmur Finsen; Vols. Ia, Ib 1852, Vol. II 1879, Vol. III 1883. Reprinted 1974, Odense: Odense University Press.

Grettis saga Ásmundarsonar, edited by Guðni Jónsson. Íslenzk fornrit, vol. VII. 1936, Reykjavík: Hið íslenzka fornritafélag.

Grænlendinga saga, edited by Einar Ól. Sveinsson & Matthías Þórðarson. Íslenzk fornrit, vol. IV. 1935, Reykjavík: Hið íslenzka fornritafélag.

GRØNLIE, SIÂN E., (ed.) 2006. *Íslendingabók, Kristni saga: The Book of the Icelanders, The Story of the Conversion*, University College, London: Viking Society for Northern Research.

GRØNVIK, OTTAR, 1985. *Runene på Eggjasteinen: En hedensk gravinnskrift fra slutten av 600-tallet*, Oslo: Universitetsforlaget.

GRØNVIK, OTTAR, 1987. *Fra Ågedal til Setre: Sentrale runeinskrifter fra det 6. århundre*, Oslo: Universitetsforlaget.

GRØNVIK, OTTAR, 1998. *Untersuchungen zur älteren nordischen und germanischen Sprachgeschichte*, Osloer Beiträge zur Germanistik 18, Frankfurt am Main: Peter Lang.

GRØNVIK, OTTAR, 2001. *Über die Bildung des älteren und des jüngeren Runenalphabets*, Osloer Beiträge zur Germanistik 29, Frankfurt am Main: Peter Lang.

GRÖNVOLD, K. *et al.*, 1995. 'Express letter: Ash layers from Iceland in the Greenland GRIP ice core correlated with oceanic and land sediments', *Earth and Planetary Science Letters* CXXXV, 1–4, 149–55.

GUÐFINNSSON, BJÖRN, 1946. *Mállýzkur I-II*, Reykjavík: Ísafoldarprentsmiðja.

GUMPERZ, JOHN J., 1977. 'The speech community', in GIGLIOLI, P. P. (ed.), *Language and Social Context*, Harmondsworth: Penguin Books, 219–30.

GUMPERZ, JOHN J., 1982. *Language and Social Identity*, Cambridge: Cambridge University Press.

GUÐMUNDSSON, HELGI, 1972. *Pronominal Dual in Icelandic*, Reykjavík: Institute of Nordic Linguistics.

GUÐMUNDSSON, HELGI, 1977. 'Um ytri aðstæður íslenzkrar málþróunar', in *Sjötíu ritgerðir helgaðar Jakobi Benediktssyni 20. júlí 1977*, Reykjavík: Stofnun Árna Magnússonar, 314–25.

GUÐMUNDSSON, HELGI, 1997. *Um haf innan: Vestrænir menn og íslenzk menning á miðöldum*, Reykjavík: Háskólaútgáfan.

GUÐMUNDSSON, VALTÝR, 1924. *Island i fristatstiden*, København: Gad.

Gunnlaugs saga ormstungu, edited by Sigurður Nordal & Guðni Jónsson. Íslenzk fornrit, vol. III. 1938, Reykjavík: Hið íslenzka fornritafélag.

GUREVICH, ARON Y., 1969. 'Space and time in the Weltmodell of the Scandinavian peoples', *Mediæval Scandinavia*, Vol. 2, 42–53.

GUREVICH, ARON Y., 1992. *Historical Anthropology of the Middle Ages*, Oxford: Blackwell Publishers.

GUÐMUNDSSON, BARÐI, 1959. *Uppruni Íslendinga*, Reykjavík: Safn ritgerða, 76–93.

HABERMAS, JÜRGEN, 1984–87. *Theory of Communicative Action*. Translated by McCarthy, T. (translated from Theorie des kommunikativen Handelns, 2 Vols, Frankfurt am Main: Suhrkamp, K. 1981), Cambridge: Polity.

HAGLAND, JAN RAGNAR, 2002. 'Dialects and written language in Old Nordic 1: Old Norwegian and Old Icelandic', in *The Nordic Languages: An*

International Handbook of the History of the North Germanic Languages, Volume 1, Berlin: de Gruyter, 1015–18.

HAGLAND, JAN RAGNAR, 2006. 'Runic writing and Latin literacy at the end of the Middle Ages: A case study', in Gillian Fellows-Jensen, Marie Stoklund, Michael Lerche Nielsen and Bente Holmberg (eds.), *Runes and Their Secrets: Studies in Runology*, Copenhagen: Museum Tusculanum Press, 141–57.

HÅKON JAHR, ERNST, 1989, 'Language planning and language change', in Leiv Egil Breivik & Ernst Håkon Jahr (eds.), *Language Change: Contributions to the Study of its Causes*, Trends in Linguistics: Studies and Monographs 43, Berlin; New York: Mouton de Gruyter, 99–113.

HALLDÓRSSON, ÓLAFUR, 1966. 'Helgafellsbækur fornar', *Studia Islandica* 24, Reykjavík: Heimspekideild Háskóla Íslands og Bókaútgáfa Menningarsjóðs.

HÁLFDANARSON, GUÐMUNDUR 1996. 'Hvað gerir Íslendinga að þjóð?', *Skírnir*, 7–32.

HÁLFDANARSON, GUÐMUNDUR, 2006. 'From Linguistic Patriotism to Cultural Nationalism: Language and Identity in Iceland'. National Languages and Language Policies: 55–67. Available at http://64.233.183.104/search?q = cache:yKjd91_yMqsJ:www.stm.unipi.it/programmasocrates/cliohnet/books/ language2/05_Halfdanarson.pdf + National + Language + and + Language + Policies + Gu%C3%B0mundur + H%C3%A1lfdanarson&hl = en&ct = clnk &cd = 1&gl = uk.

HALLBERG, PETER, 1962. *Old Icelandic Poetry: Eddic Lay and Skaldic Verse*. Translated with a foreword by P. Schach & S. Lindgrenson, S., Lincoln & London: University of Nebraska Press.

HALLDÓRSSON, HALLDÓR, 1962. 'Kring språkliga nybildingar i nutida isländska', *Scripta Islandica* 13, 3–24.

HALLDÓRSSON, HALLDÓR, 1964. *Þættir um íslenzkt mál eftir nokkra íslenzka málfræðinga*, Reykjavík: Almenna bókafélagið, 9–28.

HALLDÓRSSON, HALLDÓR, 1971. Allt er mér leyfilegt: Þátturinn Daglegt mál. Morgunblaðið, 28 November, Reykjavík.

HALLDÓRSSON, HALLDÓR, 1979. 'Icelandic purism and its history', *Word* 30, 76–86.

HALLDÓRSSON, HALLDÓR, 1981. 'Um málvöndun' in *Mál og túlkun. Safn ritgerða um mannleg fræði með forspjalli eftir Pál Skúlason*, Reykjavík: Hið íslenska bókmenntafélag, 201–20.

HAMMERICH, L. L., 1953. 'Danske tunge', *Danske Studier*, 120–1.

HANNESSON, GUÐMUNDUR, 1924–25. 'Körpermasse und Körperproportionen der Isländer', *Árbók Háskóla Íslands*, Reykjavík: Háskóla Íslands.

HARÐARSON, GUNNAR, 1999. 'Alls vér erum tungu', *Íslenskt mál* 21, 11–30.

HARRIS, ROY, 1980. *The Language-Makers*, London: Duckworth.

HARRIS, ALICE C. & CAMPBELL, LYLE, 1995. *Historical Syntax in a Cross-linguistic Perspective*, Cambridge: Cambridge University Press.

HASTRUP, KIRSTEN, 1984. 'The Icelandic free state', *Scandinavian Studies*, Vol, 56 number 3, 235–55.

HASTRUP, KIRSTEN, 1985. *Culture and Classification in Modern Iceland: An Anthropological Analysis of Structure and Change*, Oxford: Clarendon Press.

HASTRUP, KIRSTEN, 1990. *Island of Anthropology: Studies in Past and Present Iceland*, Odense: Odense University Press.

HAUGEN, EINAR, 1957. 'The semantics of Icelandic orientation', *Word* 13/3, 447–59.

HAUGEN, EINAR, 1966. 'Dialect, language, nation', *American Anthropologist* 68, 922–35.

HAUGEN, EINAR, 1972a. *First Grammatical Treatise. The Earliest Germanic Phonology: An Edition, Translation and Commentary*, 2nd edition, London: Longman.

HAUGEN, EINAR, 1972b. *The Ecology of Language*. Essays by Haugen, E. Selected and Introduced by Dil, A., Stanford: Stanford University Press.

HAUGEN, EINAR, 1973. 'The dotted runes: From parsimony to plenitude', in *Proceedings of the Seventh Viking Congress*, 83–92.

HAUGEN, EINAR, 1975. 'Pronominal address in Icelandic: From you-two to you-all', *Language in Society* 4, 323–39.

HAUGEN, EINAR, 1976. *The Scandinavian Languages: An Introduction to their History*, London: Faber & Faber.

HAZEN, KIRK, 2002. 'The family', in Jack K. Chambers, Peter Trudgill & Natalie Schilling-Estes (eds.), *The Handbook of Language Variation and Change*, Malden, MA: Blackwell, 500–25.

Hákonar saga Hákonarsonar, edited by Mundt, M. 1977. Oslo: Norsk historisk kjeldeskrift-institutt.

Heimskringla I-III, edited by Bjarni Aðalbjarnarson. Íslenzk fornrit, vol. XXVI-XXVIII. 1941–51. Reykjavík: Hið íslenzka fornritafélag.

HELGASON, AGNAR, 2000a. 'mtDNA and the origin of the Icelanders: Deciphering signals of recent population history', *American Journal of Human Genetics* 66, 999–1016.

HELGASON, AGNAR, 2000b. 'Estimating Scandinavian and Gaelic ancestry in the male settlers of Iceland', *American Journal of Human Genetics* 67, 697–717.

HELGASON, JÓN, (ed.) 1938. *Byskupa Sögur* I, Copenhagen: Munksgaard.

HELGASON, PÉTUR, 2002. *Preaspiration in the Nordic Languages: Synchronic and Diachronic Aspects*. PhD Thesis, Stockholm University.

HELLE, KNUT (ed.), 2006. *The Cambridge History of Scandinavia. Volume I, Prehistory to 1520*, Cambridge: Cambridge University Press.

HERRMANN, P., 1914. *Island, das Land und das Völk*, Leipzig; Berlin: W. Engelmann.

HESSELMAN, BENGT, 1936. 'Några nynordiska dialektformer och vikingatidens historia. En undersökning i svensk och dansk språkutveckling', in Hesselman, Bengt (ed.), *Ordgeografi och språkhistoria. Bidrag från nordiska seminariet vid Uppsala universitet* (= Nordiska texter och undersökningar 9), Stockholm: H. Gebers Förlag; Köpenhamn: Levin & Munksgaard, 127–62.

HESSELMAN, BENGT, 1948. *Huvudlinjer i nordisk språkhistoria*, Nordisk Kultur III-IV, Uppsala: Almqvist & Wiksell; Oslo: H. Aschehoug & Co; Copenhagen: J. H. Schultz, 13.

HICKEY, RAYMOND, 2000. 'Ebb and flow: A cautionary tale of language change' in Farrego, T., Méndez-Naya, B. & Seoane, E. (eds.), *Sounds, Words, Texts and Change*, Amsterdam; Philadelphia: John Benjamins, 105–28.

HICKEY, RAYMOND, 2003. 'How do dialects get the features they have?: On the process of new dialect formation', in Hickey, Raymond (ed.), *Motives for Language Change*, Cambridge: Cambridge University Press, 213–39.

HINSKENS, FRANS, 1996. *Dialect Levelling in Limburg: Structural and Sociolinguistic Aspects*, Linguistische Arbeiten, Tübingen: Max Niemeyer.

Historia Norwegiæ in Monumenta Historica Norwegiæ, edited by Storm G. 1880, Kristiania (Oslo): Bøgger.

HOFMEISTER, ADOLFUS, (ed.) 1896–1934. *Vita Lebuini Antiquior*, in Supplementa, *Monumenta Germaniae historica* (*MGH*), Scriptores (in Folio), 30, 2 Vols, Leipzig: Hierseman, 789–95.

HOGG, MICHAEL A. & ABRAMS, DOMINIC, 1988. *Social Identifications: A Social Psychology of Intergroup Relations and Group Processes*, London; New York: Routledge.

Hrafnkels saga, edited by Jón Jóhannesson. Íslenzk fornrit, vol. XI. 1959, Reykjavík: Hið íslenzka fornritafélag.

Hreiðars þáttr, edited by Björn Sigfússon. Íslenzk fornrit, vol. X. 1940, Reykjavík: Hið íslenzka fornritafélag.

HUDSON, RICHARD A., 1996. *Sociolinguistics*, 2nd edition, Cambridge: Cambridge University Press.

Hungrvaka, edited by Ásdís Egilsdóttir. Íslenzk fornrit, vol. XVI: Biskupa Sögur II. 2002, Reykjavík: Hið íslenzka fornritafélag.

HYMES, DELL, 1972. 'On communicative competence', in Pride, J. B. & Holmes, J. (eds.), *Sociolinguistics*, Harmondsworth: Penguin Books, 269–94.

HÆGSTAD, MARIUS, 1909. *Det norske maalet fyre 1350*, Kristiania: Det Norske Videnskaps-Akademi.

HÆGSTAD, MARIUS, 1942. *Vestnorske maalføre fyre 1350. II. Sudvestlandsk 2. Indre SudvestlandskFærøymaal, Islandsk, tridje bolken: Maalet paa Island.* Det norske videnskaps-akademi i Oslo II, Hist-filos. Klasse: 1941: 1, Oslo: Jacob Dybwad.

Icelandic – at once ancient and modern – pamphlet produced by the Ministry of Education, Science and Culture, Pamphlet 13. 2001. Available at http://bella.mrn.stjr.is/utgafur/enska.pdf.

INDREBØ, GUSTAV, 1951. *Norsk målsoga*, Bergen: John Grieg.

IVERSEN, RAGNVALD, 1972. *Norrøn grammatikk*, Oslo: Tano. H. Aschehoug & Co.

Ísleifs þáttr byskups, edited by Ásdís Egilsdóttir. Íslenzk fornrit, vol. XVI. 2002, Reykjavík: Hið íslenzka fornritafélag.

Íslendingabók, edited by Jakob Benediktsson. Íslenzk fornrit, vol. I. 1968, Reykjavík: Hið íslenzka fornritafélag.

JACKSON, KENNETH, 1953. 'Common Gaelic', *Proceedings of the British Academy* 37, 71–97.

JACKSON, TATJANA N., 1998. 'On the Old Norse system of spatial orientation', *Saga-Book* XXV, Part 1, Viking Society for Northern Research, 72–82.

JACOBSEN, LIS & MOLTKE, ERIK, 1941–42. *Danmarks runeindskrifter* 1–2; *under medvirkning af Anders Baeksted og Karl Martin Nielsen*, Copenhagen: Einar Munksgaards Forlag.

JACOBY, M., 1986. *Germanisches Recht und Rechtssprache zwischen Mittelalter und Neuzeit unter besonderer Berücksichtigung des skandinavisches Rechts: Gegenthese zu J. Grimm und zu romantischer Auffassung im 20. Jahrhundert*, Vol. 1, New York: Peter Lang.

JAKOBSEN, J., 1901. *Shetlandsøernes stednavne*, København: Thiele, 177–78.

JAKOBSON, ROMAN, 1929. *Remarques sur l'évolution phonologique du russe comparée à celle des autres langues slaves* (= *Travaux du Cercle Linguistique de Prague 2*). Reprinted in his *Selected Writings, I. Phonological Studies* (1962). The Hague: Mouton.

JAKOBSON, ROMAN, 1971. 'Linguistics and poetics', in *Selected Writings III*, The Hague: Mouton: 18–51.

JAKOBSSON, SVERRIR, 2005. *Við og veröldin. Heimsmynd Íslendinga 1100–1400*, Reykjavík: Háskólaútgáfan.

JENSSON, GOTTSKÁLK ÞÓR, 2003. 'Puritas nostrae linguae', *Skírnir* 177, 37–67.

JESPERSEN, OTTO, 1954. *Language: its Nature, Development and Origin*, London: George Allen & Unwin.

JOCHENS, JENNY, 1995. *Women in Old Norse Society*, Ithaca; London: Cornell University Press.

JÓHANNESSON, ALEXANDER, 1956. *Isländisches Etymologisches Wörterbuch*, Bern: A. Francke AG Verlag.

JOHNSEN, O. A. & HELGASON, JÓN, 1941. *Den store saga om Olav den hellige*, Oslo: Norsk Historisk Kjeldeskrifts-Institutt.

JOHNSTONE, BARBARA, 1999. Place, globalization and linguistic variation. Unpublished paper, presented at the Conference Methods in Sociolinguistics in Honor of Ronald K. S., Macaulay. Claremont, CA.

JÓHANNSSON, JÓHANNES L. L., 1924. *Nokkrar sögulegar athugarnir um helztu hljóðbreytingar o.fl. í íslenzku, einkum í miðaldarmálinu (1300–1600)*, Reykjavík: Bókaverzlun Sigfúsar Eymundssonar.

JÓHANNESSON, JÓN, 1941. *Gerir landnámabókar*, Reykjavík: Félagsprentsmiðjan.

JÓHANNESSON, JÓN, 1956. *Íslendinga saga*, Reykjavík: Almenna bókafélagið.

Jóhannesson, Jón, 1969. *Islands historie i mellomalderen: fristatstida.* Oversatt av Hallvard Magerøy, Oslo; Bergen: Universitetsforlaget.

Jóhannesson, Jón, 1974. *A history of the Old Icelandic Commonwealth.* Translated by H. Bessason, University of Manitoba: University of Manitoba Press.

Jómsvíkinga saga (efter Cod. AM. 510, 4:TO), edited by Carl af Petersens, 1879, Lund: Fr. Berlings Boktryckeri och Stilgjuteri.

Jones, Gwyn, 1964. *The North Atlantic Saga*, London: Oxford University Press.

Jones, Gwyn, 1968. *A History of the Vikings*, Oxford: Oxford University Press.

Jones, Gwyn, 1984. *A History of the Vikings*, Revised Edition, London: Oxford University Press.

Jónsbók. Kong Magnus Hakonssons Lovbog for Island. Vedtaget på Altinget 1281 og réttarbætr de for Island givne retterbøder af 1294, 1305 og 1314, edited by Ólafur Halldórsson, Københaven 1904, Reprinted 1970, Odense: Odense University Press.

Jones, Oscar F., 1964. 'Some Icelandic *götumál* expressions', *Scandinavian Studies* 36, 59–64.

Jones, W., 1979. 'Graphemic evidence for the diphthongisation of /e/ and /o/ in Old High German: The case re-opened', *Neophilologus* 63, Number 2, 250–59.

Jónsson, Baldur, 1976. *Mályrkja Guðmundar Finnbogasonar*, Reykjavík: Bókaútgáfa Menningarsjóðs.

Jónsson, Baldur, 1987. 'Íslensk heiti fyrir AIDS', *Málfregnir* 1, Reykjavík, 25–26.

Jónsson, Baldur, 1988. 'Isländsk språkvård', *Sprog i Norden*, Oslo: Novus Forlag, 5–16.

Jónsson, Baldur, 1997. 'Isländska språket', *Nordens språk*, Oslo: Novus Forlag, 161–76.

Jónsson, Baldur, 2006. *Þjóð og tunga: ritgerðir og ræður frá tímum sjálfstæðisbaráttunnar*, Reykjavík: Hið íslenska bókmenntafélag.

Jónsson, Finnur, 1898. 'Edda Snorra Sturlusonar. Dens oprindelige form og sammensætning', in *Aarbøger for nordisk oldkyndighed og historie* II, København: I Commission i den Gyldendalske Boghandel, 13.

Jónsson, Finnur, 1900. *Landnámabók I–III: Hauksbók, Sturlubók, Melabók*, København: Thieles Bogtrykkeri.

Jónsson, Finnur, 1901. *Det Norsk-Islandske Skjaldesprog omtr. 800–1300*, København: S. L. Møllers Bogtrykkeri.

Jónsson, Finnur, 1912–15. *Den norsk-islandske skjaldedigtning.* 4 Vols, København og Kristiania: Gyldendal, Nordisk forlag.

Jónsson, Finnur, 1921. *Norsk-islandske kultur-og sprogforhold i 9. og 10. árh.*, i Det Kgl. Danske Vid. Selsk. Meddelser III, 2, København: A.F. Høst.

JÓNSSON, FINNUR, 1927. *Óláfr Þórðarson: Málhljóða- og málskrúðsrit:* *grammatisk-retorisk afhandling*, København: A. F. Høst.

JÓNSSON, FINNUR, 1930. *Island fra sagatid til nutid*, København: Gyldendal.

JOSEPH, JOHN EARL, 1987. *Eloquence and Power: The Rise of Language Standards and Standard Languages*, London: Frances Pinter.

KALINKE, MARIANNE E., 1983. 'The second language requirement in medieval Icelandic romance', *Modern Languages Review* 78, 850–61.

KARKER, ALAN, 1977. 'The disintegration of the Danish Tongue', in *Sjötíu ritgerðir helgaðar Jakobi Benediktssyni 20. júli 1977*, Reykjavík: Stofnun Árna Magnússonar, 483.

KARRAS, RUTH MAZO, 1988. *Slavery and Society in Medieval Scandinavia*, New Haven; London: Yale University Press.

KARSTEN, T. E., 1925. *Germanerna: en inledning till studiet av deras språk och kultur*, Stockholm: Bokförlaget Natur och Kultur.

KARSTEN, T. E., 1928. *Die Germanen: eine Einführung in die Geschichte ihrer Sprache und Kultur*, Berlin: Walter de Gruyter.

KARLSSON, STEFÁN, 1967. *Sagas of Icelandic Bishops. Fragments of Eight Manuscripts. Early Icelandic Manuscripts in Facsimile 7*, Copenhagen: Rosenkilde & Bagger.

KARLSSON, STEFÁN, 1970a. 'Helgafellsbók í Noregi', *Opuscula* 4, 347–49.

KARLSSON, STEFÁN, 1970b. 'Ritun Reykjarfjarðarbókar. Excursus: Bókagerð bænda'. *Opuscula* 4, 120–140. København: Bibliotheca Arnamagnæana 30. Munksgaard. [Endurprentun: Stefán Karlsson 2000: 310–29].

KARLSSON, GUNNAR, 1975. 'Frá þjóðveldi til konungsríks', in *Saga Íslands* II, Reykjavík: Hið íslenzka bókmenntafélag: 3–54.

KARLSSON, STEFÁN, 1978. 'Om norvagismer i islandske håndskrifter', *Maal og Minne*, 87–101.

KARLSSON, STEFÁN, 1982. 'Saltarabrot í Svíþjóð með stjórnarhendi', *Gripla* 5, 320–22.

KARLSSON, STEFÁN, 1989. 'Tungan', *Íslensk þjóðmenning VI*, Reykjavík: Bókaútgáfan Þjóðsaga, 3–54.

KARLSSON, STEFÁN, 1999. 'The localisation and dating of medieval Icelandic manuscripts', *Saga-Book* 25, 138–58.

KARLSSON, STEFÁN, 2000. 'Íslensk bókagerð á miðöldum', in Guðvarður Már Gunnlaugson (ed.), *Stafkrókar-ritgerðir gefnar út í tilefni af sjötugsafmæli hans 2. desember 1998*, Reykjavík: Stofnun Árna Magnússonar á Íslandi, 225–41.

KARLSSON, STEFÁN, 2004. *The Icelandic Language*. Translated by McTurk, R. University College London: Viking Society for Northern Research.

KARLSSON, GUNNAR, 2000. *Iceland's 1100 years: The History of a Marginal Society*, London: Hurst & Company.

KARLSSON, GUNNAR, 2004. *Goðamenning: Staða og áhrif goðorðsmanna í þjóðveldi Íslendinga*, Reykjavík: Heimskringla.

KELLER, CHRISTIAN, 2006. 'Kolonisering av Island og Grønland', in A. Mortensen, A. R. Nielsen & J. T. Thor (eds.), *De vestnordiske landes fælles historie II: Udvalg af foredrag holdt på VNH-konferencerne i Ísafjörður 2003, Tórshavn 2004 og Oslo 2005*, Inussuk, Arktisk forskningsjournal 2, Nuuk: Forlaget Atuagkat, 2–19.

KELLER, RUDI, 1994. *On Language Change: The Invisible Hand in Language*, London: Routledge.

KERSWILL, PAUL, 1994. *Dialects Converging: Rural Speech in Urban Norway*, Oxford: Clarendon Press.

KERSWILL, PAUL, 1995. 'Phonological convergence and dialect contact: Evidence from citation forms', *Language Variation and Change* 7, 195–207.

KERSWILL, PAUL, 1996. 'Milton Keynes and dialect levelling in south-eastern British English', in D. Graddol, J. Swann & D. Leith (eds.), *English: History, Diversity and Change*, London: Routledge, 292–300.

KERSWILL, PAUL, 2002a. 'Models of linguistic change and diffusion: New evidence from dialect levelling in British English', in *Reading Working Papers in Linguistics* 6, 187–216.

KERSWILL, PAUL, 2002b. 'Koineisation and accommodation', in Jack Chambers, Peter Trudgill & Natalie Schilling-Estes (eds.), *The Handbook of Language Variation and Change*, Oxford: Blackwell Publishers, 669–703.

KERSWILL, PAUL, 2003. 'Dialect levelling and geographical diffusion in British English', in David Britain & Jenny Cheshire (eds.), *Social Dialectology: In Honour of Peter Trudgill*, Impact, Studies in Language and Society 16, Amsterdam; Philadelphia: J. Benjamins, 223–43.

KERSWILL, PAUL & TRUDGILL, PETER, 2005. 'The birth of new dialects', in Peter Auer, Frans Hinskens & Paul Kerswill (eds.), *Dialect Change: Convergence and Divergence in European languages*, Cambridge: Cambridge University Press, 196–220.

KERSWILL, PAUL & WILLIAMS, ANN, 2000. 'Mobility and Social Class in Dialect Levelling: Evidence from New and Old Towns in England', in K. Mattheier (ed.), *Dialect and Migration in a Changing Europe*, Frankfurt am Main: Peter Lang, 1–13.

KERSWILL, PAUL & WILLIAMS, ANN, 2002. '"Salience" as an explanatory factor in language change: Evidence from dialect levelling in urban England', in Mari C. Jones & Edith Esch (eds.), *Language Change: the Interplay of Internal, External and Extra-linguistic Factors*, Berlin; New York: Mouton de Gruyter, 81–110.

KLOSS, HEINZ, 1952. *Die Entwicklung neuer germanischer Kultursprachen seit 1800 bis 1950*, München: Pohl.

KLOSS, HEINZ, 1967. 'Abstand languages and Ausbau languages', *Anthropological Linguistics* 9 (7), Harvard: Harvard Press, 29–41.

KNIRK, JAMES, E., 1993. 'Runes and runic inscriptions', in P. Pulsiano *et al* (eds.), *Medieval Scandinavia: An Encyclopedia*, New York & London: Garland Publishing, 545–52.

KNUDSEN, T., 1962. *Gammelnorsk Homiliebok: etter AM 619 qv./ med en innledning av T. Knudsen*, Oslo: Selskapet til utgivelse av gamle norske handskrifter.

KNÚTSSON, PÉTUR, 2004. *Intimations of the Third Text: An Enquiry into Intimate Translation and Tertiary Textuality*. PhD Thesis, Det Humanistiske Fakultet, Københavns Universitet.

KOCK, E. A., 1946–49. *Den norsk-isländska skaldediktningen*, Lund: C. W. K. Gleerups Förlag.

Konungs skuggsjá. 1983. Edited by L. Holm-Olsen, Oslo: Norsk Historisk Kjeldeskrift-Institutt.

KRESS, B., 1937. *Die Laute des modernen Isländischen*, Institut für Lautforschung an der Universität Berlin, Leipzig: Otto Harrassowitz.

KRISTMANNSSON, GAUTI, 2004. 'Will Icelandic language policy corner the Icelandic language?', in Ari Páll Kristinsson & Gauti Kristmannsson, *Málstefna – Language Planning*, Reykjavík: Íslensk málnefnd, 155–62.

KRISTINSSON, ARI PÁLL, 2000. 'Islandsk språkpolitikk', *Språk og litteratur i Vest-Norden*. Available at < http://www.ismal.hi.is/islpolitikk.htm >.

KRISTINSSON, ARI PÁLL, 2001. Utredning om de nordiske språkenes domener og det siste tiårs språkpolitiske initiativ – Island – for Nordisk ministerråds språkpolitiske referansegruppe, 16 November 2001 'Det islandske språkets dag'. Unpublished presentation. Available at < http://www.ismal.hi.is/utredning.html >.

KRISTIANSEN, TORE & VIKØR, LARS, S., 2006. *Nordiske språkhandlingar. Ei meiningsmåling*, Oslo: Novus Forlag.

KRISTJÁNSSON, JÓNAS, 1988. *Eddas and Sagas: Iceland's Medieval Literature*. Translated by Foote, Peter, Reykjavík: Hið íslenska bókmenntafélag.

KRISTJÁNSSON, JÓNAS, 1997. *Eddas and Sagas: Iceland's Medieval Literature*, 2nd edition, Reykajvík: Hið íslenska bókmenntafélag.

Kristni saga, edited by Sigurgeir Steingrímsson, Ólafur Halldórsson & Peter Foote. Íslenzk fornrit, vol. XV: Biskupa Sögur I, síðari hluti. 2003, Reykjavík: Hið íslenzka fornritafélag.

KUHN, HANS, 1935. 'Die sprachliche Einheit Islands', *Zeitschrift für Mundartforschung* XI, 21–39.

KUHN, HANS, 1955. 'Zur Gliederung der germanischen Sprachen', *Zeitschrift für deutsches Altertum und deutsche Literatur* 86, 1–47.

Kulturhistorisk Leksikon for Nordisk Middelalder fra Vikingetid til Reformationstid. 1956–78. I-XXII. Edited by J. Danstrup & L. R. Jacobsen, København; Stockholm; Oslo: Rosenkilde og Bagger.

KVARAN, GUÐRÚN, 2004. 'Is Icelandic language policy legitimate?', in ARI PÁLL KRISTINSSON & GAUTI KRISTMANNSSON (eds.), *Málstefna – Language Planning*, Reykjavík: Íslensk málnefnd, 163–9.

LABOV, WILLIAM, 1963. 'The social motivation of a sound change', *Word* 19, 273–309.

LABOV, WILLIAM, 1966. *The Social Stratification of English in New York City*, Washington DC: Centre for Applied Linguistics.

LABOV, WILLIAM, 1972. *Sociolinguistic Patterns*, Philadelphia: University of Philadelphia Press.

LABOV, WILLIAM, 1982. *The Social Stratification of English in New York City*, Third Edition, Washington DC: Centre for Applied Linguistics.

LABOV, WILLIAM, 1994. *Principles of Linguistic Change, Vol. 1: Internal Factors*, Language in Society 20, Oxford, UK; Cambridge, USA: Basil Blackwell.

LABOV, WILLIAM, 2001. *Principles of Linguistic Change, Vol. 2: Social Factors*. Language in Society 29, Oxford, UK; Cambridge, USA: Basil Blackwell.

LAGMAN, SVANTE, 1990. *De stungna runorna: Använding och ljudvärden i runesvenska steinnskrifter* (= Runrön 4). Uppsala: Uppsala universitet.

LAKOFF, ROBIN, 1972. 'Another look at drift', in R. P. Stockwell & R. K. S. Macaulay (eds.), *Linguistic Change and Generative Theory*, Bloomington, Indiana: Indiana University Press, 172–98.

Landnámabók, edited by Jakob Benediktsson. Íslenzk fornrit, vol. I & II. 1968. Reykjavík: Hið íslenzka fornritafélag.

LARSEN, AMUND, B. 1917. 'Naboopposition Knot', *Maal og Minne* 34, 46.

LÁRUSSON, ÓLAFUR, 1944. *Byggð og saga*, Reykjavík: Ísafoldarprentsmiðja H. F.

LÁRUSSON, ÓLAFUR, 1958. *Lög og saga*, Reykjavík: Hlaðbúð.

LÁRUSSON, ÓLAFUR, 1960. *Lov og ting: Islands forfatning og lover i fristatstiden*. Translated by K. Helle, Bergen-Oslo: Universitetsforlaget.

LASS, ROGER, 1980. *On Explaining Language Change*, Cambridge: Cambridge University Press.

LASS, ROGER, 1997. *Historical Linguistics and Language Change*, Cambridge: Cambridge University Press.

LAUR, W., 1983. 'Zur Schwedenherrschaft in Haithabu und neuere Überlegungen zur Frühgeschichte des Schleswiger Raumes', in *Beiträge zur Schleswiger Stadtgeschichte* 28, 9–25.

Laxdæla saga, edited by Einar Ól. Sveinsson. Íslenzk fornrit, vol. V. 1934, Reykjavík: Hið íslenzka fornritafélag.

LEACH, EDMUND, 1982. *Social Anthropology*, Oxford: Oxford University Press.

LEEUW VAN WEENEN, ANDREA, 1993. *The Icelandic Homily Book, Perg. 15 4 in the Royal Library, Stockholm*, Reykjavík: Stofnun Árna Magnússonar á Íslandi.

LEFEBVRE, HENRI, 1991. *The Production of Space*, Translated by D. Nicholson-Smith, Oxford: Blackwell Publishers.

LEHMANN, WINFRED PHILIP, 1986. *A Gothic Etymological Dictionary*, Leiden: E. J. Brill.

LEITH, DICK, 1983. *Social History of English*, London: Routledge.

LENKER, U. 2000. 'The monasteries of the Benedictine reform and the "Winchester School": Model cases of social networks in Anglo-Saxon England?' *European Journal of English Studies* 413, 225–38.

LE PAGE, ROBERT B., 1980. 'Projection, focusing, diffusion or steps towards a sociolinguistic theory of language, illustrated from the sociolinguistic survey of multilingual communities, stages I: Cayo District, Belize (formerly British Honduras), and II: St Lucia', *York Papers in Linguistics* 9, 9–32.

LE PAGE, ROBERT B. & TABOURET-KELLER, ANDREE, 1985. *Acts of Identity: Creole-based Approaches to Language and Ethnicity*, Cambridge: Cambridge University Press.

LEVINSON, STEPHEN C., 1983. *Pragmatics*, Cambridge: Cambridge University Press.

LIPSKI, JOHN M., 1994. *Latin American Spanish*, London: Longman.

Ljósvetninga saga, edited by Björn Sigfússon. Íslenzk fornrit, vol. X. 1940, Reykjavík: Hið íslenzka fornritafélag.

LOCKWOOD, W. B., 1955/77. *An Introduction to Modern Faroese*, Tórshavn: Føroya Skúlabókagrunnur.

LOMNITZ, LARISSA, 1977. *Networks and Marginality*, New York: Academic Press.

LÖNNROTH, LARS, 1964. 'Tesen om de två kulturerna. Kritiska studier i den isländska sagaskrivningens sociala förutsättningar', *Scripta Islandica* 15, 1–97.

LUND, NIELS, (ed.) 1994. *Fra vikingeriger til stater. Træk af Skandinaviens politiske udvikling 700–1200*, København: Museum Tusculanum Press, 9–26.

LYONS, JOHN, 1977. *Semantics*, Vols. 1 & 2, Cambridge: Cambridge University Press.

MAGERØY, HALLVARD, 1965. *Norsk-islandske problem*, Gjøvik: Universitetsforlaget.

MAGERØY, HALLVARD, 1993a. 'Soga om austmenn. Nordmenn som siglde til Island og Grønland i mellomalderen', in *Det Norske Videnskaps-Akademi II. Hist-Filos. Klasse. Skrifter. Ny Serie. No. 19*, Oslo: Det Norske Samlaget, 33–57.

MAGERØY, HALLVARD, 1993b. 'Diplomatics', in P. Pulsiano *et al.* (eds.), *Medieval Scandinavia: An Encyclopedia*, New York; London: Garland Publishing, 137–8.

MÁR LÁRUSSON, MAGNÚS, 1959. 'Um hina ermsku biskupa', *Skírnir* 133, 81–94.

MAKAEV, E. A., 1996 [1965]. *The Language of the Oldest Runic Inscriptions: A Linguistic and Historical Philological Analysis*, Translated from Russian by J. Meredig in Consultation with E. H. Antonsen, Stockholm: Kungl. Vitterhets Historie och Antikvitets Akademien.

MARSTRANDER, CARL J. S., 1915. *Bidrag til det norske sprogs historie i Irland*. Videnskapsælskapets Skrifter II. Hist-Filos. Klasse No.5, Kristiania: Jakob Dybwad.

MARSTRANDER, CARL, J. S., 1932. 'Okklusiver og substrater', *Norsk Tidsskrift for Sprogvidenskab* 5, 258–314.

MASSEY, DOREEN, 1994. *Space, Place and Gender*, Cambridge: Polity Press.

MATRAS, CHRISTIAN, 1965. 'Írsk orð í føroyskum', *Almanakki 1966*, København, 22–32.

MAURER, KONRAD, 1867. *Über die Ausdrücke: altnordische, altnorwegische & isländische Sprache*, München: Verlag der K. Akademie, in Commission bei G. Franz, 48–49.

MAURER, KONRAD, 1874. *Island von seiner ersten Entdeckung bis zum Untergange des Freistaats*, München: C. Kaiser.

MAURER, KONRAD, 1877. *Die Berechnung der Verwandtschaft nach altnorwegischem Rechte*, München: Sitzungsberichte der philosophisch-philologischen und historischen Classe der k. b. Akademie der Wissenschaften zu München.

MAURER, KONRAD, 1878. *Die Freigelassenen nach altnorwegischem Rechte*, München: Die königliche bayerische Akademie der Wissenschaften.

MAURER, KONRAD, 1906–10. *Vorlesungen über altnordische Rechtsgeschichte*, Leipzig: Biblio-Verlag.

McDOUGALL, D., 1993. 'Homilies (West Norse)', in P. Pulsiano *et al.* (eds.), *Medieval Scandinavia: An Encyclopedia*, New York; London: Garland Publishing, 290–2.

McMAHON, APRIL M. S., 1994. *Understanding Language Change*, Cambridge: Cambridge University Press.

MEAD, GEORGE HERBERT, 1934. *Mind, Self and Society from the Standpoint of a Behaviourist*, Chicago: University of Chicago Press.

MELBERG, HÅKON, 1951. *Origin of the Scandinavian Nations and Languages*, 2 parts, Halden, Norway: H. Aschehoug & Co; Ejnar Munksgaard.

MELSTEÐ, BOGI TH., 1903. *Íslendinga saga*, København: Hinu íslenska bókménntafjélagið.

MELSTEÐ, BOGI TH., 1914. 'Töldu Íslendingar sig á dögum þjóðveldsins vera Norðmenn?', in *Afmælisrit til Dr. Phil. Kr. Kaalunds bókavarðar við safn Árna Magnússonar 9 águst 1914*, Copenhagen: Möller, 16–33.

MELSTEÐ, BOGI TH., 1916. *Handbók í Íslendinga sögu* I, Kaupmannahöfn: S. L. Møller.

MERRILL, R. T., 1964. 'Notes on Icelandic kinship terminology', *American Anthropologist*, New Series 66, No. 4, Part I, 867–872.

MESTHRIE, RAJEND, 1992. *Language in Indenture: A Sociolinguistic History of Bhojpuri-Hindi in South Africa*, London: Routledge.

MEULENGRACHT SØRENSEN, PREBEN, 1993. *Saga and Society*, Translated by J. Tucker, Odense: Odense University Press. [Revised, English version of *Saga og samfund*, Copenhagen: Berlingske Forlag, 1977].

MEULENGRACHT SØRENSEN, PREBEN, 2000. 'Social institutions and belief systems', in Margaret Clunies Ross (ed.), *Old Icelandic Literature and*

Society, Cambridge Studies in Medieval Literature 42, Cambridge: Cambridge University Press, 8–29.

MILROY, JAMES, 1992. *Linguistic Variation and Change: On the Historical Sociolinguistics of English*, Language in Society 19, Oxford, UK & Cambridge, MA: Basil Blackwell.

MILROY, JAMES, 1993. 'On the social origins of language change', in Charles Jones (ed.), *Historical Linguistics: Problems and Perspectives*, London: Longman, 213–36.

MILROY, JAMES & MILROY, LESLEY, 1985. 'Linguistic change, social network and speaker innovation', *Journal of Linguistics* 21, 339–84.

MILROY, LESLEY, 1980. *Language and Social Networks*, Language in Society 2, Oxford: Basil Blackwell.

MILROY, LESLEY, 1999. Mobility and emergence of levelled dialects. Presented at *Workshop on Social History and Sociolinguistics*, Centre for Metropolitan History, University of London.

MILROY, LESLEY, 2002. 'Social networks', in Jack K. Chambers *et al.* (eds.), *The Handbook of Language Variation and Change*, Malden, MA.: Blackwell, 549–72.

MILROY, LESLEY, 2003. 'Social and linguistic dimensions of phonological change', in David Britain & Jenny Cheshire (ed.), *Social Dialectology: In Honour of Peter Trudgill*, Impact, Studies in Language and Society 16, Amsterdam; Philadelphia: J. Benjamins, 155–72.

MOAG, RODNEY, 1977. *Fiji Hindi*, Canberra: Australia National University Press.

MOLTKE, ERIK, 1985. *Runes and their Origin: Denmark and Elsewhere*, Copenhagen: National Museum of Denmark.

MONTGOMERY, MICHAEL, 2000. 'Isolation as a linguistic construct', *Southern Journal of Linguistics* 24, 41–53.

Monumenta Germaniae historica. Scriptores perum Langobardicarum et Italicarum saec. 1841. Vol. IV. Hannoverae.

MORTENSEN, ANDRAS & ARGE, SÍMUN, 2005. *Viking and Norse in the North Atlantic: Select Papers from the Proceedings of the Fourteenth Viking Congress*, Tórshavn 19–30 July, 2001, Tórshavn: Føroya Fróðskaparfelag.

MUFWENE, SALIKOKO S., 2001. *The Ecology of Language Evolution*, Cambridge: Cambridge University Press.

MUNCH, P. A., 1852. *Det norske folks historie* 1: 1, Christiania: Tonsbergs Forlag.

MÜHLHÄUSLER, PETER, 1977. *Pidginisation and Simplification of Language*, Canberra: Pacific Linguistics.

MÜHLHÄUSLER, PETER & HARRÉ, ROM, 1990. *Pronouns and People: The Linguistic Construction of Social and Personal Identity*, (Language in Society), Oxford: Blackwell.

MYERS-SCOTTON, CAROL, 1980. 'Bilingualism, multilingualism, code-switching: Introduction', in Howard Giles et al. (ed.), *Language: Social Psychological Perspectives*, Oxford: Pergamon Press, 327–28.

MYHRE, BJØRN, 2003. 'The Iron Age', in Knut Helle (ed.), *The Cambridge History of Scandinavia, Volume 1, Prehistory to 1520*, Cambridge: Cambridge University Press, 60–93.

MÆHLUM, BRIT, 1992. 'Dialect socialization in Longyearbyen, Svalbard (Spitsbergen): A fruitful chaos', in Ernst Jahr Håkon (ed.), *Language Contact: Theoretical and Empirical Studies*, Berlin: Mouton de Gruyter, 117–30.

MÆHLUM, BRIT, 1993. 'Hva er "Identitet"?' Rapport fra et tverrfaglig seminar ved Institutt for språk og litteratur, Universitetet i Tromsø, 7–8. mai 1992. B. Mæhlum (red.). ISL & Norges forskningsråd, Tromsø.

MÆHLUM, BRIT, 1994. 'Tradering eller Utradering? Østnorske Innflyttermål i Nord-Norge', in U.-B. Kotsinas & J. Helgander (eds.), *Dialektkontakt, språkkontakt och språkforändring i Norden: föredrag från ett forskarsymposium*, Stockholm: Meddelanden från Institutionen för nordiska språk vid Stockholms universitet, 232–41.

MÆHLUM, BRIT, 1997. *Dølamål: dialektene i Bardu og Målselv*, Målselv: Målselv Mållag.

MÆHLUM, BRIT, 1999. *Mellom Skylla og Kharybdis: forklaringsbegrepet i historisk språkvitenskap*, Oslo: Novus forlag.

MÆHLUM, BRIT, 2002. 'Hvor går vi – og hvorfor? Et forsøk på å trekke noen store linjer i utviklingen av norsk talemål', *Målbryting* 6, 67–93.

MÆHLUM, BRIT, 2003. 'Normer', in Brit Mæhlum et al. (eds.), *Språkmøte: innføring i sosiolingvistikk*, Oslo: Cappelen Akademisk Forlag, 86–102.

MÆHLUM, BRIT, SLETTAN, DAGFINN, & STUGU, OLA, (eds.) 1999. *Stedet som kulturell konstruksjon*, Skriftserie fra Historisk institutt nr. 27, Trondheim: Historisk institutt, NTNU.

NÄSMAN, ULF, & LUND, JØRGEN, (eds.) 1988. *Folkevandringstiden i Norden: en krisetid mellom ældre og yngre jernalder*, Århus: Århus Universitetsforlag.

NEVALAINEN, TERTTU & RAUMOLIN-BRUNBERG, HELENA, 1996. *Sociolinguistics and Language History: Studies based on the Corpus of Early English Correspondance*, Amsterdam: Rodopi.

NICHOLS, JOHANNA, 1992. *Linguistic Diversity in Space and Time*, Chicago: The University of Chicago Press.

NIELSEN, HANS FREDE, 2000. *The Early Runic Language of Scandinavia*, Heidelberg: C. Winter.

NIELSEN, K. M., 1984. 'Svenskevældet og Haddeby-stenene', *Danske Studier*, København: Schubotheske forlag, 17–25.

NORDAL, GUÐRÚN, 2001. *Tools of Literacy: The Role of Skaldic Verse in Icelandic Textual Culture of the Twelfth and Thirteenth Centuries*, Toronto; Buffalo; London: University of Toronto Press.

NORDAL, SIGURÐUR, 1942. *Íslenzk menning 1 (Arfur Íslendinga)*, Reykjavík: Mál og menning.

NORDAL, SIGURÐUR, 1990. *Icelandic Culture*. Translated by Vilhjálmur T. Bjarnur, Ithaca: Cornell University Library.

NORDENSTAM, KERSTIN, 1979. *Svenskan i Norge*, Gothenburg: Gothenburg University Press.

NOREEN, ADOLF, 1903. *Altisländische und altnorwegische Grammatik: unter Berücksichtigung des Urnordischen*, Halle: Niemeyer.

NOREEN, ADOLF, 1904. *Altnordische Grammatik 1. Altschwedische Grammatik mit Einschluss des Altgutnischen*, Sammlung kurzer Grammatiken germanischer Dialekte 8, Halle: Niemeyer.

NOREEN, ADOLF, 1923. *Altnordische Grammatik 2. Altisländische und altnorwegische Grammatik (Laut und Flexionslehre) unter Berücksichtigung des Urnordischen* (4th edition), Sammlung kurzer Grammatiken germanischer Dialekte 4, Halle: Niemeyer.

Norges gamle love indtil 1387. 1846–95. Edited by Keyser, R. & Munch, P. A. *et al.* 5 Vols. Christiania: Trykt hos C. Gröndahl.

NYGAARD, MARIUS, 1906. *Norrøn syntax*, Oslo: Aschehoug.

ÓLADÓTTIR, HANNA, 2005. Pizza eða flatbaka? Unpublished M.A. thesis submitted to the University of Iceland in June 2005.

ÓLAFSSON, EGGERT & PÁLSSON, BJARNI, 1943. *Ferðabók*, 2 Vols, Reykjavík: Ísafoldarprentsmiðja (Originally published in Danish in 1772).

ÓLAFUR HANSSON, GUNNAR, 1997. Aldur og útbreiðsla aðblásturs í tungumálum Norðvestur-Evrópu [The age and distribution of preaspiration in the languages of Northwestern Europe]. Unpublished M.A. Thesis, University of Iceland.

ÓLAFUR HANSSON, GUNNAR, 2001. 'Remains of a submerged continent: Preaspiration in the languages of northwest Europe', *Historical Linguistics 1999: Selected Papers from the 14th International Conference on Historical Linguistics, Vancouver, 9–13 August 1999*, Amsterdam: Benjamins, 151–73.

ÓLASON, VÉSTEINN, 1992. *Íslensk bókmenntasaga*, Vol. 1, Reykjavík: Mál og menning.

ÓLASON, VÉSTEINN, 1998. *Dialogues with the Viking Age: Narration and Representation in the Sagas of the Icelanders*. Translated by A. Wawn, Reykjavík: Heimskringla, Mál og menning Academic Division.

ÓLASON, VÉSTEINN & TÓMASSON, SVERRIR, 2006, in D. Neijmann (ed.), *A History of Icelandic Literature*, Lincoln; London: University of Nebraska Press, 1–64.

OLRIK, J. & RÆDER, H., 1931. *Saxonis Gesta Danorum*, København: Hauniae: Levin & Munksgaard.

OLSEN, MAGNUS, 1941–80. *Norges innskrifter med de yngre runer I-V*, Oslo: Norsk historisk kjeldeskrift-institutt, i kommisjon hos J. Dybwad A/S Bokcentralen.

ÓLSEN, BJÖRN M., 1884. *Den tredje og fjærde grammatiske afhandling i Snorres Edda: tilligemed de grammatiske afhandlingers prolog og to andre tillæg/udgivne for samfundet til udgivelse af gammel nordisk literatur af Björn Magnússon Ólsen*, København: Fr. G. Knudtzon.

OLSON, EMIL, 1912. *Yngvars saga víðförla*, København: S. L. Møllers Bogtrykkeri.

OMDAL, HELGE, 1977. 'Høyangermålet – en ny dialekt', *Språklig Samling* 1, 7–9.

ONIONS, CHARLES TALBUT, 1966. *Oxford Dictionary of English Etymology*, Oxford: Clarendon Press.

O'RAHILLY, THOMAS F., 1988. *Irish Dialects Past and Present: With Chapters on Scottish and Manx*, Dublin: Dublin Institute for Advanced Studies.

Orkneyinga saga, edited by Finnbogi Guðmundsson. Íslenzk fornrit, vol. XXXIV. 1965, Reykjavík: Hið íslenzka fornritafélag.

OTTÓSSON, KJARTAN G., 1987. 'An archaising aspect of Icelandic purism: The revival of extinct morphological patterns', in Lilius, P. & Saari, M. (eds.), *The Nordic Languages and Modern Linguistics* 6, Helsinki: Helsinki University Press, 311–24.

OTTÓSSON, KJARTAN G., 1990. *Íslensk málhreinsun*, Reykjavík: Íslensk málnefnd.

OTTÓSSON, KJARTAN G., 2002. 'Old Nordic: A definition and delimitation of the period' in Oscar Bandle *et al.* (eds.), *The Nordic Languages: An International Handbook of the History of the North Germanic Languages*, Vol. 1, Berlin; New York: Walter de Gruyter, 787–93.

OTTÓSSON, KJARTAN G., 2003. 'Heimenorsk innverknad på islandsk språk i mellomalderen, særleg i morfologien', in Kristján Árnason (ed.), *Útnorður: West Nordic Standardisation and Variation*, Reykjavík: University of Iceland Press, 111–52.

OSGOOD, CHARLES E. & SEBEOK, THOMAS A., (eds.) 1954. *Psycholinguistics*, Baltimore. (= Supplement to *IJAL* 20: 4.).

Óláfs saga Tryggvasonar en mesta. 1958–2000. Edited by Ólafur Halldórsson, Copenhagen: Ejnar Munksgaard.

ÓLAFSSON, ÓLAFUR M. & HALLDÓRSSON, ÓSKAR Ó., 1964. 'Um íslenzkan framburð: Mállýzkur II', *Studia Islandica* 23, 118–33.

PÁLSSON, ÁRNI, 1924. 'Íslendingar og Norðmenn', *Skírnir,* Reykjavík: Ísafoldaprentsmiðja, 199–204.

PÁLSSON, GÍSLI, 1979. 'Vont mál og vond málfræði', *Skírnir* 153, 175–201.

PÁLSSON, GÍSLI, 1989. 'The ethnolinguistics of Icelanders', in Paul E. Durrenberger, & Gísli Pálsson (eds.), *The Anthropology of Iceland*, Iowa City: University of Iowa Press.

PÁLSSON, GÍSLI, 1992. 'Text, life, saga', in Gísli Pálsson (ed.), *From Sagas to Society: Comparative Approaches to Early Iceland*, Enfield Lock: Hisarlik, 1–25.

PÁLSSON, GÍSLI, 1995. *The Textual Life of Savants: Ethnography, Iceland and the Linguistic Turn*, Studies in Anthropology and History Vol. 18, Chur: Harwood Academic Publishers.

PÁLSSON, GÍSLI & DURRENBERGER, PAUL E., 1992. 'Icelandic dialogues: Individual differences in indigenous discourse', *Journal of Anthropological Research* 48, No.4 (Winter), 301–16.

PÁLSSON, HERMANN, 1996. *Keltar á Íslandi*, Reykjavík: Háskólaútgáfan.

PÁLSSON HERMANN & EDWARDS, PAUL G., 1972. *The Book of Settlements: Landnámabók*, Winnipeg: University of Manitoba.

PAPAZIAN, ERIC, 1997. 'Dialektdød i Numedal? Om språkutviklinga i Nore og Uvdal', *Maal og Minne*, 161–190.

PAUL, HERMANN, 1880. *Prinzipien der Sprachgeschichte*, Halle: Niemeyer.

PAUL, HERMANN, 1937. *Prinzipien der Sprachgeschichte*. 2nd edition, Halle: M. Niemeyer.

PEDERSEN, INGE LISE, 1994. 'Linguistic variation and composite life modes', in Nordberg, B. (ed.), *The Sociolinguistics of Urbanization: The Case of the Nordic Countries*, Berlin; New York: Walter de Gruyter, 87–115.

PEDERSEN, INGE LISE, 2001. 'Talesprog som identitetsskaber og identitetsud-tryk'. *Nordlit* 10, Det humanistiske fakultet, Universitet i Tromsø, 41–55.

PENNY, RALPH, 1987. *Patterns of Language-Change in Spain*, London: University of London, Westfield College.

PETERSON, LENA, 1992. 'Hogastenen på Orust', *Blandade runstudier 1* (= *Runrön 6*). Uppsala: Uppsala Universitet, 81–111.

PHELPSTEAD, CARL, (ed.) 2001. *A History of Norway and the Passion and Miracles of the Blessed Óláfr*, translated by D. Kunin, Text Series 13, London: Viking Society for Northern Research.

PHILLPOTTS, BERTHA SURTEE, 1913. *Kindred and Clan in the Middle Ages and After: A Study in the Sociology of the Teutonic Races*, Cambridge: Cambridge University Press.

PINSON, ANN, 1979. 'Kinship and economy in modern Iceland: A study in social continuity', *Ethnology* 18, 183–197.

PINSON, ANN, 1985. 'The Institution of friendship and drinking patterns in Iceland', *Anthropological Quarterly*, 75–82.

POIRIER, C., 1994. 'La langue parlée en Nouvelle-France: vers une convergence des explications', in R. Mougeon & É. Beniak (eds.), *Les origins du français québecois*, Sainte-Foy: Laval University Press, 237–74.

PRESTON, DENNIS R., 1991. 'Sorting out the variables in sociolinguistic theory', *American Speech* 66, 33–56.

PULGRAM, ERNST, 1958. *The Tongues of Italy*, Cambridge, Mass.: Harvard University Press.

PULSIANO, P. *et al*, 1993. *Medieval Scandinavia: An Encyclopedia*, New York; London: Garland.

RAFNSSON, SVEINBJÖRN, 1974. *Studier i Landnámabók*. *Kritiska bidrag till den isländska fristatstidens historia*, Lund: (Bibliotheca Historica Lundensis 31).

RAFNSSON, SVEINBJÖRN, 1979. 'Um kristnitökufrásögn Ara prests Þorgilssonar', *Skírnir*, 153, 167–74.

RASCHELLÀ, F. D., (ED.) 1982. *The so-called Second Grammatical Treatise, Edition, Translation and Commentary*. (Filologia Germania Testi e Studi II), Florence: Felice le Mannier.

Reykdæla saga ok Víga-Skútu, edited by Björn Sigfússon. Íslenzk fornrit, vol. X. 1940, Reykjavík: Hið íslenzka fornritafélag.

RICH, GEORGE W., 1976. 'Changing Icelandic kinship', *Ethnology* 15, 1–20.

RICH, GEORGE W., 1980. 'Kinship and friendship in Iceland', *Ethnology* 19, 475–49.

RÖGNVALDSSON, EIRÍKUR, 1983. 'Þágufallssýkin og fallakerfi íslensku', *Skíma* 16, 3–6.

RÖGNVALDSSON, EIRÍKUR, 1988. 'Islandsk sprogpolitik', *Sprog i Norden*, 56–63.

RÖGNVALDSSON, EIRÍKUR, 2005. *Íslensk tunga III. Setningar*. Handbók um setningafræði. Aðalhöfundur og ritstjóri Höskuldur Þráinsson, meðhöfundar: Eiríkur Rögnvaldsson, Jóhannes Gísli Jónsson, Sigríður Magnúsdóttir, Sigríður Sigurjónsdóttir og Þórunn Blöndal. Almenna, Reykjavík: bókafélagið.

ROMAINE, SUZANNE, 1982. *Socio-historical Linguistics: Its Status and Methodology*, Cambridge: Cambridge University Press.

ROMAINE, SUZANNE, 2005. 'Historical sociolinguistics', in U. Ammon *et al* (eds.), *Sociolinguistics: An International Handbook of the Science of Language and Society*. Second completely revised and extended edition. Vol. 2, 1696–1703.

ROMAINE, SUZANNE & TRAUGOTT, ELIZABETH L., 1985. Papers from the Workshop on Socio-historical Linguistics. Folio Linguistica 6.

ROSS, A. S. C., 1981. *The Terfinnas and Beormas of Ohthere*, London: Viking Society for Northern Research.

ROSS, MALCOLM, 1997. 'Social networks and kinds of speech-community event', in R. Blench & M. Spriggs, *Archaeology and Language 1: Theoretical and Methodological Orientations*, London; New York: Routledge, 209–61.

RØYNELAND, UNN, 2005. *Dialektnivellering, ungdom og identitet: Ein komparativ studie av språkleg variasjon og endring i to tilgrensande dialektområde, Røros og Tynset*. Dr. art. avhandling. Institutt for nordistikk og litteraturvitskap, Det historisk-filosofiske fakultet, Universitetet i Oslo.

Saga Óláfs Tryggvasonar af Oddr Snorrason munk, edited by Finnur Jónsson. 1932, Copenhagen: Gad.

SAMUELS, MICHAEL L., 1972. *Linguistic Evolution with Special Reference to English*, Cambridge Studies in Linguistics, 6, Cambridge: Cambridge University Press.

SANDØY, HELGE, 1985. *Norsk dialektkunnskap*, Oslo: Novus.

SANDØY, HELGE, 1994. 'Utan kontakt og endring?', in *Dialektkontakt, språkkontakt och språkforändring i Norden: föredrag från ett forskarsymposium*, (edited by U.-B. Kotsinas & J. Helgander), Stockholm: Meddelanden från Institutionen för nordiska språk vid Stockholms universitet, 38–52.

SANDØY, HELGE, 2001. 'Færøysk i vestnordisk språkhistorie' in K. Braunmüller & J. Lon Jacobsen (eds.), *Moderne lingvistiske teorier og færøysk*, Oslo: Novus Forlag, 125–54.

SANDØY, HELGE, 2003. 'Types of society and language change in the Nordic countries', in B-L. Gunnarson (ed.), *Language Variation in Europe*, Uppsala: Uppsala University, Dept. of Scandinavian Languages, 53–76.

SANDØY, HELGE, 2005. 'Sociolinguistic structures chronologically IV: Icelandic and Faeroese', in Oscar Bandle *et al.* (eds.), *The Nordic Languages: An International Handbook of the History of the North Germanic Languages*. Vol. 2, 1923–32.

SANDVE, BJØRN HARALD, 1976. Om talemålet i industristadene Odda og Tyssedal. Generasjonsskilnad og tilnærming mellom dei to målføra. Hovudoppgave i norsk, Universitetet i Bergen.

SANKOFF, GILLIAN, 1980. *The Social Life of Language*, Philadelphia: University of Pennsylvania Press.

SANTINI, C., 1993. 'Historia Norwegiæ', in P. Pulsiano *et al.* (eds.), *Medieval Scandinavia: An Encyclopedia*, New York; London: Garland Publishing, 284–5.

SAPIR, EDWARD, 1921. *Language: An Introduction to the Study of Speech*, New York: Harcourt, Brace and Company.

SAPIR, YAIR, 2003. 'Linguistic purism in the shadow of satellites: The cases of post-standardisation Finnish, Hebrew and Icelandic', in Kristján Árnason (ed.), *Útnorður: West Nordic Standardisation and Variation*, 33–46.

SAPIR, YAIR & ZUCKERMANN, GHIL'AD, in press. 'Phono-semantic matching in Icelandic', in J. Rosenhouse & R. Kowner (eds.), *Globally speaking: English vocabulary in World languages. Multilingual Matters*, Available at < http://www.zuckerman.org >.

DE SAUSSURE, FERDINAND, [1915] 1998. *Course in General Linguistics*, C. Bally & A. Sechehaye (eds.), Translated by R. Harris, La Salle, Illinois: Open Court.

SAWYER, PETER, H., 1982. *Kings and Vikings: Scandinavia and Europe, A.D. 700–1100*, London: Methuen.

SAWYER, PETER, H., 1997. 'The age of the Vikings and before', in *The Oxford Illustrated History of the Vikings*, Oxford: 1–18.

SAWYER, PETER, H., 2003. 'The Viking expansion', in Knut Helle (ed.), *The Cambridge History of Scandinavia, Volume 1. Prehistory to 1520*, Cambridge: Cambridge University Press.

SAYERS, WILLIAM, 1994. 'Management of the Celtic fact in *Landnámabók*', *Scandinavian Studies* 66, 129–153.

SCHIER, KURT, 1975. 'The rise of literature in "Terra Nova": Some comparative reflections', *Gripla* 1, 168–81.

SCHIFFMAN, HAROLD F., 1996. *Linguistic Culture and Language Policy*, London; New York: Routledge.

SCHILLING-ESTES, NATALIE, 2002. 'On the nature of isolated and post-isolated dialects: Innovation, variation and differentiation', *Journal of Sociolinguistics* 6/1, 64–85.

SCHIRMUNSKI, VIKTOR, 1930. 'Sprachgeschichte und Siedlungsmundarten', *Germanisch-Romanische Monatsschrift* 18, 113–22 (Part I); 171–88 (Part II).

SCHMEIDLER, BERNHARD (ed.), 1917. Adam of Bremen, *Gesta Hammaburgensis Ecclesiæ Pontificum. Adam von Bremen, Hamburgische Kirchengeschichte.* 3rd ed., Hannover & Leipzig: Hahnsche Buchhandlung.

SCHREIER, DANIEL, 2001. *Non-Standard Grammar and Geographical Isolation: The Genesis, Development and Structure of Tristan da Cunha English*, PhD dissertation, University of Fribourg, Switzerland.

SCHREIER, DANIEL, 2003. *Isolation and Language Change: Contemporary and Sociohistorical Evidence from Tristan da Cunha English*, New York: Palgrave Macmillan.

SCHULTE, MICHAEL. 2002. 'The phonological systems of Old Nordic 1: Old Icelandic and Old Norwegian' in Oscar Bandle *et al.* (eds.), *The Nordic Languages: An International Handbook of the History of the North Germanic Languages*, Volume 1. Berlin: de Gruyter, 882–96.

SEBBA, MARK, 1997. *Contact Languages: Pidgins and Creoles*, Basingstoke: Macmillan.

SEIP, DIDRIK ARUP, 1955. *Norsk språkhistorie til omkring 1370*, Oslo: Aschehoug.

SEIP, DIDRIK ARUP, 1971. *Norwegische Sprachgeschichte, bearbeitet und erweitert von Laurits Saltveit*, Berlin; New York: Walter de Gruyter.

SIEGEL, JEFF, 1985. 'Koines and koineization', *Language in Society* 14, 357–78.

SIEGEL, JEFF, 1987. *Language Contact in a Plantation Environment*, Cambridge: Cambridge University Press.

SIEGEL, JEFF, 1993. 'Dialect contact and koineization', *International Journal of the Sociology of Language* 99, Berlin; New York: Mouton de Gruyter, 105–21.

SIGURJÓNSDÓTTIR, SIGRÍÐUR, & MALING, JOAN, 2001. 'Ný setningafræðileg breyting? Um hina svokölluðu nýju þolmynd í íslensku', *Íslenskt mál* 23, 123–80.

SIMPSON, SAM, 1996. Dialect Contact in Telford New Town, unpublished BA Project. University of Essex.

Skarðsárbók: Landnámabók Björns Jónssonar á Skarðsá. 1958. Edited by Jakob Benediktsson, Reykjavík: Háskóli Íslands.

Skautrup, Peter, 1944. *Det danske sprogs historie* 1, Københaven: Gyldendal.

Skúli Kjartansson, Helgi, 1979. 'Eignarfallsflótti: Uppástunga um nýja málvillu', *Íslenskt mál* 1, 88–95.

Smith, Henry, 1996. *Restrictiveness in Case Theory*, Cambridge: Cambridge University Press.

Solheim, Randi, 2006. *Språket i smeltegryta: sosiolingvistiske utviklingsliner i industrisamfunnet Høyanger*. NTNU: Det skapende universitetet.

Solvason, Birgir T. R., 1993. 'Institutional evolution in the Commonwealth Period', *Constitutional Political Economy*, Vol. 4, Number 1, December 1993, 97–125.

Sveinsson, Sölvi, 1991. *Íslensk málsaga*, Reykjavík: Iðunn.

Spurkland, Terje, 2005. *Norwegian Runes and Runic Inscriptions*, Rochester: Boydell Press.

Spurkland, Terje, 2006a. 'From Tune to Eggja – the ontology of language change', in Gillian Fellows-Jensen, Marie Stoklund, Michael Lerche Nielsen & Bente Holmberg (eds.), *Runes and their Secrets: Studies in Runology*, Copenhagen: Museum Tusculanum Press, 333–45.

Spurkland, Terje, 2006b. 'Literacy and the Viking Age runes', in Steinsland, G. (ed.), *Transformasjoner i vikingtid og norrøn middelalder*, Oslo: Unipub forlag.

Steenstrup, Johannes C. H. R., 1878 (reprint 1972). *Normannerne*. Vol. II, Kjobenhavn: R. Klein.

Stefánsson, Magnús, 1993. 'Iceland: Economy', in P. Pulsiano *et al.* (eds.), *Medieval Scandinavia: An Encyclopedia,* New York; London: Garland Publishing, 312–13.

Stefánsson, Magnús, 2003. 'The Norse island communities of the western ocean', in Knut Helle (ed.), *The Cambridge History of Scandinavia, Vol. 1 Prehistory to 1520*, Cambridge: Cambridge University Press, 202–20.

Steffensen, Jón, 1966–69. 'Aspects of life in Iceland in the heathen period', *Saga-Book* 17, 177–205.

Steffensen, Jón, 1975. *Menning og meinsemdir: ritgerðarsafn um mótunarsögu íslenskrar þjóðar og baráttu hennar við hungur og sóttir*, Reykjavík: Ísafoldarprentsmiðja.

Stoklund, Marie, 1996. 'The Ribe cranium inscription and the Scandinavian transition to the younger reduced Futhark', in T. Looijenga & A. Quak (eds.), *Frisian Runes and Neighbouring Traditions*, (Amsterdamer Beiträge zur älteren Germanistik 46). Amsterdam: Rodopi, 199–209.

Storm, Gustav, 1880. *Monumenta historica Norvegiæ: latinske kildeskrifter til Norges historie i middelalderen*, Kristiania: A. W. Brogger.

Sturlunga saga. 1946. Edited by Jón Jóhannesson, Magnús Finnbogason & Kristján Eldjárn. Vol. 1, Reykjavík: H. F. Leiftur Prentaði.

SUDBURY, ANDREA, 2000. Dialect contact and koineisation in the Falkland Islands: development of a southern hemisphere variety, unpublished PhD thesis, University of Essex.

SUDBURY, ANDREA, 2001. 'Falkland Islands English: A southern hemisphere variety?', *English World-Wide* 22, 1, 55–80.

SUTTON, PETER, 2008. Mobility, sedentism, identity and mechanisms of language shift in aboriginal Australia. Seminar Paper, Department of Linguistics, SOAS, University of London, 9 December 2008.

Svarfdæla saga, edited by Jónas Kristjánsson. Íslenzk fornrit, vol. IX. 1956, Reykjavík: Hið íslenzka fornritafélag.

SVARSDÓTTIR, ÁSTA, 1982. 'Þágufallssýki: breytingar á fallnotkun í frumlags-sæti ópersónulegra setninga', *Íslenskt mál* 4, 19–62.

SVENONIUS, PETER, 2006. Icelandic Particles in *-an*. *CASTL*, University of Tromsø.

SIGURÐSSON, GÍSLI 1988. *Gaelic Influence in Iceland: Historical and Literary Contacts: A Survey of Research*, Reykjavík: Bókaútgáfa Menningarsjóðs.

Sverris saga, edited by Þorleifur Hauksson. Íslenzk fornrit, vol. XXX. 2007, Reykjavík: Hið íslenzka fornritafélag.

SWANTON, M. J., 1996. *The Anglo-Saxon Chronicle*, London: J. M. Dent.

SYKES, BRYAN, 2006. *Blood of the Isles: Exploring the Genetic Roots of our Tribal History*, London: Bantam.

SYRETT, MARTIN, 1994. *The Unaccented Vowels of Proto-Norse*, Odense: Odense University Press.

TABOURET-KELLER, ANDREE, 1989. 'Language contact in focused situations', in Leiv Egil Breivik & Ernst Håkon From Linguistic Patriotism to Cultural Nationalism: Language and Identity in Iceland Jahr (eds.), *Language Change: Contributions to the Study of its Causes*, Trends in Linguistics Studies and Monographs 43. Berlin: Mouton de Gruyter, 179–94.

TABOURET-KELLER, ANDREE, 1997. 'Language and identity', in Florian Coulmas (ed.), *The Handbook of Sociolinguistics*, Oxford: Basil Blackwell, 315–26.

TAJFEL, H. & TURNER, J. C., 1986. 'The social identity theory of inter-group behavior', in S. Worchel & L. W. Austin (eds.), *Psychology of Intergroup Relations*, Chicago: Nelson-Hall, 7–24.

TAYLOR, LAURA A., 2005. The representation of land and landownership in medieval Icelandic texts. Unpublished D.Phil thesis.

TENBRINK, THORA, 2007. *Space, Time, and the Use of Language: An Investigation of Relationships*. Berlin; NewYork: Mouton de Gruyter.

THELANDER, MATS, 1979. *Språkliga variationsmodeller tillämpade på nutida Burträsktal I/II*. Acta Universitatis Upsaliensis 14, Uppsala.

THOMAS, GEORGE, 1991. *Linguistic Purism*, London; New York: Longman.

THOMASON, SARAH G., 2001. *Language Contact*, Edinburgh: Edinburgh University Press.

THOMASON, SARAH G., & KAUFMAN, TERRENCE, 1988. *Language Contact, Creolization, and Genetic Linguistics*, Berkeley: University of California Press.

THUEN, TROND, 2001. 'Sted og identitet', *Nordlit* 10, Universitetet i Tromsø: Det humanistiske fakultetet, 79–93.

THUEN, TROND, 2003. 'Steder, grenser, tilhørigheter. Noen innledende betraktinger', in T. Thuen (ed.), *Sted og tilhørighet*, Kulturstudier 27, NFR, Kristiansand: Høyskole Forlaget, 11–39.

TIERNEY, J. J., 1967. *Dicuili Liber de mensura orbis terrae*, in J. J. Tierney (ed.) with contributions by L. Bieler, Dublin: Institute for Advanced Studies.

TOMASSON, RICHARD, 1980. *Iceland: The First New Society*, Minneapolis: University of Minnesota Press.

TÓMASSON, SVERRIR, 1998. *Málvöndum á miðöldum*. Greinar af sama meiði helgaðar Indriða Gíslasyni sjötugum. Reykjavík: Rannsóknarstofnun Kennaraháskóla Íslands, 293–300.

TORP, ARNE, 2002. 'The Nordic languages in a Germanic perspective', in Oscar Bandle *et al.* (eds.), *The Nordic Languages: An International Handbook of the History of the North Germanic Languages*, Volume 1, Berlin: de Gruyter, 13–25.

TORP, ARNE & VIKØR, LARS S., 1993. *Hovuddrag i norsk språkhistorie*, Oslo: Ad Notam Gyldendal.

TOWNEND, MATTHEW, 2002. *Language and History in Viking Age England*, Turnhout, Belgium: Brepols.

TOYNBEE, ARNOLD J., 1962. *A Study of History*. Vol. 2, London; New York; Toronto: Oxford University Press.

TRUDGILL, PETER, 1986. *Dialects in Contact*, Language in Society 10, Oxford: Basil Blackwell.

TRUDGILL, PETER, 1989. 'Contact and isolation in linguistic change', in Leiv Egil Breivik & Ernst Håkon Jahr (eds.), *Language Change: Contributions to the Study of its Causes*, Trends in Linguistics Studies and Monographs 43, Berlin: Mouton de Gruyter, 227–38.

TRUDGILL, PETER, 1992. 'Dialect typology and social structure', in Ernst Håkon Jahr (ed.), *Language Contact: Theoretical and Empirical Studies*, Trends in Linguistics Studies and Monographs 60, Berlin: Mouton de Gruyter, 195–210.

TRUDGILL, PETER, 1994. 'Language contact and dialect contact in linguistic change', in U.-B. Kotsinas & J. Helgander (eds.), *Dialektkontakt, språkkontakt och språkforändring i Norden: föredrag från ett forskarsymposium*, Stockholm: Meddelanden från Institutionen för nordiska språk vid Stockholms Universitet, 13–22.

TRUDGILL, PETER, 1998. 'The chaos before the order: New Zealand English and the second stage of new-dialect formation', in Ernst Håkon Jahr (ed.), *Advances in Historical Sociolinguistics*, Berlin: Mouton de Gruyter, 1–11.

TRUDGILL, PETER, 2001. 'On the irrelevance of prestige, stigma and identity in the development of New Zealand English phonology', *New Zealand English Journal* 15, 42–6.

TRUDGILL, PETER, 2002. 'Language and social typology', in Jack Chambers, Peter Trudgill & Natalie Schilling-Estes (eds.), *Handbook of Variation and Change*, Malden/Oxford: Blackwell, 707–28.

TRUDGILL, PETER, 2004. *New-dialect Formation: The Inevitability of Colonial Englishes*, Edinburgh: Edinburgh University Press/Georgetown.

TRUDGILL, PETER *et al.*, 2000. 'Determinism in new-dialect formation and the genesis of New Zealand English', *Journal of Linguistics* 36, 299–318.

TULINIUS, TORFI, 2000. 'The matter of the North: Fiction and uncertain identities' in Margaret Clunies Ross (ed.), *Old Icelandic Literature and Society*, Cambridge: Cambridge University Press, 242–65.

TURNER, VICTOR W., 1971. 'An anthropological approach to the Icelandic saga', in Beidelman Thomas O. Beidelman (ed.), *The Translation of Culture: Essays to E. E. Evans-Pritchard*, London: Tavistock, 349–74.

TURVILLE-PETRE, E. O. G., 1951. *The Heroic Age of Scandinavia*, London: Hutchinson.

TURVILLE-PETRE, E. O. G., 1953. *Origins of Icelandic Literature*, Oxford: Clarendon Press.

TURVILLE-PETRE, E. O. G., 1976. *Scaldic Poetry*, Oxford: Clarendon Press.

TURVILLE-PETRE, JOAN, 1978–79. 'The genealogist and history: Ari to Snorri', *Saga Book of the Viking Society* 20, 7–23.

TUTEN, DONALD, 2003. *Koineisation in Medieval Spanish*, Berlin; New York: Mouton de Gruyter.

ULVESTAD, B., 1964. Review of 'Icelandic-Norwegian Linguistic Relationships' by Kenneth G. Chapman, *Language* 40, 601–04.

UNGER, C. R., 1862. *Stjórn: Gammelnorsk bibelhistorie fra verdens skabelse til det babyloniske fangenskab*, Christiania: Feilberg & Landmarks Forlag.

Valla-Ljóts saga, edited by Jónas Kristjánsson. Íslenzk fornrit, vol. IX. 1956, Reykjavík: Hið íslenzka fornritafélag.

VANNEBO, K. I., 2005. 'Written language and oral colloquial language in the 20th century: A survey', in Oscar Bandle *et al.* (eds.), *The Nordic Languages: An International Handbook of the History of the North Germanic Languages*. Vol. 2, 1682–91.

Vatnsdæla saga, edited by Einar Ól. Sveinsson. Íslenzk fornrit, vol. VIII. 1939, Reykjavík: Hið íslenzka fornritafélag.

VESTERGAARD, T. A., 1988. 'The system of kinship in early Norwegian law', *Mediæval Scandinavia* 12, 160–193.

VÉSTEINSSON, ORRI, 1998. 'Patterns of settlement in Iceland: A study in prehistory', *Saga-Book* 25/1, 1–29.

VÉSTEINSSON, ORRI, 2000. *The Christianization of Iceland: Priests, Power and Social Change 1000–1300*, Oxford: Oxford University Press.

VIÐAR SIGURÐSSON, JÓN, 1999. *Chieftains and Power in the Icelandic Commonwealth*, Odense: Odense University Press.

VIÐAR SIGURÐSSON, JÓN, 2006. 'Landnåmsgården og den første bosetningen på Island', in A. Mortensen, A. R. Nielsen, & J. T. Thor (eds.), *De vestnordiske landes fælles historie II: Udvalg af foredrag holdt på VNH-konferencerne i Ísafjörður 2003, Tórshavn 2004 og Oslo 2005*, Inussuk. Arktisk forskningsjournal 2, Nuuk: Forlaget Atuagkat, 56–79.

Víga-Glúms saga, edited by Jónas Kristjánsson. Íslenzk fornrit, vol. IX. 1956, Reykjavík: Hið íslenzka fornritafélag.

VON SEE, KLAUS, 1964. *Altnordische Rechtswörter: philologische Studien zur Rechtsauffassung und Rechtsgesinnung der Germanen*, Tübingen: M. Niemeyer.

Vöðu-Brands þáttr, edited by Björn Sigfússon. Íslenzk fornrit, vol. X. 1940, Reykjavík: Hið íslenzka fornritafélag.

WEINREICH, URIEL, 1954. 'Is a structural dialectology possible?', *Word* 10 (2/3), 388–400.

WEINREICH, URIEL, 1963. *Languages in Contact: Findings and Problems*, The Hague: Mouton.

WEINREICH, URIEL, 1968. *Languages in Contact: Findings and Problems*. 6th Printing, The Hague: Mouton & Co.

WEINREICH, URIEL, LABOV, WILLIAM & HERZOG, MARVIN, 1968. 'Empirical foundations for a theory of language change', in W. Lehmann & Y. Malkiel (eds.), *Directions for Historical Linguistics: a Symposium*, Austin: University of Texas Press, 95–188.

WELLS, JOHN C., 1990. *Althochdeutsches Glossenwörterbuch*, Heidelberg: Carl Winter Universitätsverlag.

WESSÉN, E., 1957. *De nordiska språken*. Acta Universitatis Stockholmiensis. Stockholm Studies in Scandinavian Philology, Stockholm: Filologiska Föreningen vid Stockholms Högskola.

WHALEY, DIANA, 2000. 'A useful past: Historical writing in medieval Iceland', in Margaret Clunies Ross (ed.), *Old Icelandic Literature and Society*, Cambridge: Cambridge University Press, 161–203.

WHELPTON, MATTHEW, 2000. 'Að tala íslensku, að vera íslenskur: mál og sjálfsmynd frá sjónarhóli útlendings', *Málfregnir* 19, 17–22.

WHITNEY, WILLIAM DWIGHT, 1867. *Language and the Study of Language: Twelve Lectures on the Principles of Linguistic Science*, New York: Charles Scribner & Co.

WIDMARK, GUN, 1994. 'Birkasvenskan – fanns den?', *Arkiv för nordisk filologi* 109, 173–216.

WIDMARK, GUN, 2001. *Det språk som blev vårt: ursprung och utveckling i svenskan*, Uppsala: Gustav Adolfs akad.

WILLIAMS, ANN & KERSWILL, PAUL, 1999. 'Dialect levelling: Change and continuity in Milton Keynes, Reading and Hull', in P. Foulkes & G. J. Docherty (eds.), *Urban voices: Accent Studies in the British Isles*, London: Arnold, 141–162.

WOODS, NICOLA J., 2000. 'Archaism and innovation in New Zealand English', *English World-Wide* 21, 109–50.

WYLIE, JONATHAN & MARGOLIN, DAVID, 1981. *The Ring of Dancers: Images of Faroese Culture*, Philadelphia: University of Pennsylvania Press.

Ynglinga saga, edited by Bjarni Aðalbjarnarson. Íslenzk fornrit, vol. XXVI. 1979, Reykjavík: Hið íslenzka fornritafélag.

ZACHRISSON, ROBERT EUGEN, 1913. *Pronunciation of English Vowels 1400– 1700*, Göteborg: Wald. Zachrissons Boktryckeri A. B.

ZELINSKY, WILBUR, [1973] 1992. *The Cultural Geography of the United States, a Revised Edition*, Englewood Cliffs, NJ: Prentice Hall.

ÞRÁINSSON, HÖSKULDUR & ÁRNASON, KRISTJÁN, 1984. 'Um reykvísku', *Íslenskt mál* 6, 113–34.

ÞRÁINSSON, HÖSKULDUR & ÁRNASON, KRISTJÁN, 1986. 'Um skagfirsku', *Íslenskt mál* 8, 31–62.

ÞRÁINSSON, HÖSKULDUR, & ÁRNASON, KRISTJÁN, 1992. 'Phonological variation in 20th Century Icelandic', *Íslenskt mál* 14, 89–128.

ÞRÁINSSON, HÖSKULDUR, et al., 2004. *Faroese: An Overview and Reference Grammar*, Tórshavn: Føroya Fróðskaparfelag.

ÞÓRA BJÖRK HJARTARDÓTTIR, 2004. 'Icelandic in a new language environment', in Ari Páll Kristinsson & Gauti Kristmannsson (eds.), *Málstefna – Language Planning*, Reykjavík: Íslensk málnefnd, 113–21.

ÞORLÁKSSON, HELGI, 1979. 'Kaupmenn i þjónustu konungs', in *Mímir. Blað stúdenta í íslenzkum fræðum* 13, 5–12.

ÞORLÁKSSON, HELGI, 1989. 'Mannfræði og saga', *Skírnir* 163, 231–48.

ÞORSTEINSSON, BJÖRN, 1953. *Íslenska þjóðveldið*, Reykjavík: Prentsmiðjan Hólar.

ÞORSTEINSSON, BJÖRN & ÁSA GRÍMSDÓTTIR, GUÐRÚN, 1989. 'Norska öldin', in Sigurður Líndal (ed.), *Saga Íslands* IV, Reykjavík: Hið íslenska bókmenntafélag & Sögufélagið, 61–258.

ÞÓRÓLFSSON, BJÖRN, K. 1925. *Um íslenskar orðmyndir á 14. og 15. öld og breytingar þeirra úr fornmálinu: með viðauka um nýjungar í orðmyndum á 16. öld og siðar*, Reykjavík: Fjelagsprentsmiðjan.

ØYE, I., 2006. 'Vestnorsk og vestnordisk landbruk i vikingetid og middelalder', in A. Mortensen, A. R. Nielssen & J (eds.), *De vestnordiske landes fælleshistorie II: Udvalg af foredrag holdt på VNH-konferencerne i Ísafjörður 2003, Tórshavn 2004 og Oslo 2005*, MortensenInussuk Arktisk forskningsjournal 2. Nuuk: Forlaget Atuagkat, 33–56.

Örvar-Odds saga. 1888. Edited by Boer, R. C. Altnordische Saga-Bibliothek Ser. 2, Leiden: Brill.

INDEX